Praise for *Th[e Brilliant Abyss]*

"Written by a highly articulate ex[pert . . . The Brilliant Ab]yss is] so comprehensive and insightfu. ...at it will be a long time before it's surpassed . . . It is hard to imagine a more timely or important book than *The Brilliant Abyss*. Carefully conceived and luminously written, it is certain to be a bestseller, which gives me hope that its urgent message might help save the world."

—Tim Flannery, *New Statesman*

"Helen Scales offers up an abundance of wondrous revelation and wise warnings in this mesmerizing consideration of the vibrant world of darkness under the sea. This is essential, unforgettable reading about our marvelous blue planet."

—Aimee Nezhukumatathil, bestselling author of *World of Wonders*

"Helen Scales is one of those rare scientists who can capture the excitement of science. *The Brilliant Abyss* has a thrill on every page as she explores the deep and little-known ocean. But this comes with a warning. Man's destruction is now reaching the remotest corners of the planet and our survival depends on stopping it."

—Mark Kurlansky, bestselling author of *Salmon: A Fish, the Earth, and the History of Their Common Fate* and *The Unreasonable Virtue of Fly Fishing*

"Mind-blowing! From vampire squids to translucent octopuses, from marine snow to sea butterflies, from Yeti crabs who farm their microbial meals on their own hairy claws, to snails who build shells of iron in hydrothermal vents, Helen Scales blitzes us again and again with the deep sea's staggering strangeness and arresting beauty. Studded with wonder on every page, *The Brilliant Abyss* is proof that, even as we consume and ruin our beautiful Earth in our greed, we hardly know our planet *at all*!"

—Sy Montgomery, author of the national bestseller *The Soul of an Octopus*

"An enjoyable and accessible introduction to the deep sea, told with a passion that I found infectious. The stories of life's struggle for survival beneath the waves are compelling and Scales is particularly evocative when describing hydrothermal vents . . . Scales brings to life this important part of our planet." —*New Scientist*

"Marine biologist Scales tours the lightless depths of the ocean and showcases its denizens in this show-stopping work . . . This vivid survey hits the mark as an awe-filled paean to the mysteries of the deep." —*Publishers Weekly* (starred review)

"It is the author's lush descriptive language and the breadth of her knowledge that truly stand out . . . The questions, Scales insists in this compelling title, should not be so much what the deep can do for us (feed us, cure us, save us), but rather what we must be willing to do for the oceans and every wondrous thing that lives there, given that our very existence depends on the health of the planet's seas." —*Booklist* (starred review)

"Scales introduces readers to the deep ocean, which begins where photosynthesis stops, 660 feet below the surface. Humans have interacted almost exclusively with the ocean's surface and edges, but the deep comprises far more of the ocean's volume and is likely more vital to the continuation of life on earth, Scales writes . . . A fascinating international glimpse of Earth's last frontier that will draw in readers concerned for the health of our oceans."
—*Library Journal* (starred review)

"[A] beguiling journey into the ocean's deep, a wondrous landscape full of mystery and adventure . . . Scales offers crisp, engaging prose, linking everything together in an accessible, entertaining manner. With plenty of scientific research to back her up, the author displays legitimate concerns about a wide variety of maladies . . . A captivating nature tour and a convincing warning that 'the deep needs decisive, unconditional protection.'" —*Kirkus Reviews* (starred review)

"The author lucidly explains not only the geological contours of the deep but also the animals that inhabit it . . . Scales bids us to think of the deep not merely as a place to exploit for resources, but as a wondrous abode that we are compelled to protect—a precious realm that we should all care about." —*Christian Science Monitor*

"In *The Brilliant Abyss*, Helen Scales, a marine biologist whose previous books explored the shallower reaches of the sea, dives deep and revealingly into the realm below." —*Economist*

"Extraordinary . . . So marvellous, astonishing, remarkable and compelling that readers can't help but embrace Scales's vision of a majestic and mysterious world mostly unsullied by humans . . . An important, powerful and hypnotizing tale of the deep, one that can't be recommended enough . . . Scales is a brilliant writer." —*Winnipeg Free Press*

"Scales writes beautifully of the ocean floor while at the same time instilling rage for the damage wrought by deep-sea fishing and mining . . . It is the author's gift to leave us both enthralled and angry, but angered to action and not to despair." —*Air Mail*

"In *The Brilliant Abyss*, the erudite Helen Scales explains why the ocean is so important and valuable an asset to our planet and to our survival . . . Scales joins activists around the world in demanding that the way the world does business has to change . . . If we do it the right way, Scales suggests that we will also be able to preserve the oceans as sanctuaries filled with wonder and beauty." —*Arts Fuse*

"Scales's enthusiasm for her subject is matched by a gift for visual evocation . . . The book also has a crusading message, which is that we depend on the ocean more than we realise, and are harming ourselves the more we harm it." —*Daily Telegraph*

Also by Helen Scales

The Great Barrier Reef
Octopuses
Eye of the Shoal
11 Explorations into Life on Earth
Spirals in Time
Poseidon's Steed

THE BRILLIANT ABYSS

EXPLORING the MAJESTIC
HIDDEN LIFE of the DEEP OCEAN and the
LOOMING THREAT THAT IMPERILS IT

HELEN SCALES

Grove Press
New York

Published simultaneously in Canada
Printed in the United States of America

This book was designed by Norman Tuttle at Alpha Design & Composition. This book was set in 12-pt. Bembo by Alpha Design & Composition of Pittsfield, NH.

First Grove Atlantic hardcover edition: July 2021
First Grove Atlantic paperback edition: June 2022

Library of Congress Cataloging-in-Publication data is available for this title.

ISBN 978-0-8021-5823-9
eISBN 978-0-8021-5824-6

Grove Press
an imprint of Grove Atlantic
154 West 14th Street
New York, NY 10011

Distributed by Publishers Group West

groveatlantic.com

22 23 24 25   10 9 8 7 6 5 4 3 2 1

For Josh, Sam, and David.

ZHEMCHUG
Canyon

KURILE-KAMCHATKA
Trench

JAPAN
Trench

PHILIPPINE
Trench

IZU-OGASAWARA
Trench

CENTRAL INDIAN
Ridge

HAWAIIAN-EMPEROR
Seamount Chain

MARIANA
Trench

JAVA
Trench

SOLITAIRE
Vent Field

KAIREI
Vent Field

TONGA
Trench

LONGQI
Vent Field

KERMADEC
Trench

GRAVEYARD
Seamounts

SOUTHEAST INDIAN
Ridge

SCALY-FOOT
SNAIL

YETI
CRAB

YETI
CRAB

PACIFIC-ANTARCTIC
Ridge

Contents

PRELUDE

Standing on the mid-deck of the research vessel *Pelican*, I stayed well out of the way while I watched proceedings unfold below. The 116-foot ship had left port a day and a half before and wound its way in the dark night through the salt marshes of southern Louisiana and out into the warm, rolling waves of the Gulf of Mexico. Immediately, my world had shrunk. I was one of ten marine scientists on board to run a series of studies in the deep sea, alongside eleven crew who ensured the smooth running of the ship. We all gathered in the galley at mealtimes and sporadically to watch TV. There was also a small research lab, plus several staterooms, a grandiose term for the cramped, four-person cabins, where I had a coffin-like bunk, which I learned to roll into and out of. There was also a shared bathroom, or head, as mariners are supposed to call it, with a sturdy horizontal bar to grab onto and hold yourself steady in a heaving swell. Waking up on the first morning, all that was visible outside, stretching to a horizon that encircled the ship, was the gulf and its waves. Soon enough, though, the view would begin to reach much farther.

The vital machine was hanging from a crane above the back deck, waiting to be sent into the deep. Roughly the size of a small car, the deep-diving submersible was built around a tubular metal frame with bright yellow floats and an impressive payload of electronic gadgets and sensors strapped all over it. At the front end, two close-set glassy eyes gave the submersible the endearing face of an anxious robot. Those were the stereo camera lenses that would become our eyes in the deep. It had a pair of arms too. One was fancy, with seven-way jointed movements that would mirror the gestures of a skilled human pilot controlling it from the ship. The second was operated by push buttons, giving it the simple instructions to rotate, grab, and let go. A long, ridged plastic tube, like a vacuum cleaner pipe, known as the slurp gun, could be used to gently suck up things from the deep and bring them back to the surface. A series of small propellers would maneuver the submersible up and down, left and right. And a cable as thick as my wrist connected it to a quarter-ton stack of electronics, the clump weight, which in turn was connected via a very long cable to the ship, supplying power and instructions to the sub and relaying video footage in real time of everything it was seeing. There was no room inside for a human. All personnel would be staying on the ship.

Four people wearing yellow hard hats were hanging on ropes looped around each corner of the submersible, and like animal tamers, they wrestled it under control as it swung across the deck and over the side of the ship, where it dangled expectantly in midair. If it had been a living animal, it would have known what was coming and strained at its leash, eager to return to the place where it feels most agile and free. Then the crane dipped its head and lowered the sub down until it floated on the sea surface and, in a satisfying sigh of bubbles, wallowed a short distance away from the ship. Looking down from my vantage point, I watched as the enormous winch clicked into gear and began to unspool the cable, lowering millions of dollars of sophisticated hardware into the deep.

Monitor screens stationed around the ship showed the submersible's video feed and tracked its progress: first through bubbling blue water with golden sargassum fronds floating by, then green water growing darker as the numbers ticked away, measuring the steady descent until the sub's headlights shone through the permanent dark.

The submersible needed an hour to reach the seabed, a little more than 6,600 feet down. On the way, enticing glimpses of deep-sea life flashed past—hints of jellyfish and squid—but the submersible pilots had not been instructed to stop the vessel and watch. The first animal I got a good look at was swimming just above the seabed. It was a translucent, scarlet creature, sometimes called the "headless chicken monster" because it is roughly the shape of a plucked carcass on a supermarket shelf, one that's been reanimated and flung into the deep sea.* Officially called *Enypniastes*, it's a sea cucumber and, unusually for a holothurian, is a part-time swimmer. Unlike its more sluggish relatives that loll around on the bottom, this one occasionally leaps into action and glides gracefully along, just above the seabed, with sinuous undulations of its body, flapping what looks like a flamenco dancer's ruffled skirt. *Enypniastes* will drift with the current, then land back down to continue its ponderous walking and feeding. Its burst of swimming can be an escape response—this one may have got scared by the sub or, alternatively, it was setting off in search of a freshly fallen flurry of food from above. With nutrition hard to come by in the deep, it pays to have ways of finding as much food as possible. And like many inhabitants of the deep ocean, *Enypniastes* has evolved the ability to glow in the dark. When disturbed, it shucks off an outer layer of illuminated skin, probably to confuse an intruder, creating a shining ghost of itself while the real sea cucumber makes a getaway. But the sub's lights were too bright for us to spot that phenomenon, and besides there wasn't time on the schedule for watching sea cucumbers.

For the next twelve hours, the scientists on board the *Pelican* took it in turns, two or three at a time, to step into the control room—a large metal box out on deck—and direct the submersible pilots as we set about our scientific tasks. All the while we gazed via the monitor

---

* The stump where the chicken's head would have been cut off is in fact the sea cucumber's mouth, surrounded by a ring of short tentacles.

screens at the scene beaming up from a mile and a quarter beneath our feet, each of us becoming remote explorers of the deep.

∽

The oceans have always shaped human lives, but the surface and the very edges have so far mattered the most. People have walked the coastlines and settled along the boundary between land and sea; they've sailed across the waves to gather food and reach distant lands, to send armies and claim colonies, and to fetch exotic riches. Still today, a great deal of food comes from the shallow, surface seas where highways transport many of the everyday goods that have come to dominate the global economy. And people still retreat to the edges of the sea to seek tranquility, to stare into the wild waves and escape busy lives. What lies far below the surface has long remained out of sight and usually out of mind. Now, though, humanity's close ties to the oceans are sinking deeper.

This is without a doubt a golden era for deep-sea exploration. Assisted by new technological tools, such as deep-diving submersibles, scientists are opening up a more expansive and intricate view of the deep than we've ever had before. Not so very long ago, it was thought no life existed there at all, but in fact the deep is home to countless unimaginable life-forms. This is the domain of jelly creatures so fragile they would fall straight through your fingers if you tried to pick one up, and yet they remain unperturbed by pressure so extreme it would squash your body's cells and molecules lethally out of shape. Here live billions and trillions of small, glowing fish that spend their daily lives rushing skyward then back down to the depths. Here lie entire ecosystems shut away in the dark that are based around the chemical powers of microbes, where worms are nine feet long, crabs dance, and snails grow suits of shiny metal armor.

Studies of the deep are transforming the very notion of life on Earth, rewriting the rules of what's possible. This could well be where life began in the first place and where it grew more elaborate and complex before moving off to inhabit all the shallower and drier parts of the planet. Not only that—as scientists look longer and harder into the deep, they're seeing just how much it matters. Invisible connections lead far and wide from the deep sea, keeping balance in the atmosphere and climate, storing away and pouring out vital substances, all processes without which life on Earth would become unbearable or impossible. Every living thing needs the deep.

While deep-sea scientists are busy making remarkable discoveries, there is a growing urgency to know and understand the deep. What was once considered the very paradigm of untouched wilderness is increasingly feeling the influence and impacts of human lives, as we collectively tighten our grip on the planet.

At the same time, people are starting to ask more of the deep. Some are asking whether it can solve the problems facing humanity today. Can the deep feed us? Can it cure us? Will it save us from the climate crisis?

Others are asking whether the deep can make them rich. Beneath the surface are substances and animals that until now have remained too distant and costly to extract, but that is swiftly changing. As shallow seas have become overfished and exhausted, fishing fleets have been pushing deeper, year after year, depleting populations of typically slow-growing, long-lived fish. Plans are also underway to begin mining the seabed. This brand-new industry would sweep aside fragile, deep-sea ecosystems and in time could tread the single biggest ecological footprint on the planet, all to extract the metal ores that lie in the abyss and use them to make the electronic devices on which the modern age increasingly depends.

One way or another, the future ocean is the deep ocean. Decisions and choices being made now will determine what that future will look like. If industrialists and powerful states have their way, and the deep is opened up to them, then it raises the ironic and dismal prospect that the deep sea will become empty and lifeless, just as people once thought it was.

History tells us that exploration and exploitation of the earth and its resources have always gone hand in hand, with little care for what the consequences might be. New regions are discovered and surveyed; new frontiers are opened up, containing new resources to be extracted and ultimately exhausted: crude oil and minerals, forests and fish, whales and sea otters, elephants for their tusks and tigers for their bones.

But there is another option.

We now face the possibility of forging a new relationship with the living planet, and we have the chance to decide there are things we just don't need and places that are special, unique, and important enough to leave alone—and one of those places is the deep.

PART ONE

EXPLORE

Here Is the Deep

Watch Earth from afar as it spins through space, and it shows itself to be a water planet. Seven-tenths of the surface is covered in what we see as blue ocean. Blue light from the sun seeps down through the seawater, leaving all the other colors behind in the shallows, where they're absorbed by vibrating molecules of H_2O. The tenacity of those shorter wavelengths of light, 450 nanometers and under, gives Earth its particular shade of blue. But even those deepest-diving photons can go only so far. Below the first 660 feet—roughly the long side of a Chicago city block—weak remnants of dim blue sunlight remain. Below that depth, physical conditions shift and oceanic life becomes distinct from the shallower, surface seas. This is where the deep sea officially begins.

On average, the oceans are around 12,500 feet deep, or close to two and a half miles, ten times the height of the Empire State Building in New York. Below 3,300 feet there are no sunbeams at all, which means that a huge portion of the planet is untouched by sunlight. Far more permanent night fills up our world than day, but most of us don't see those dark parts or what lies within them.

Often it's said that more is known about the surface of the moon than the bottom of the sea, and there is truth in this. The whole of the moon has been mapped to a resolution of twenty-three feet. Meanwhile, the best map of the entire deep seabed shows only features larger than three miles across. But the astronomical comparison rather misses the point, partly because of the gaping size difference between the lunar and abyssal maps. If the moon's surface could be peeled off and laid out on the deep seabed, it would fit almost ten times over. And even though it lies a lot farther away than the deep seabed, the moon is also a great deal easier to map than the deep, because it's bone-dry, with no oceans or lakes in the way. With a telescope and a clear night, any of us can get a reasonable idea of what the near side of the moon looks like (accessing the dark side is rather more involved). Try doing the same for the deep seabed.

Were our view not blocked by its cloak of water—blue above, black below—Earth would look very different. We would see the complex topography of the deep ocean floor laid out in a spectacular terrain.

Most obviously, our planet would look like it had exploded and been crudely stitched back together again. Great jagged scars across the deep seabed mark the world's longest, most dramatic mountain range. Composed of geological formations known as mid-ocean ridges, the mountain range threads for 34,000 miles, its underwater peaks up to 2 miles high and in places almost 1,000 miles wide. Portions of this mountain range are named mostly for their geographical locations: the Mid-Atlantic Ridge bisects the Atlantic from Greenland all the way south toward Antarctica; slicing across the Indian Ocean are the Southwest, Central, and Southeast Indian Ridges; skirting south of Australia and New Zealand, the mountain range continues as the Pacific–Antarctic Ridge, then veers north as the East Pacific Rise toward California. Other segments connect to the great mountain chain: the Aden Ridge is located between Somalia and the Arabian Peninsula; the Chile Rise stretches through the eastern Pacific toward the tip of South America; the 300-mile-long Juan de Fuca Ridge passes offshore from the Pacific coast of North America between Oregon and Vancouver Island. All these peaks form at the edges of seven major and numerous minor tectonic plates, the giant jigsaw puzzle pieces of the earth's outermost rigid layer, the crust, which glide around on the viscous mantle beneath them. Wherever submerged tectonic plates pull apart, lava erupts from deep within the mantle, pushing up the mid-ocean mountain peaks and oozing brand-new seafloor that spreads sideways, forming a basaltic, oceanic crust between three and six miles thick.

Frequently, the mountain range doesn't stretch in smooth lines across the seabed but is broken and offset in giant corrugations. Fracture zones form when sections of rifting tectonic plates slip past each other, triggering earthquakes and sending tsunamis racing across the oceans.

Moving away in various directions, the abyssal plains begin to either side of the soaring peaks of mid-ocean ridges—to the east and west of the Mid-Atlantic Ridge, north and south of the Pacific-Antarctic Ridge. Lying between 10,000 and 16,400 feet below the sea surface, these prairies of the deep go on and on. With their horizontal spread, they collectively form the biggest feature of the seabed and cover more than half of the earth's surface; even the vast Eurasian Steppe, the belt of grasslands ranging between Hungary and China, is dwarfed by the abyssal plains. These swaths of the abyss are soft underfoot, should you decide to go for a walk there; in most places you would have to dig through a mile of mud before hitting rock on the seafloor beneath, and in some places more like six miles. A map of the globe's seafloor sediments, newly updated in 2019, suggests there is 30 percent more mud than previous studies had estimated. The sediments are a mix of flecks of eroded rock washed out in rivers, dropped by glaciers, or blown in the wind, together with the minute bodies of planktonic creatures that sprinkle down from the surface and settle in great seabed slicks.

Abyssal plains are not simply endless, flat tracts of mud. They are intersected by undulating hills and winding valleys, burping mud volcanoes and fizzing Jacuzzis of methane bubbles; and dotted across the plains stand thousands of tall volcanoes, active or inactive, cone-shaped or flat-topped if they were worn away by waves in past times when they reached the sea surface. Known as seamounts, these isolated peaks are distinct from the ranges of mid-ocean ridges, although they can form nearby. The biggest mounts are generally located in the central regions of tectonic plates, in places where chambers of molten magma bubble up in hot spots through the oceanic crust. As tectonic plates slide over these hot spots, chains of seamounts form one after another, like cakes being made on a factory conveyor belt.

Journey across an abyssal plain, skirting the seamounts and facing away from a mid-ocean ridge, and you will pass over gradually older and older seabed until eventually you reach the brink of the very deepest parts of the ocean. Tectonic plates collide at subduction zones, where one plate gets thrust under another. Here, as old seafloor is dragged down into the earth's molten interior, to be melted and recycled, oceanic trenches are formed, reaching to depths of 20,000 feet and more. Principally formed from twenty-seven trenches worldwide, this is the hadal zone, named after Hades, the ancient Greek god of the underworld.

In cross section, trenches are V-shaped and can stretch horizontally for thousands of miles. The Atlantic and Indian Oceans each contain a single trench, the Puerto Rico Trench, north of Puerto Rico and the Virgin Islands,★ and the Java Trench, skirting south of the Indonesian islands of Java and Sumatra, respectively. In the Southern Ocean beyond the tip of Tierra del Fuego lie the South Sandwich and the South Orkney Trenches. The remaining trenches are all located around the Ring of Fire, a horseshoe-shaped region fringing the east, north, and west of the Pacific, where multiple tectonic plates meet, causing intense seismic activity and 90 percent of the world's earthquakes. A string of trenches running from Russia to

---

★ The Cayman Trench, also in the Caribbean, is a trench fault formed not at a subduction zone but by the fracturing of the Mid-Cayman spreading center.

New Zealand are all more than 32,000 feet deep: the Kurile-Kamchatka, Philippine, Tonga, and Kermadec Trenches, plus the deepest of all, the Mariana Trench, which spikes below 36,000 feet.

Seismologists make sure to listen very carefully to trenches. Located at subduction zones, where tectonic plates push and shove each other, the steep trench walls regularly heave and shake with the world's most powerful earthquakes. An array of sensors strung through the Japan Trench is poised to detect rumbles that could foretell the next mega-earthquake, like the one that caused the devastating 2011 tsunami, which killed eighteen thousand people and flooded the Fukushima Daiichi power station, causing the worst nuclear accident since Chernobyl. In April 2020, a panel of advisers to the Japanese government warned that a massive earthquake and tsunami could strike the northern region, around Hokkaido, at any time. While they can't say exactly when it will happen, the advisers studied ancient sediments and discovered that a huge quake has hit every three hundred to four hundred years—and the last time was in the seventeenth century.

Retreating from the shuddering hadal zone, back across the calm and quiet abyssal plains and toward land, the deep seafloor comes to an end where the continental shelves begin. To get up onto the shallow plateaus, those familiar parts of the ocean that reach the coast, great piles of sediments must be clambered over, an area called the continental rise. Then come the escarpments of the continental slopes like giant cliff faces, which are sliced through with nine thousand or so steep-walled canyons. Many great rivers, including the Amazon, Congo, Hudson, and Ganges, lead toward underwater canyons formed not by persistent water flow, as river channels are, but sculpted by underwater landslides as sediments build up and slump off the edges of the continental shelves. On average, submarine canyons are twenty-five miles long and a mile and a half deep, and many are even more dramatic. Nazaré Canyon is Europe's largest, running 130 miles toward the Portuguese coast, where it funnels the wild Atlantic swell into record-breaking waves. It was here, in 2017, that Brazilian big-wave rider Rodrigo Koxa surfed the biggest wave anyone ever had (80 feet), and in 2020 his compatriot, Maya Gabeira, set the women's record (73.5 feet), which was also the biggest wave surfed by anyone during that winter season, a first for women in professional surfing. On the other side of the planet, in the Bering Sea off Alaska, Zhemchug Canyon is sixty miles wide, compared to the Grand Canyon's eight miles. And America's iconic terrestrial canyon is half the height of the oceans' most impressive equivalent, the Great Bahama Canyon, whose walls tower 14,060 feet (almost three miles) up from the abyss.

But this grand panorama of the ocean floor is hidden away beneath so much seawater. The total volume of the deep ocean water, everything below 660 feet, is roughly 240 million cubic miles. To put this in perspective, the Amazon River pours out a single cubic mile's worth of water every five and a half hours. At that rate, it would take approximately 150,000 years to fill up the entire deep.

That isn't how the ocean basins originally came to be full of water, however. For almost as long as Earth has existed, there have been oceans, although how so much water ended up here has been an enduring mystery among cosmologists. Many consider it likely that water was imported from the outer reaches of the solar system when icy comets bombarded the early Earth. Traces of water detected in dust particles from a peanut-shaped stony asteroid called Itokawa indicated that half of Earth's water supply may have come from this common form of space rock. Earth may also have come preloaded with some of its own primordial water, lodged deep within rocks that coalesced and formed the planet 4.55 billion years ago. Conditions were much hotter back then, and minerals rich in hydrogen and oxygen would have melted and reacted together, and spewed the resulting water from the planet's crust; the water would then have evaporated and risen into the newly forming atmosphere. Subsequently, as Earth cooled, the water vapor condensed, clouds formed, and it started to rain—perhaps as early as 4.4 billion years ago—beginning to form the oceans.

The ancient history of the oceans is difficult to tell because their geological record is continually wiped clean.★ Oceanic crust is thin, young, and short-lived compared to the thick, primeval continents floating above the rest; seafloor exists for tens or maybe hundreds of millions of years (not long, in geological terms), before getting dragged back into the earth at subduction zones, to be melted, recycled, and squeezed back out as new oceanic crust. Occasionally, a slab of ancient seafloor has been pushed up onto a continent, where it remains for geologists to inspect and reconstruct what happened long ago. One such chunk of primordial seabed found in the Outback of Western Australia has offered a glimpse into the past, hinting that more than three billion years ago, most of the planet was covered in water. Chemical traces in these rocks point toward the existence of a water world, devoid of enormous, soil-rich continents but with microcontinents peeping up above the waves here and there, little more than rocky islets. In time, the full-size continents emerged, and as the eons passed, they began to perform a slow, shuffling dance around the planet, and around them the shape of the global ocean has continually changed.

Partially enclosed basins have formed, and ancient oceans have come and gone. Superoceans formed at times when the continents were all clustered together, surrounding them with water. A billion years ago, a vast ocean called Mirovia is thought to have encircled the supercontinent Rodinia. The continents split apart, then came together again, most recently 355 million years ago, forming Pangaea, encircled by the superocean Panthalassa, which eventually

★ I say "oceans" but really the earth has only ever had one interconnected mass of water. Throughout this book I will heedlessly switch between the words "sea," "ocean," and "oceans." Unless I give a specific name—such as Pacific, Atlantic—you should take it that I mean to refer in a general way to the earth's body of salt water, which strictly speaking is the global ocean.

fragmented into the oceans we know today. The oldest, biggest, and deepest is the Pacific, which is at least 250 million years old; next the Atlantic, Indian, and Arctic Oceans formed; and finally, 30 million years ago, the Antarctic and South American continents pulled apart, and the Southern Ocean began its clockwise swirl around the bottom of the planet.

❧

The expanses of the deep seabed, the abyssal plains and seamounts, canyons and trenches, plus all the water above them, constitute the single biggest living space on the planet. More than 95 percent of the earth's biosphere—the volume of habitats available for living organisms to occupy—is made up of the deep sea. Everything else—the forests and grasslands, rivers and lakes, mountains, deserts, and shallow coastal waters—is collectively outstripped in terms of sheer volume by those colossal reaches of the oceans that lie below the blue surface.

If you were to sail out into the open ocean and drop a glass marble over the side of the boat, for the first six or seven minutes it would fall through the uppermost layer of water, the part where the sun still shines. Some call this the epipelagic or euphotic zone, or simply the sunlit zone. It's the most familiar part of the oceans, where most of the known species live, and it's where all the oceans' photosynthesis takes place. The sun-catchers come in the form of large seaweeds as well as microscopic, single-celled creatures, collectively known as phytoplankton,★ which all suck in carbon dioxide and turn it into food for almost all the rest of ocean life.

As the marble drops, the sunlight fades until, at around 660 feet, there is just enough dim blue light to see by but not enough to power

---

★ Once thought to be plants and still variously referred to as algae, phytoplankton in fact comprise a motley collection of organisms from different superkingdoms and phyla spread across the tree of life, including such life-forms as diatoms, coccolithophores, dinoflagellates, and cyanobacteria.

photosynthesis, and phytoplankton venture no deeper (at least not while they're still alive). Here the marble enters the deep. Below, horizontal zones are laid out one above the other, like layers of Jell-O poured into a tall sundae glass. The uppermost layer, reaching downward from 660 feet, is the twilight zone (also known as the mesopelagic). The falling marble takes almost a half hour to pass through this zone of indigo dusk, until, at 3,300 feet, the twilight zone gives way to the permanent dark of the midnight zone (or bathypelagic). At this depth, the temperature, which has been falling, begins to level off. So far, the marble has been passing through the thermocline, where seawater rapidly cools, from the sun-warmed surface into the oceans' dark interior. Within the midnight zone, across most of the planet, water stays at a steady thirty-nine degrees Fahrenheit.★ It takes the marble another hour and a half to pass all the way through the midnight zone, at which point it reaches the next great portion of the deep, between around 13,000 and 20,000 feet down, the part of the deep sea now officially known as the abyss.†

All through its journey toward the seafloor, the marble passes living creatures. Flashing lights glint in the glass sphere, not from sunlight but from the many light-making animals, the glowing worms and flashing lanternfish, which might wonder what kind of creature is blinking back at them. The marble would collect a dusting of organic matter, and tiny shrimp might take a ride while scraping up those particles of food. In open waters of the midnight zone, the marble could get knocked aside by the swish of a sperm whale's tail as it chases after a squid. It might bounce down the steep rocky walls of a canyon or land in a soft abyssal plain, perhaps next to a herd of sea cucumbers that look like small, pale piglets with too many legs,

★ Ocean temperatures drop to 35.6 degrees Fahrenheit at the greatest depths, lower still at the poles.

† While deep-sea scientists classify the abyss as seabed deeper than 13,000 feet (4,000 meters), the term continues to be more generally applied to the deep sea. Open waters between 13,000 and 20,000 feet (4,000 and 6,000 meters) are referred to as the abyssopelagic.

some with a spiny, red crab riding on their backs because there's nowhere else for it to hide. The marble could land on the flank of a seamount and get lost in tangled forests of immobile animals that have been living there for centuries, or it could fall next to a scorching hot spring gushing from cracks at a mid-ocean ridge and land among clusters of giant clams and huge worms with scarlet feathers.

Or, if your aim was good, the marble could plunge down into a trench and reach the hadal zone, the oceans' deepest layer. Even there, the glass sphere would pass living things, the blur of ghostly white fish. Then, eventually—six hours after you let it go at the surface—the marble would land at the very bottom, just shy of seven miles down, where it might attract a hungry swarm of pale crustaceans, eager to have a go at eating it.

A total tally of the number of deep-sea species is, of course, a long way out of reach given the deep's vast size, and systematic surveys have revealed glimpses of what is still to be found. In 1984, two American scientists, Fred Grassle and Nancy Maciolek, used a box corer, a tool like a giant cookie cutter, to extract chunks of mud from the deep seabed off the coasts of New Jersey and Delaware, between 4,900 and 8,200 feet down. Carefully sifting through the mud and picking out every tiny living thing—every worm, crustacean, starfish, sea cucumber, clam, and snail—they identified 798 species, over half of them new to science. Based on an average of three new species per square mile of seabed, Grassle and Maciolek estimated that abyssal plains across the planet could be home to thirty million species. The duo acknowledged that some regions of the deep may support a lower density of species, so they dialed down their estimate to a more cautious ten million.

More than thirty-five years after Grassle and Maciolek's groundbreaking study, the task continues of knowing all that lives in the deep. In 2019, a team of seventeen lead scientists published the results of a three-year survey of the Pacific in an area of deep sea bigger than the state of California, involving hundreds of hours of dive time using remote-operated submersibles. In all, they photographed 347,000 animals, and only one in five of them were known species. Some were too small, or the pictures too blurry, to identify, but the majority were animals that nobody had ever seen before. The diversity of life is prolific in the deep, rivaling the shallow, familiar seas—perhaps even life on land.

A central inventory of deep-sea life, the World Register of Deep-Sea Species, has been growing since 2012, a cataloguing job that is far from complete, as more species are constantly being added. By 2020, there were 26,363 listed species. All these organisms, and multitudes more besides, have evolved ways to survive and thrive in the extreme conditions of the deep, something that until relatively recently was thought to be impossible.

∽

For the longest time, the only things people thought lived in the deep ocean were monsters, demons, and deities. Mythmakers hid these powerful beings in sunken isolation, away from prying eyes. Occasional glimpses of them at the surface, often by homesick, hallucinating sailors, helped to ensure people kept believing they were real.

Sharing the oceans with famous beasts and gods such as the Kraken, Leviathan, Triton, and Poseidon are scores of others, let loose in and put in charge of this water realm by cultures around the world. Umibōzu is a Japanese sea monk with a humanoid form, coal-black skin, and sometimes tentacles, who unleashes great storms at sea. Swimming through Scottish Gaelic myths is the sea serpent Ceirean, and in Icelandic sagas a giant sea monster, Hafgufa, disguises itself as islands. Tangaroa is a Maori god of the sea who fathered many sea creatures. The ancient Finnish sea goddess Vellamo had many daughters, personified in the waves, who raised cattle and crops on the seafloor. Tiamat was the ancient Babylonian goddess of the sea, often depicted as a sea serpent. In Norse mythology, Jörmungandr, also known as the Midgard Serpent, was thrown into the sea by the god Odin and grew so big it encircled the Earth and bit its own tail; if ever Jörmungandr were to let go of its tail, the great battle of Ragnorök would begin.

While all these imagined beings have deep oceanic links, not all writings and stories of the abyss are necessarily related to the ocean depths. The word *abyss* has meant many other things. It stems from the Latin *abyssus*, meaning "bottomless pit," or the Ancient Greek ἄβυσσος, "great deep." The abyss has referred to the primordial chaos from which Earth and the heavens were created, and also an endless chasm or the infernal pits of hell, as featured in the Old Testament's angel of the abyss, and of which John Milton wrote in *Paradise Lost* in 1667:

> His dark materials to create more Worlds,
> Into this wild Abyss the warie fiend
> Stood on the brink of Hell and look'd a while,
> Pondering his Voyage: for no narrow frith
> He had to cross.

The abyss can be anything that is boundless, incomprehensible, or unfathomable. As the seventeenth-century German philosopher Jakob Böhme wrote in his book *The Signature of All Things*, there is "an eye of eternity, an abyssal eye, that stands or sees in the nothing." Countless authors have sent their protagonists toward the edge of the abyss, to stare or jump right into a literal or figurative place they don't expect to come back from. In her 1723 novel *A Patchwork Screen for the Ladies*, Jane Barker included a poem with the lines:

> To trace but out the follies of mankind,
> Whether in the common-mass, or else disjoin'd,
> Is an abyss, wherein to drown the mind.

The metaphorical abyss is certainly a good fit for the real ocean depths. It's easy to imagine that the oceans could be bottomless. To many, the deep is inscrutable and incomprehensible, and if you toss something in, it's unlikely to ever come back out. But not until the mid-nineteenth century were the deepest parts of the ocean referred to specifically as "the abyss," around the time sailors and scientists were starting to determine just how deep the sea can be. They were the first generation of deep-sea explorers, and they took on the painstaking task of lowering lead weights over the side of ships and paying out wire until they touched down on the seabed.

Popularizing the notion of the oceans' abyss was a man who was also responsible for banishing monsters from these depths, along with every other living thing. Edward Forbes, a young British naturalist, set off in 1841 on a deepwater survey of the Aegean Sea, the Mediterranean embayment between Greece and Turkey, with the aim of understanding the forces that sculpt the seas' living underworld. For a year and a half, sailing on the ship HMS *Beacon*, Forbes dredged up animals from as deep as 230 fathoms, or 1,380 feet.★

It was a formidable task, using only wind and manpower to drag nets across the seabed and haul them back up. Forbes amassed a huge collection of animals, and using the captain's cabin as part museum, part laboratory, he dissected, preserved, and illustrated his specimens. His interest lay not simply in identifying the different types of animals but in carefully scrutinizing where he had found them. Forty years previously, the German naturalist Alexander von Humboldt had formulated his theory of the zones of life on land, noticing that different plants grow up the sides of mountains compared to forests at sea level and that plant life decreases from the equator toward the poles. Forbes was searching for equivalent vertical patterns descending into the depths of the oceans.

★ A fathom is six feet, originally measured as the distance between an adult person's outstretched arms.

His studies revealed many important ecological ideas about sea life. He showed that the type of animals he found depended on the consistency of the seabed—sandy, rocky, or muddy—and he showed that some animals live only in certain places. Crucially, he noted how life began to run out at depth; the deeper he looked, the fewer living creatures he saw.

Forbes took his Aegean findings to their logical conclusion, extrapolating to a point where, he presumed, there was no life at all. This led him, in 1843, to a general rule that nothing in the sea lives deeper than 300 fathoms, or 1,800 feet. He drew a line near the upper reaches of the twilight zone and declared it the limit to life on earth.

In his time, Forbes was highly influential, and his ideas caught on. Had he lived longer, he may well have gone on to make many other scientific discoveries about the deep. In 1852, he was the first to apply the term *abyss* to the deep sea, specifying a zone deeper than 100 fathoms. But two years later, at age thirty-nine, he died while partway through writing his book *The Natural History of European Seas*. His friend Robert Godwin-Austen finished the book, which included Forbes's idea of the lifeless deep.

> *As we descend deeper and deeper in this region, its inhabitants become more and more modified, and fewer and fewer, indicating our approach towards an abyss where life is either extinguished, or exhibits but a few sparks to mark its lingering presence.*

What came to be known as the azoic theory was widely popular, partly because Forbes had data to support his reasoning that the dark, cold, crushing depths must be inhospitable to life. But those data were flawed on three counts. Firstly, his dredging equipment was far from ideal. The device he used was essentially a canvas bag with small eyelet holes. When Forbes and the crew of HMS *Beacon* dragged the dredge across the seabed, the bag would have quickly filled with mud, and the holes would have become clogged. Whatever animals it caught were the ones that happened to get scooped up in the first few moments of dredging.

Secondly, the Aegean Sea is not a good study site for making wider claims about the oceans. This part of the Mediterranean is unusually empty of sea life, both shallow and deep. The surface waters lack nutrients, and the entire ecosystem is essentially starving. If he had looked elsewhere in the Mediterranean and used more suitable dredging equipment that didn't get choked with mud, Forbes would have seen that life can indeed carry on well below the 300-fathom mark.

Forbes also failed to consider what some other people had been finding, as did most of the scientific establishment at the time. More than thirty years earlier, in 1818, Captain John Ross was commanding HMS *Isabella* in search of the Northwest Passage between the Atlantic and Pacific Oceans. In Baffin Bay off the Canadian coast, members of his crew were measuring the depth of the water, lowering down a mechanical device with snapping jaws at the end, which grabbed a sample of mud when it hit the bottom. As well as mud, the jaws brought up living worms and a large basket star. This animal is an echinoderm, a relative of the starfish, with five branching, lacy arms, and it's large enough to make an elaborate hat. Ross and his team had caught this newly discovered species at around 600 fathoms, or 3,600 feet. The discovery should have put an end to the azoic theory once and for all, but it was not widely disseminated because of controversies and arguments that flared up on the ship's return to Britain; several crew members quarreled over the subsequent reports, which, they claimed, didn't fully acknowledge their contributions to the expedition, and Ross was discredited after making false claims about a range of mountains in Lancaster Sound, off Baffin Bay.

Meanwhile, other reports of life from less extreme depths were also accumulating. At the same time that Forbes was dredging the

Aegean, John Ross's nephew, James Clark Ross, was captain of a scientific expedition to Antarctica. There he brought up corals from 400 fathoms. Many more deep-sea corals were dredged from waters around Norway in the 1850s by zoology professor Michael Sars, who helped to show that these animals don't build reefs only in the tropical shallows but also thrive in the dark deep, at least 200 or 300 fathoms down. Nevertheless, most naturalists demanded solid evidence that life is common at far greater depths.

In 1860, the scientific establishment dismissed further proof of deep life, following reports from British surgeon and naturalist George Charles Wallich on an expedition to Iceland and Greenland on HMS *Bulldog*. He watched as a sounding line was hauled up with thirteen starfish clinging to the end; being seabed-dwelling species, they couldn't have grabbed hold in midwater. The line had reached the seabed and picked up those starfish at 1,260 fathoms, or 7,560 feet. But still this finding was ignored, and Forbes's azoic theory lived on. Most naturalists stuck firm to the belief that life was impossible at great depths, and they refused to accept contradictory evidence. Wallich's discovery was overlooked because the gear he used was not a purpose-built piece of scientific equipment and also because he was shunned by the scientific establishment, seen by many as a foul-tempered megalomaniac. In particular, he made archenemies of Charles Wyville Thomson and William Carpenter, influential fellows at the Royal Society in London. Those two decided instead to search the deep themselves, leading Royal Society expeditions from 1868 to 1870 on the naval ships HMS *Lightning* and HMS *Porcupine*. They adapted the dredging nets, tying on lengths of rope called hempen tangles, which snagged starfish, basket stars, and hundreds of other seabed species. Finally, in the closing decades of the nineteenth century, Forbes's azoic theory was thoroughly disproved.

∽

The unfathomable size of the oceans, and the extreme conditions this brings, were what made people like Edward Forbes doubt that anything could live in the deep. Firstly, there's the immense pressure, which any being would have to cope with. Walking around on land, terrestrial animals are unaware of the column of air constantly pressing down from above. Jump in the sea, hold your breath, and swim down, and very quickly you'll feel the pressure squeezing inward. At just thirty-three feet down, a human free diver's lungs will compress to half the normal size, and by ninety-eight feet they shrink by three-quarters. People would not do at all well in the twilight zone or deeper. In the abyss, the water pressure is 400 times greater than at the surface, or more than 150 times the pressure inside a car tire.

Two other great challenges await creatures in the deep. Being so very big and dark, the abyss is a lonely, hungry place. It's not easy to find a mate, either roaming the wide seafloor or especially in boundless open waters. And with no photosynthesis taking place, no new food is being made (with some notable exceptions). Instead, most deep-sea animals ultimately rely on a thin trickle of organic matter that falls down from surface seas.

Japanese scientists in the 1950s were the first to watch particles falling through the open ocean, as they peered out the window of a cramped metal sphere, the undersea observation chamber called *Kuroshio*. The observing scientists, Noboru Susuki and Kenji Kato, named these particles "marine snow" and suggested they were part of a cycle in the oceans of "transmuting from water, to living matter and then to the earth." In other words, oceangoing animals could be eating marine snow. And indeed they do, although the fluffy particles are not nearly as nice as the name suggests, being made primarily of dead phytoplankton, zooplankton,★ and their droppings, glued together with a sticky substance formed from molecules secreted by plankton and bacteria—but food is food.

★ Zooplankton are the animal component of the plankton, including tiny, larval stages of fish and crustaceans.

Across most of the deep sea, marine snow is the only source of food for animals feeding at the bottom of the food web. Herds of sea cucumbers march across the abyssal plains searching for fresh flurries of marine snow; starfish and brittle stars are also among the snow-eating echinoderms of the abyss. Meanwhile, in open water, animals catch the snow as it falls. Munnopsid isopods are crustaceans with long, hairy arms, many times their body length, which they use to comb the water for snow. Tiny swimming snails known as sea butterflies cast wide sticky webs to catch falling flakes. And an unlikely addition to the guild of snow-catchers is an animal whose name conjures a terrifying vision. The vampire squid, *Vampyroteuthis infernalis*,★ has blood-red skin, domed red eyes, and a bone-white beak. When threatened, it wraps its eight arms around its body, like an umbrella turned inside out by a gust of wind, displaying rows of fearsome-looking hooks. Vampires are small cephalopods, less than one foot long, and most of the time they hold themselves perfectly still in deep midwater, unfurling a long, coiled filament that reaches eight times their body length. This narrow appendage could perhaps be mistaken for a lure or a sticky trap or a sensitive feeler like a tripwire, checking for the presence of nearby prey. But in fact, the filament just hangs there while snow particles trickle down and stick to it. From time to time, the vampire squid slowly reels in its filament and carefully wipes it over its arms. It packs the particles together and, using the dexterous hooks on its arms, passes snowballs toward its mouth and swallows. Then the vampire squid, with a diet unlike that of any other cephalopod, unfurls its filament and continues its peaceful business of gathering snow.

The problem is that only a very gentle shower of marine snow reaches the deep. At most, 2 percent of the food produced at the surface seas will sink to the deep seabed. For an equivalent situation on land,

---

★ Technically speaking this is not a squid but the only known species in the obscure cephalopod order Vampyromorpha.

there would be no grasses, trees, flowers, seeds, or fruit, just a scattering of crumbs falling from the sky—and the occasional dead whale.

༄

The enormous size of the deep ocean also means deep-sea biologists have their work cut out for them, in what is still a relatively new and small field of research. Perhaps five hundred people currently identify as full-time deep-sea biologists, and they share the task of studying this unthinkably huge and little-known space. If the entire deep-sea realm were divided up equally between them, each would get roughly half a million cubic miles of ocean to study.

Gaining access to the deep depends on technologies the likes of which were not even dreamed of in the days of Edward Forbes and the other Victorian biologists. Automatons fly through the unreachable deep like mechanical whales, using beams of sound to see through the dark; none have yet encountered a demon or deity, but they always find real living marvels. Technically known as autonomous underwater vehicles, or AUVs, these untethered submersibles commonly look like torpedoes, ten or fifteen feet long, fitted out with measuring devices, sonar, and cameras, and with guidance systems similar to those used in missiles. For the rare occasions these diving robots get lost, a message is usually written on the side reading: HARMLESS SCIENTIFIC INSTRUMENT. Scientists program AUVs with a planned mission, then let them go, unable to communicate directly through the seawater with the machines until they return from their dives. Other deep-diving submersibles are remotely operated via long cables and so offer a real-time view of the deep together with the ability to carefully gather and bring back samples of water, animals, and seabed rocks and sediments. Generally known as remote-operated underwater vehicles, or ROVs,* these machines were originally developed by the oil and gas industry to

---

* Throughout this book I refer to ROVs as submersibles, or subs.

build and maintain offshore drilling platforms and pipelines, with various designs rated as deep as 20,000 feet. There are also a few brave and lucky souls who get to go into the deep in person; submariners likely remain within the upper reaches of the twilight zone (although exact depths naval submarines descend to is classified), and scientists go much deeper.

There are far more astronomers than astronauts, and the same applies to deep-sea biologists and deep-sea aquanauts. Only a few submersibles in operation are capable of taking humans below the first 1,000 feet of ocean.★ Most famous is *Alvin*, the US Navy submersible run by the Woods Hole Oceanographic Institution in Massachusetts, which has been in operation in various guises since the 1960s, taking scientists into the abyss, two at a time, plus a pilot. The Japan Agency for Marine-Earth Science and Technology (JAMS-TEC) operates *Shinkai 6500*, which can bring researchers 21,325 feet, or 6,500 meters, down. The Chinese named their submersible *Jialong*, after an aquatic dragon who causes floods. Keeping humans alive in the deep sea is a far more expensive operation than deploying remotely operated and automated machines. That's why the relatively limited budgets committed to deep-sea research are generally spent on sending robots in place of humans to explore the deep.†️ Even so, deep-sea explorers have generally been a few steps ahead of their equivalents in space. People went into the deep before they went off planet. In the 1930s, American naturalist William Beebe and American inventor Otis Barton climbed inside a cramped metal bathysphere and had themselves lowered a half mile down into the twilight zone off the island of Bermuda, twenty years before Soviet

---

★ Should you have cash to spare, private submersibles are now commercially available that are rated to a few hundred feet. They look like spacecraft as imagined in the 1960s and are compact enough to fit on the deck of a superyacht.

†️ In 2019, the total budget for the National Oceanic and Atmospheric Administration (NOAA), which oversees American scientific research in all the earth's oceans, waterways, and atmosphere, was US$5.4 billion (an 8 percent drop from the previous year); meanwhile NASA's budget saw a 3.5 percent increase to $21.5 billion.

cosmonaut Yuri Gagarin was flung out of Earth's atmosphere into lower orbit. In 1960, humans reached the deepest point of the oceans for the first time, when Swiss oceanographer Jacques Piccard and US Navy lieutenant Don Walsh descended into the Mariana Trench inside the bathyscaphe *Trieste*. And while billionaires today still dream of going into space, some have already paid their way into the deep. In 2012, Canadian film director James Cameron ventured into the Mariana Trench in his one-person vessel *Deepsea Challenger*, followed seven years later by the American financier Victor Vescovo, who completed a personal mission to reach the deepest point in each of the five major ocean basins.

Astronauts do, however, regularly live for months in space, something that aquanauts have yet to equal, their brief visits to the deep lasting less than twenty-four hours at a time. Deep-sea research stations have not become a reality, and for now the chief way to visit and study the vast deep sea is to set off on large ships. Functioning as mobile research platforms, they float above the deep and support teams of biologists, geologists, chemists, physicists, and engineers, all working together to understand what lies below. Research cruises, as they're known, typically last weeks and months, as scientists explore wild, remote seas. And all the while, deep-sea biologists must leave their assumptions behind, learning to see what they weren't looking for and notice things that nobody was expecting.

The Whale and the Worm

"It always surprises me that they're not gone," said Craig McClain, executive director of the Louisiana Universities Marine Consortium (LUMCON), and co–chief scientist on the expedition to the Gulf of Mexico on the *Pelican*. Together we were watching the live footage beaming up from 6,600 feet below, showing the submersible picking up a chunk of wood from the deep seabed. You certainly couldn't leave something like that on a coral reef or a seagrass meadow and expect to come back and find it in the same spot; a strong current or a storm-stirred wave would have picked it up and swept it away. And yet, there was a log right where McClain had put it eighteen months previously, along with dozens more, down in the quiet, still deep.

Leaving blocks of wood at the bottom of the sea is something McClain has done before and for good reason. Previously, off the California coast, he threw thirty-six logs into the deep, 10,500 feet down, and five years later went back to pick them up. He found they were riddled with *Xylophaga*, deep-sea clams that have evolved a specialized diet consisting, as their scientific name suggests, entirely of wood.★ The clams dig their way into solid logs with the sharp edge of their shells, then eat the wood splinters, probably with the help of symbiotic bacteria living inside them. These bivalves pave

---

★ *Xylo* means "wood," and *phaga* is derived from *phagus*, "glutton."

the way for other animals to crawl into the bore holes: snails, worms, starfish, sea cucumbers, and crustaceans, many of them feeding on the clams' droppings or the clams themselves. In time, a unique wood-based ecosystem assembles. Most of the species, including the *Xylophaga* clams, are thought to live nowhere else and have come to rely entirely on rotting wood.

Down in the hungry deep, nothing goes to waste. Major rivers across the world sweep all manner of debris out to sea, including dead trees and fallen branches, which float away offshore before they eventually get waterlogged and sink. These sporadic lumps of carbon form connections between the land and the deep. They boost biodiversity, feeding the wood-only species, and form stepping-stones across the deep for creatures to hop between.

Working with Clifton Nunnally, a specialist in the Gulf's deep ecosystems, McClain has designed experiments to understand more about how these woody ecosystems operate. Larger wood blocks contain more food, but how is that food used? Do more species move in and form a more complex food web, or do a few bullish species muscle in and grow bigger? How does proximity between blocks influence the animals that live there? Knowing more about the fate of wood in the deep will help forecast what might happen to deep-sea biodiversity as changes take place above—if, for example, deforestation leads to less sunken wood, or if the climate crisis brings more hurricanes and increases flooding, which sweeps more trunks and branches into the deep.

To conduct these experiments on land would be a fairly straightforward affair, involving laying out logs of different sizes in particular arrangements. But McClain and Nunnally were doing this from a distance of more than a mile, in the pitch dark, using the submersible to deploy and recover logs, a laborious and time-consuming task.

Watched on the monitor screen in the ship's galley, the sub's robotic arms looked so space age. When the metal gripper fumbled and dropped one of the logs, it sank to the seabed slowly, as if gravity were a little weaker.* The submersible had to carefully pick up each log and place it in a fine mesh bag to catch all the animal hitchhikers; the bag then needed to be closed with a toggle, then carried over to the large metal cage—the benthic elevator—which would be winched up at the end of each twelve-hour dive to deliver the wood blocks to the *Pelican*.

In the meantime, I was in the ship's lab, writing tiny labels for masses of plastic, screw-capped jars, ready to receive and preserve little animals from the logs. I was focusing on the satisfying task of making my handwriting as small and neat as possible, when one of the crew poked his head around the door and announced that whale spouts had been spotted off the starboard bow. I climbed up to the bridge and joined First Mate Brennon Carney, who lent me his binoculars and pointed in the direction I should look. As my eyes adjusted to the bright sunshine, I scanned the waves and saw nothing, assuming I was already too late. Then there it was, a bushy puff of vapor. Whale breath.

More spouts went up closer to the ship, followed by gray bodies that peeped above the waves, each one with a short, knobbly dorsal fin. Closer still, I could see the vapor puffing to one side, the distinctive lopsided spout identifying the pod as sperm whales, which breathe through one nostril, on the left side of their snout.

One of the whales then jumped, its head blunt and square, small pectoral fins held flat against its flanks, as if they were hands stuffed in pockets, and the whale headbutted the sky. At roughly twenty feet long, dainty for a sperm whale, this was probably a female. She landed with a splash. A moment later the whale jumped again, and then a third and final time we saw her, as her tail fluke tipped up and slid straight down, into the water and out of sight.

---

* Earth's gravitation field varies from place to place (for several reasons, including the fact that our planet is not a perfect sphere), but it is not uniformly weaker in the deep sea. The simulated effect of low gravity comes from the buoyancy of salt water.

I darted back to the lab, where the video feed was showing the submersible picking up another block of wood, hoping the sperm whale might appear on-screen and peer into the camera at 6,600 feet, by no means an impossible depth for a sperm whale. One of the deepest-diving species of cetaceans,★ sperm whales, as adults, make regular dives for an hour or longer and spend more than three-quarters of their lives hunting, down in the twilight and midnight zones. They are denizens of a realm far from ours and yet, for centuries, sperm whales forged a close connection between human lives and the deep sea.

∽

Whale hunters were the first people to comprehend just how deep sperm whales can go. They would watch harpooned whales charge downward, dragging great loops of rope after them. In the nineteenth century, American whalers commonly used ropes 225 fathoms (1,350 feet) long. Often, they needed to join three or four such lengths together before the whale succumbed. Even if these fleeing sperm whales didn't dive directly downward, this was still a mile or more of rope. English naturalist George Wallich recounted in 1862 the true story from Captain William Scoresby of a harpooned whale dragging a whaleboat down so deep, all the air was squeezed from the wood and after it was hauled to the surface it no longer floated but sank back down like a stone.

In Herman Melville's *Moby Dick*, Captain Ahab converses with the decapitated head of a sperm whale as it hangs from the side of the whaling ship *Pequod*.

★ A few species of marine mammals join sperm whales at immense depths, including the record holders, Cuvier's beaked whales, originally discovered by French anatomist Georges Cuvier in 1823 as a fossilized skull from the Mediterranean. In 2014, a Cuvier's beaked whale was reported to dive to 9,816 feet off the southern California coast.

Speak, though vast and vulnerable head . . . tell us the secret thing that is in thee. Of all divers, thou hast dived the deepest. That head upon which the upper sun now gleams, has moved amid this world's foundations.

In the process of killing and butchering whales, hunters learned what tempts the kin of the mysterious white whale to swim so deep underwater. Opening up their stomachs has revealed that sperm whales will eat various types of fish, including sharks, but their favorite food by far is squid. Great quantities of hard, indigestible beaks accumulate inside sperm whales from many different squid species, including the two biggest—the giant and the colossal squid— although the most common ones are medium-size, at most five feet long. All the squid sperm whales eat, large and small, spend much of their time in the deep.

In order to hunt squid in the midnight and twilight zones, sperm whales bring their own supplies of oxygen, although not in their lungs—which reversibly collapse under the pressure at 1,000 feet underwater, aided by their folding rib cage—but stashed in their muscles and blood. One-fifth of a sperm whale's body weight is made up of the enormous volume of blood, which oozes, thick as molasses, through arteries and veins so big you could easily push your arm into one. The stickiness comes from masses of red blood cells packed with the oxygen-binding protein hemoglobin. Another protein, myoglobin, darkens their muscles to almost black. This too locks onto oxygen and releases it when and where it is needed. Whales, as well as otters, seals, dolphins, and other diving mammals, have ten times as much myoglobin in their muscles as an average human, so much that it should, in theory, clump together and stiffen their bodies into solid blocks. But these swimmers stay supple because they evolved a form of myoglobin with a slight positive charge that causes the molecules to repel each other. Marine mammals have a nonstick version of myoglobin.

Additional strategies help sperm whales eke out their oxygen supply. During dives, their heart rate slows to five thuds per minute, a reflex common to many diving mammals but taken to an extreme in sperm whales. (Immerse your face in a basin of cold water and your heart rate will also drop a little.) Such a low pulse rate slows the depletion of oxygen reserves and reduces the amount of oxygen used by the sperm whale's heart. Blood vessels close and shunt flow away from organs that are not needed during dives—kidneys, liver, intestines, and stomach—saving oxygen for the brain and the muscles.

Bringing so much oxygen with them on their dives is not just a matter of survival in the deep; it also gives sperm whales a major advantage. In their hunting grounds, typically around 3,300 feet down, oxygen in the water is in short supply. These regions across the oceans are known as the oxygen minimum zone or the shadow zone. To survive there, water-breathing animals like fish and squid must grasp whatever oxygen they can through their gills, but there can be so little, they become temporarily slow and stupid, limiting their ability to escape predators. Sperm whales, on the other hand, carry their own private oxygen supply, allowing them to operate at ease in these suffocating depths, outswimming and outsmarting their prey.

Getting themselves into the deep is one thing, but exactly how sperm whales hunt has long presented whale biologists with a conundrum. The whales push their gigantic heads through the water and catch prey in their narrow, underslung jaws, an unlikely setup for such successful hunters; sperm whales subdue between one hundred and five hundred prey animals a day, a take weighing, on average, a ton. Various theories have been put forward over the years for how sperm whales operate in the deep, among them that they hang motionless head down waiting to ambush a passing squid, or they lure prey in with their pale-colored mouths or maybe listen for them. Eventually, early twenty-first century studies, involving pressure sensors, motion detectors, and hydrophones fixed to diving whales, confirmed that sperm whales are not ambush predators, waiting stock-still for prey to come by, but they actively chase their targets and track them with their own particular, noisy way of seeing through the dark.

In contrast to the lyrical, haunting song of a humpback whale, the sperm whale's sound is more like the crackle of a roll of adhesive tape being unwound, and it makes an impressive racket. This is the most powerful sound in the animal kingdom, emanating from the sperm whale's huge, block-shaped head, which is, in fact, an overgrown nose. The sources of its noises are snorts of air, pushed along the right nostril tube, which isn't connected to the outside; the air flows past a pair of fleshy flaps, known as the monkey lips, which vibrate like a human larynx. Sound pulses then bounce around inside the giant nose, where a series of fluid-filled chambers shape and focus the vibrations and direct them into the water. In the 1980s, the so-called biological big bang hypothesis suggested that sperm whales hunt with sound, acoustically debilitating their prey, but subsequent studies have shown the calls are not loud enough for that. Instead, sperm whales search for and pursue their prey using bursts of echolocating sound, like giant, aquatic versions of bats.

When a sperm whale's hunt begins, it sends volleys of clicks through the deep, one or two per second. This long-range sonar interrogates the darkness, leaving any squid within thousands of feet nowhere to hide. The whale listens for echoes bouncing off hard body parts, such as a squid's snapping, parrot-like beak and the rings of teeth arranged on suckers all along eight arms and at the end of two tentacles.* Approaching a target, the hunting whale quickens its clicks until they blend together into a creak, like a rusty door hinge. Bats do a similar thing, adjusting their acoustic gaze as they prepare to swoop for an insect and generating more sound beams to make out extra details of their fluttering prey.

Squid seem oblivious to the whales' clicks and creaks but might sense ripples in the water, and so as it approaches the sperm whale stops beating its tail and glides onward through the dark, stalking its

---

* The tough protein that makes up squid sucker teeth has been named suckerin. Further evidence that sperm whales hunt giant squid are the circular sucker scars, several inches across, sometimes found on whale skin.

prey. When the moment comes to attack, the whale puts on a burst of speed, moving up to twenty-three feet per second. It twists and turns, firing more shots of sound and chasing the squid as it tries to escape; once within striking distance, the whale brakes and sharply turns, sucking in the squid and swallowing it whole.

Hunting continues for an hour or longer as sperm whales go from squid to squid until their oxygen begins to drain away. When the time comes to recharge their reserves, they swim silently upward, breach the waves with their noses, breathe out and in, shedding carbon dioxide and letting oxygen soak back into their muscles and blood. And then, after only eight or nine minutes, sperm whales are ready to go back down.

∽

Around the era when *Moby Dick* was set, in the mid-nineteenth century, the commercial whale hunt gathered pace through the world's oceans, driven by demand from the oil industry. Blubber from shallow-swimming baleen whales—the fins, humpbacks, seis, and blues—was flensed from their carcasses, boiled down, and used as cheap lamp oil that stank when it burned. Sperm whales were targeted not for their fatty skin but for the more lucrative contents of their noses. One of the nasal chambers through which echolocation sounds pass is the spermaceti organ. Whalers would cut a hole in sperm whales' heads and scoop out gallons of spermaceti, the valuable liquid gold encased inside.* Spermaceti made the cleanest, brightest candles. It lit the streets of Europe and North America and powered

---

* This is the material that gave the sperm whale its erroneous common name; both male and female sperm whales have noses filled with this stuff, which is definitely not sperm but plays a role in shaping beams of sound. Whalers also checked sperm whales' stomachs for the congealed remains of squid beaks smothered in waxy secretions. A mature version of this substance will occasionally wash up on coasts, long after a sperm whale expelled it and it floated for years through the ocean, altering chemically in the sun and waves, forming the unlikely but incredibly valuable perfumery ingredient ambergris.

the bright beams of lighthouses. All this light was a distillation of energy harnessed in the deep. Via their squid-based diet, sperm whales linked the lighthouses that illuminated the surface waves and the dark depths below, the "world's foundations" as Melville put it.

Vast quantities of whale oil and spermaceti have flowed from the deep into the human world. Up until 1900, the total number of sperm whales killed globally was three hundred thousand, each individual providing 500 gallons or so of spermaceti. Then the industry entered its most aggressive phase, abandoning sail power and hand-thrown spears in favor of steam-powered ships and explosive harpoons. Twentieth-century demand for whale oil remained strong, even after kerosene overtook it as a source of domestic lighting. Whale oil was used as an industrial lubricant, as automatic transmission fluid in North American cars, in lipsticks, glues, and crayons. During the First World War, soldiers smeared their feet with whale oil, hoping to waterproof them to stave off the misery of trench foot. And in 1930s Europe, almost half of all margarine spreads were made from hydrogenated whale oil. Spermaceti also kept its uses, as a superior lubricant that doesn't go rancid or corrode metal and that stays slippery at high temperatures, allowing machinery to operate at ever faster speeds.

Not until the late 1970s did people begin to turn into whale advocates. The Save the Whales campaign was one of the most successful efforts in history to shift public opinion about wild species. Within a few short years, whales were transformed from an industrial resource into treasured, protected wildlife. The success of the campaign was thanks in large part to discoveries of intricate whale behaviors and recordings of the entrancing songs of humpbacks, which convinced people to love them.

A global moratorium on commercial whaling came into force in 1986, but before then, in the twentieth century alone, hunters killed 2.9 million whales. Of those, 761,523 were recorded as sperm whales.

It's hard to say exactly how well sperm whale populations have recovered in the decades since the commercial whale hunt was called off, given the difficulties of conducting a head count on animals that spend so long deep underwater. In 2002, the world's leading sperm whale expert, Hal Whitehead, took the best estimates of sperm whale numbers, based on counts that marine biologists made across a quarter of the species' global range. Then he tested three different ways of scaling up those data: by total habitat area, by the availability of whale food in the oceans (i.e., squid), and by analyzing the number of whales hunted in the nineteenth century. All three methods led Whitehead to a similar estimate, pinning the number of living sperm whales at roughly 360,000. In the twentieth century, humans killed more than twice the number of sperm whales that remain alive today.

∼

Whales are no longer killed by humans in the hundreds of thousands, but their deaths can still draw them closer to human lives, bringing with them secrets of the deep. When whales become trapped in shallow waters or stranded by the tide on a beach, human spectators gather around to watch and size themselves up against the biggest animals that have ever evolved. And with a whale fully exposed on land, details are revealed that were hidden before.

A stranded sperm whale on a beach lies on its side, one eye pressed into the sand, the other staring up at the sky. It appears flattened, its body squashed. You couldn't roll a beached sperm whale onto its belly, as it would flop right back over; in their natural realm, supported by water, they can, of course, float upright with ease. The body is elephant gray, smooth at the front and wrinkled farther along, as if excess skin had been cinched backward. If the whale is a male, you will know it: as the innards decompose and inflate with gases, the huge penis is pushed out and dangles onto the sand.

The whale's pink and white jaw hangs open. You can peer into the dark throat where so many squid have vanished. The lower jaw, you'll see, has a row on each side of stubby teeth that splay outward like caterpillar feet. The upper jaw has a row of holes and no teeth. They haven't fallen out; they were never there in the first place. What sperm whales use their lower teeth for is not exactly clear. Toothless individuals still appear to be well fed, so perhaps eating is not their purpose. Male sperm whales are commonly covered in scratches and scars, hints that they fight rivals with their teeth.

When stranded live whales can't be coaxed back to sea, scientists arrive to learn what they can from the dead bodies. The key question to ask is, *why is it here?*

Sometimes the cause of death is obvious. In 1997, a dead sperm whale drifted into a Scottish estuary, the Firth of Forth. An autopsy revealed the whale had a ruptured penile urethra, an injury grave enough to have killed him. Increasingly, dead whales are found with their guts stuffed with plastic. In 2018, a male pilot whale got in trouble in a canal in Thailand and coughed up five plastic bags before dying in the arms of his human rescuers; he was later found to have eighty bags in his stomach. More often, though, some mystery remains as to why a whale, a masterful swimmer and ocean navigator, becomes stranded in water too shallow to keep it afloat.

The noisy ocean may contribute to whale stranding. Thundering clamor from military sonar and the seismic search for oil and gas below the seabed seems to cause deep-diving whales to panic and flee to the surface. Like human scuba divers who come up too quickly, whales can suffer decompression sickness, or the bends, with nitrogen bubbles forming in their tissues, blocking blood vessels and choking lungs.

A natural phenomenon that begins far from the oceans could also lead whales astray. In 2015, around Christmastime, a spectacular aurora borealis lit up the northern skies. Over the following month, twenty-nine sperm whales stranded on coasts fringing the North Sea. This enclosed sea, a notorious sperm whale trap, shallows progressively to the south and seems to confuse the animals, and the

Christmas stranding was the biggest such event ever recorded. Their giant bodies were found on beaches in Germany, Britain, the Netherlands, and France. A researcher at Kiel University in Germany, Klaus Vanselow, wondered whether phenomena above and beneath the waves were linked. Violent solar storms had been raging, with coronal mass ejections from the sun sending out volleys of charged particles that knocked the earth's magnetic field out of kilter and created the stunning northern lights that Christmas.

It's not known for sure whether whales navigate by sensing magnetic fields, as bees, pigeons, and sea turtles do, but it seems likely. Assuming they do, Vanselow and colleagues worked out that the 2015 solar storms shifted the earth's magnetic field by enough to trick whales into thinking they were hundreds of miles from their actual location. This could explain why so many young, fit male sperm whales veered into the North Sea instead of heading for the deep, squid-rich Norwegian Sea, where they normally spend time hunting. By the time the magnetic field returned to normal, the whales would not have been able to retrace their path easily.

It's an explanation that can't be fully tested, but many experts agree the theory is valid. Other navigating animals seem to get confused by solar storms. Pigeon races take longer, and fewer honeybees make it back to their hives. And in an earlier study, Vanselow found that in years with stronger solar activity and more solar storms, more sperm whales stranded in the North Sea than at other times.

∽

Most whales never know what it feels like to leave their buoyant realm and collapse under their own weight on a beach, because they die at sea, far from shore. Commonly, whales die from disease or starvation, and their bodies are depleted of oily reserves, so they readily sink. When a descending carcass reaches about 330 feet, the pressure is enough to compress any gases released by decomposing bacteria, and there is no more risk it will float back up. From there, a dead whale goes on one final dive into the deep, where a very different fate awaits it.

"Nobody will ever give you money to go searching the bottom of the ocean for a dead whale," says Bob Vrijenhoek, an evolutionary biologist retired from the Monterey Bay Aquarium Research Institute (MBARI)★ in California. But as Vrijenhoek knows, sometimes a dead whale is found by accident.

In 2002, he led a team of researchers that made an unexpected discovery in the deep canyon of Monterey Bay. They were searching for beds of clams using sonar on a remote-operated submersible. At around 10,000 feet, the sub's cameras showed something that was obviously not a clam bed but the skeleton of a large whale lying on the seabed. The scientists gazed at the bones, which looked to be covered in a red shag-pile carpet. The sub's pilot reached in with a robotic arm and took a piece of fuzzy red vertebra to bring back to the ship. Later on, the team called the whale Ruby.

"Among us, we had a hundred years of experience combined of looking at the seafloor," says Shana Goffredi, at the time a Research Associate at MBARI. Yet none of the team's deep-sea experts could identify the creatures carefully dissected from one of Ruby's bones. Somewhat wormy in appearance, each one had a pink, inch-long body nestled inside a cylindrical tube made of mucus. Sticking out of one end of the tube was a crown of red feathery tentacles, creating the fuzzy carpet effect. At the other end, hidden inside the bone, was something far stranger: a clump of vivid green branching roots. Closer inspection revealed that these animals had no mouth, no guts, and no anus. If these were worms, they were unlike any the scientists had ever seen before.

Back in the lab, Goffredi removed tissue samples for DNA sequencing, which classified these animals as polychaetes,† members of a

---

★ Generally pronounced *embaree*.

† Pronounced *polly-keets*.

large class of marine worms that includes common species from beaches and coasts such as sandworms and lugworms. The genetic code was an unmistakable match. Next the team at MBARI packaged up some of Ruby's preserved worms and sent them to Greg Rouse, a leading polychaete expert, then at the South Australia Museum in Adelaide. He at first found nothing to convince him these animals were indeed polychaetes. They were all females, with ovisacs stuffed with eggs, and they all lacked typical polychaete features, including a body divided into distinct segments.

Eventually, Rouse noticed the females were holding a secret that gave away their true identity and made the story of these green-rooted worms even stranger. Peering inside the females' tubes, he found what he at first thought were packages of sperm, but then he realized they were tiny males that never grow up, equipped with tiny hooks, called chaetae—not a feature of sperm but a distinctive character of these worms (hence *poly*chaetes). Inside her tube, each female has her own resident harem of dwarf males, tens or hundreds of them, hooked on with their chaetae and waiting to fertilize her eggs.

Two years after the discovery, Rouse, Goffredi, and Vrijenhoek, published a paper in the journal *Science* describing a new genus of deep-sea polychaete worms, with dwarf males, red feathers, and green roots. They named the genus *Osedax*, from Latin words *os*, meaning "bone," and *edax*, meaning "devourer," because they were convinced the worms weren't just sitting on Ruby's skeleton but that those green roots were somehow helping them to eat her bones.

Early on, the new species was nicknamed the zombie worm, a label that Rouse doesn't think makes much sense. "I understand it's catchy," he says, "but zombies eat brains. They're not interested in your bones." Nevertheless, the name caught on, and soon *Osedax* was picked up by the media and became notorious as the bone-eating zombie worm.

❧

By the time the rest of the world came to hear about *Osedax*, biologists already knew that dead whales give rise to their own unique ecosystems, materializing like ephemeral islands on the seabed. In the 1990s, these came to be known as "whale falls," although for a whale carcass, the falling part is just the start of things.

Whenever dead whales sink into the deep, they bring with them tremendous consignments of food. As whale hunters have known for centuries, much of a whale carcass is made of energy-rich oils, in the blubber and deep inside the bones. For abyssal animals to scavenge the same amount of nourishment as is carried in a forty-ton whale carcass (and whales can be much bigger than that), they would need to roam a couple of acres of regular deep seabed for a century or two. Despite being such a rich feast, a whale fall is not a jumbled free-for-all but an orderly meal. Separate courses are eaten by distinct groups of dining companions among the hundreds of species that take their turn at the banquet.

First, the scavenging animals swim and march in, mostly fish and crustaceans with keen senses that let them sniff out distant food. Three-foot-long hagfish look as small as leeches as they squirm across a giant whale. Sleeper sharks tear off chunks of blubber. Crabs join this first wave of whale scavengers, which together can strip 100 pounds of blubber and muscle in a day.

When the flesh is gone and the skeleton clean, a second company of animals arrives. These snails, crabs, and worms feed on scraps littered across the seabed by the sloppy-eating scavengers. *Osedax* worms settle on bare bones. After several years, a whale fall has become a busy, bustling ecosystem, home to tens of thousands of animals.

Much of what is known about these ecosystems and the waves of feasting animals that arrive comes from whale falls that scientists make for themselves. Rather than hoping to bump into a dead whale in the deep, it's a lot easier to refloat and deliberately sink one that has stranded and died on shore, creating an "implanted" whale fall.⋆ To help find the sunken whale later, a sonar beacon is fixed to it, which responds to a sonar ping from the ship, sending a return signal. "It's a hotter-colder type of game," says Vrijenhoek. Once it's found, a deep-diving submersible allows the scientists to observe the great feast unfolding.

꩜

With the creation and study of implanted whale falls, scientists have discovered more than 120 previously unknown animals, including dozens of species of *Osedax*. The discovery of these bone-eating worms is a classic case of how deep-sea science often proceeds. Typically, scientists operate with a degree of confirmation bias, seeking to understand more about what they already know exists. It just happened that the skeleton of Ruby the whale was infested with one of the biggest species of *Osedax*, at an inch long. Following that chance encounter, scientists knew what they were looking for. The oceans, it turns out, are full of bone-eating worms, many of them far smaller and harder to spot than the original species. There is a bone-eating snot flower, *Osedax mucofloris*, found off Sweden, and *Osedax jabba*, originally found on bone fragments scattered around Ruby the whale, which has a twist in its plump trunk resembling the tail of Jabba the Hutt from the Star Wars movies. Other new species have been found off New Zealand, Australia, Costa Rica, Antarctica, Japan, and Brazil.

Finding *Osedax* has done more than merely add to the catalogue of known species in the deep. From the beginning, the people studying these polychaetes have been filling in details of their lives. These peculiar worms face the same challenges as all deep-sea animals: to find food and a mate in the hungry, lonely depths. Their situation is even more challenging because they rely on dead carcasses that

---

⋆ A standard technique for sinking a dead whale involves fixing to the carcass a giant metal T-bar stacked with iron railway wheels.

drop sporadically and unannounced from above. But as many other species of the deep have done, *Osedax* worms have evolved some especially unusual ways to survive.

✍

Nobody yet knows exactly how bone-eating worms move through the deep sea or how they locate a skeleton. One thing we do know is that when an *Osedax* larva does find a bone, timing is everything.

Those that happen to arrive first and land on a piece of bare bone will transform into females; they grow bigger, sprout roots, drill into the bone, start eating, make eggs, and wait for males to find them. Larvae that find a bone already fully occupied will likely land on the body of a female worm that got there first. These latecomers become males. They halt their growth, crawl inside a female's tube, hook themselves in place with their chaetae, and settle in with any other males already there. Never again will these males venture outside; they will live out their short lives, not eating but running down the yolk supplied by their mothers, converting the energy into sperm. Once the yolk is all used up the males die.

Dwarf males have evolved in other animals, usually when food is scarce and mates are tricky to find. Deep-sea anglerfish have taken this option, with pinky-size males clamped to the outside of football-size females. This limits the number of young a male can produce, because he can't fertilize eggs from multiple females. But the payoff for sticking with one mate is a guarantee of at least some offspring, rather than the far riskier option of wandering around the deep in the vague hope of encountering more partners.

✍

To survive on an all-bone diet is an intricate procedure. First, the worms secrete acid from their green roots, melting the bones. Then the roots release an enzyme that digests the bone's protein matrix, made of collagen, providing them with the bulk of their nutrition.

When Shana Goffredi, now a professor at Occidental College in Los Angeles, first examined *Osedax* from Ruby the whale, she immediately suspected something else might be going on inside those green roots. Goffredi specializes in symbionts, the organisms that live in close association with one another, often animals with single-celled microbes living inside them. A tip-off she has learned to spot is when an animal has no obvious way to feed itself. With no mouth or guts, *Osedax* definitely ticked that box. Another hallmark of a symbiotic animal is an unusual body tissue that could be a storehouse for microbes. Sure enough, when Goffredi looked inside the peculiar green roots, she found them loaded with bacteria. More than fifteen years later, though, it's still not entirely clear what exact role those bacteria play in the lives of *Osedax* worms.

A strong possibility is that the bacteria provide a vital nutrient that's otherwise missing in a diet of bones. Various animals use symbiotic microbes as an inbuilt source of vitamin tablets. Aphids, for example, get plenty of carbohydrates from the sap they suck out of plants but not enough protein; they obtain two key amino acids from bacteria housed in pouches in their abdomen. Goffredi thinks the bacteria inside *Osedax* could provide the missing amino acid tryptophan, helping these bone-eating worms get a full and balanced diet.

∽

The bone-devouring habits of *Osedax* have helped to provide an answer to the question of which came first, the worm or the whale.

The first animals with backbones (broadly referred to as fish) evolved in water; they breathed it, swam in it, raised their young in it. Eventually, some left the water, giving rise to all the vertebrates that fly, hop, trot, and crawl across land today, the amphibians, reptiles, birds, and mammals. Then, around fifty million years ago, one group of mammals, which originally looked rather like large wolves with hooves, embarked on an evolutionary pathway leading right back to where their ancestors came from. For the subsequent ten million years, this lineage of mammalian species became increasingly adapted to an aquatic life: some had otter-like webbed feet and swam in shallow coastal seas; later species lost their back legs and evolved flippers and fluked tails and took to open waters; their ears evolved modifications to hear underwater, and their nostrils moved to the top of the skull and became blowholes. In one of evolution's greatest U-turns, with these vertebrates' return to the water, the era of great whales began.

Osedax may have evolved at around the same time, in response to the arrival of so many large skeletons on the seabed. It's a theory backed up by another genetic study carried out by Bob Vrijenhoek and colleagues. Comparing DNA sequences of *Osedax* and other worms, the team constructed a molecular clock. This virtual chronometer winds back time and indicates when species may have split apart. "Calibrating a molecular clock is extremely tricky," Vrijenhoek says. Without fossils to pin dates on branches of the evolutionary tree, it's difficult to know how fast the molecular clocks have been ticking.

One version of the *Osedax* clock sets the genus's origins at around forty-five million years ago, not so long after the first whales appeared. This whales-then-worms hypothesis makes for a tempting story. But the story of the bone-eating worms is more complex. A second *Osedax* clock, calibrated with a different set of living species, ticks much more slowly.* It's been running more than eighty million years longer and pushes back the origin of *Osedax* into the Cretaceous period. This offers up the enticing possibility that *Osedax* was already there by the time whales and their skeletons showed up, in which case *Osedax* had previously been eating the bones of other giant vertebrates that roamed the oceans long before whales arrived.

---

* The species used to calibrate the first clock were shallow marine invertebrates; the second used deep-sea hydrothermal vent worms.

Paleontologists couldn't hope to find fossils of soft *Osedax* worms, but in museum collections of old bones lay the chance of finding telltale holes the worms left behind. Plesiosaurs were promising candidates, the extinct oceangoing reptiles that looked like Loch Ness monsters, with long necks, small heads, and four paddles for fins. In 2015, a hundred-million-year-old plesiosaur humerus bone was placed in a CT scanner, a machine more often used in hospitals to produce three-dimensional scans of living human bodies. Sure enough, the intricate scans showed in exquisite detail the distinctive *Osedax*-like holes punched in the surface of the ancient bone, as well as lumpy cavities inside of the right shape to match those made by the living worms' acid secretions. It's unlikely that *Osedax* would have colonized old bones that had already fossilized, because there would have been no collagen left for them to eat, just bones turned to stone. These holes must have been made shortly after the plesiosaur died and fell to the seabed.

The truth about the origins of bone-eating worms had been there all along. It took a prediction based on cutting-edge genetic tools combined with the latest scanning technology to decode this ancient secret, locked up in bones. The slow-ticking clock is likely telling the correct evolutionary time. When whales evolved, *Osedax* worms were already there, and they had been waiting for a while.

A final twist in the story is what has come to be known as the *Osedax* effect. Each individual worm is tiny, but the worms have lived in such huge numbers and for so many millions of years that *Osedax* have left an indelible but invisible mark on the fossil record. The worms not only punched holes in ancient bones but demolished entire skeletons, shrinking the pool of bones that could undergo the unlikely process of rapid burial and fossilization. Today, the halls of natural history museums would perhaps have more ancient aquatic skeletons on display if it hadn't been for these abundant bone-eating worms.

An unusual deep-sea visitor came into view on the monitor screens of the *Pelican* in the Gulf of Mexico. I walked across the ship's back deck and stepped into the submersible's control room, the nerve center of the activities on the seabed. Inside it was cool, dark, and a little humid after a long day's work. "More Than a Feeling," by Boston, was playing on the stereo. Two submersible pilots, Travis Kolbe and Jason Tripp, were sitting in ergonomic office chairs in front of a bank of six screens. Behind them, Craig McClain and Clifton Nunnally were giving instructions. Kolbe twisted his arm in the control, and more than six and a half thousand feet below, a jointed, rotating robot arm moved in synchrony.

On the screens, a scaly body swung into view, suspended by a rope harness. "Just taking an alligator for a walk," said Tripp, who was controlling the sub's position with a second set of controls. The dead six-and-a-half-foot alligator came to a rest belly-down on the seabed, a rope fixed to a forty-pound metal weight anchored it in place.

Several days previously, when the ship's chef saw three dead alligators in the *Pelican*'s walk-in refrigerator, nestled in with two weeks' worth of provisions, she had inhaled a long gasp and said, "I *love* science." The reason we brought the alligators with us was to study what happens to their carcasses when they fall into the deep sea. After hurricanes and floods in the Mississippi Delta, alligators often drown and get swept away in the deluge, like branches and trees, and they've been spotted miles offshore. McClain and Nunnally wanted to discover the fate of the dead gators and find out whether a particular entourage of scavengers and bone eaters assembles on the bodies of big, dead reptiles. American alligators,★ as well as caimans, saltwater crocodiles, and various other reptilian coastal dwellers, send considerable parcels of carbon into the deep when

---

★ Specimens of these American alligators (*Alligator mississippiensis*) were obtained by special permit from a humane culling program in Louisiana.

they die. They also happen to be the closest living analogies to ichthyosaurs, plesiosaurs, and mosasaurs, the giant marine reptiles that once roamed the oceans, and thus offer scientists the chance to glimpse at ecosystems from the ancient abyss.

Less than twenty-four hours after deploying the first alligator, we sent back the submersible to view it and saw something dramatic had clearly happened. Giant isopods, at least ten of them, were busy eating the alligator. Picture a close relative of the pill bug that hides under rocks or garden pots, but pale pink and the size of a football. Giant isopods evolved their size precisely so they could take advantage of the kind of large, unpredictable meal that an alligator provides. The crustaceans' bodies store massive fat reserves, in the manner of a camel's hump, which see them through lean times. One specimen kept in a Japanese aquarium didn't eat for four years, despite the food on offer.

In almost no time at all, giant isopods had sniffed out the alligator carcass we had left on the deep seabed, swum in, and begun to chew through the softer areas of hide, in the armpits and belly. And clearly there was a lot of food to be had. We watched as one isopod gorged itself silly and swam off in a daze, crashing headfirst into the seabed.

A month later, the team went back to check on the second alligator. By that time, the scavengers had stripped it down to a clean skeleton, and it had grown red and fuzzy, colonized by bone-eating worms. A bone retrieved from that skeleton later revealed the worms to be two new species of *Osedax*, the first to have been discovered in the Gulf of Mexico. These could be the descendants of worms that long ago specialized in chewing on the bones of ancient, reptilian sea monsters.

When McClain and Nunnally went back to check on the third alligator, it was nowhere to be seen. Just eight days after it had been laid to rest on the seabed, there was no sign of it, except for a depression in the sediment and drag marks leading across the abyss.

Thirty feet away lay the metal weight, and the thick rope that had tied it to the alligator was bitten clean through.

The alligator-grabbing scavenger could have been either of the two large, deepwater sharks known to be in the Gulf, a sixgill or a Greenland shark. At least thirteen feet long as adults, both are large enough to tackle a whole alligator and have strong enough jaws to have bitten through the rope.

There's also another possibility. Shortly after the alligator went missing, a different research team was working not far away, using a drop-down camera to hunt for another predator that operates in the deep. After watching hours of footage, Edith Widder, chief executive officer of the Ocean Research and Conservation Association in Florida, finally spotted what she had been looking for, when something long and pale reached into view. It splayed out and revealed a cluster of enormous tentacles and arms covered in suckers, belonging to an animal at least ten feet long. There's no way we'll ever know for sure, but perhaps the third alligator was grabbed in those strong arms, and the rope sliced in two by the sharp beak of that very same giant squid.

Caught in a Jelly Web

Several days into the research expedition to the Gulf of Mexico on the *Pelican*, I no longer had to make a conscious effort to stay standing upright. I even began to enjoy the feeling of being much heavier and then lighter, in turns, as the waves rolled by. There was a peaceful efficiency of this small, simple world, where the only other signs of human life were the oil rigs perched on the horizon like giant, metal mosquitoes. In quiet moments when I wasn't needed elsewhere, I would climb up to the bow, hang my head over the side, and check on the textures and colors of the ocean, which changed hour by hour. A gentle crosswind would etch the surface into a pattern like tree bark in motion, or smooth it over to a sheeny gloss. The offshore colors were always more intense than those of coastal seas, with the subtropical sun soaking through 3,000 feet of pellucid blue and no seabed within reach to reflect off, just the black water below.

The submersible's cable, looped over the pulley and plunging straight down, reminded me of dioramas of fishing scenes in museums, the way the intricate model boats float on a transparent resin sea, cut away to show their miniature fishing lines and nets lowered down to catch tiny model fish. A scaled version of the *Pelican* would need a display case stretching through several stories of the building to show how far down our submersible roamed. In the water, there would be model sperm whales chasing model squid, and jellyfish that glow by themselves when the lights in the room are switched off. And perhaps there would be a miniature version of me out on deck, contemplating the seabed so far beneath my feet, and all the water in between.

෴

Midwater can be the hungriest and loneliest place in the deep. It's not easy finding food and mates in the enormous, three-dimensional space of the water column between the surface and the abyss. Down on the seabed, animals at least have a surface to explore and a chance to find accumulated piles of fallen food. In open water there is much more searching to be done or waiting patiently for prey and mates to come by.

Common in midwater are animals with delicate, gelatinous bodies. Some look like flying saucers, some like tangled feather boas, and some like round-bodied spiders with too many spindly legs; there are glistening spheres with rainbows flickering across them and elaborate glass chandeliers complete with glittering lights.

The stillness of the deep encourages these gossamer bodies to evolve. Here they thrive beyond the reach of waves and tides, where only gentle currents flow by. Being made of jelly is a winning strategy for all these members of the plankton, the wandering organisms that never touch a solid surface and spend their whole lives afloat, supported by their watery world.★ Tissues made of jelly, or gelatin, a thin mix of water and the protein collagen, constitute a simple way of making a body: it's efficient to operate because it floats and comes with a low metabolic cost. Jelly-based creatures take an energy-saving approach to life, cutting their need to feed and raising their chances of survival in the hungry expanses of the deep.

★ The term *plankton* stems from the Ancient Greek word *planktos*, meaning "wandering," and refers generally to species that live in open water and are unable to swim against strong tides and currents.

This flimsy life does, however, have its drawbacks. In midwater, some animals are so dainty that a nearby swish of a fish's tail is enough to make them fall apart. And their frailty makes them difficult for scientists to study. Finding and catching these delicate animals is rather like chasing ghosts. When caught in nets, jelly animals get shredded and collapse. And with deep-adapted cells, they don't do well when brought to the surface where the pressure is hugely reduced; they can simply melt away.

Despite the difficulty of catching them intact, many major groups of gelatinous animals were first discovered in deep midwater more than a hundred years ago. One scientist's name appears next to the monikers of the numerous fragile, deep-sea animals that he described and named. He made a great many contributions to science but is perhaps best remembered today for his artwork, which brought these ethereal creatures firmly into the public eye.

∼

Ernst Haeckel was born in Germany in 1834. He trained as a physician in Berlin, but his passions lay in exploring the natural world and also in art. During his medical training, he took classes on Helgoland, a small island off the German coast. Years later, looking back on that trip, Haeckel wrote that "nothing exerted such a powerful force of attraction on me amongst the myriad animal forms, of which I had not seen living specimens until then, as the medusae." These medusae, otherwise known as jellyfish, continued to captivate him, scientifically and artistically, and in time they helped to draw his attention into the deep.

Haeckel worked for a short while as a doctor in Berlin but soon turned instead to zoology. Initially he specialized in radiolarians, microscopic sea creatures—not animals nor plants nor fungi—that live inside glassy skeletons sculpted from silica. Radiolarians were the first marine species to unite Haeckel's love of science and art. In 1862, he published a long scientific monograph on them, including dozens of exquisitely detailed drawings depicting these creatures, like living snowflakes.

The following decade, diaphanous, gelatinous animals floated back into Haeckel's life. In 1876, the British ship HMS *Challenger* returned from its global, two-year oceanographic voyage, led by chief scientist Charles Wyville Thomson of the Royal Society in London, and brought back yet more evidence disproving Edward Forbes's azoic theory of the deep. Haeckel had not been on board the *Challenger*, but he took on the task of studying the collection of gelatinous animals that had been carefully collected with nets towed through the water and buckets dipped below the waves.

With hundreds of preserved specimens to work with from all around the world, Haeckel opened up a whole new view of the ocean and uncovered a multitude of delicate life-forms that waft through the deep. He named some six hundred species of gelatinous plankton, some so unique he assigned them new branches on the evolutionary tree of life.* He revealed that many deep-dwelling animals, while looking like jellyfish, are in fact something altogether different. And he brought many of these previously unseen, unknown animals of the deep to the public's attention.

In 1899, Haeckel began publishing his most famous, nonscientific work, a series of booklets called *Kunstformen der Natur* (published in English as *Art Forms in Nature*). Each booklet featured ten ornate illustrations of animals, plants, or fungi. His aim was to connect people with nature by offering a glimpse of what scientists and naturalists saw when they discovered these organisms in the wild or watched them under a microscope, or in the case of the gelatinous creatures, what he imagined they looked like as they drifted through the deep sea. Across many pages, Haeckel depicted assemblies of animals he discovered in the *Challenger* collection, reimagining them in their

---

* Haeckel named numerous orders, classes, and genera of gelatinous animals that are still considered scientifically valid today.

living state, before their delicate forms collapsed and their colors were sapped in preserving fluids.

Only some, strictly speaking, are true jellyfish—the scyphozoans—including familiar varieties that inhabit shallow, coastal seas and others that roam much deeper. A page of scyphozoans in *Kunstformen der Natur* depicts among them *Desmonema annasethe*, which Haeckel discovered and named after his first wife, Anna Sethe. It has a large blue and red body, a fringe of arms like lacy petticoats, and trailing tentacles, their movement frozen, but you might easily imagine it will continue to twirl and pulse its way off the page and into your lap. What Haeckel's drawing doesn't show is that there is more to life for a true jellyfish than just this flamboyant stage, known as the medusa. Scyphozoans spend a lot of time looking completely different, as a small polyp stuck to the seabed. Resembling tiny flowers, the polyps show their affinity to their close relatives, the corals and anemones (all belong to the same phylum of animals, the Cnidaria★). Over the course of years or even decades of seabed life, polyps periodically shed scores of tiny swimming medusae. These quickly grow into full-size adults that hunt and eat and mate with each other. Female and male medusae live for a few months, during which time they release eggs and sperm into the water, sometimes on a daily basis when conditions are favorable, with enough food. Their fertilized eggs develop into minute larvae, which settle onto the seabed and transform into new polyps. And so, the scyphozoan life cycle goes round and round, from medusa to polyp and back again.

Other, more obscure varieties of cnidarian jellies that Haeckel discovered and named appear in *Kunstformen der Natur*. Narcomedusae and trachymedusae, both new orders of cnidarians Haeckel described, are depicted with smooth-domed bodies, tentacles like strands of beads, and a tube mouth hanging down, blooming into flowerlike lips. Differing from the more cosmopolitan scyphozoans,

---

★ Pronounced *nigh-daria* and derived from the Ancient Greek word for "nettle."

these animals live almost exclusively in deep midwater, where they skip the seabed-bound polyp stage entirely and their fertilized eggs transform directly into mini medusae. But these tiny jellies aren't always immediately ready for life on their own. For a while, some young hitchhike inside the body of an adult medusa, stealing its food and waiting until the time comes to swim off through midwater alone.

Siphonophores comprise another group of cnidarians that Haeckel studied and illustrated in his booklets. One drawing shows a siphonophore with a body like a spire of flowers spinning around, trailing an elegant whorl of tentacles; one looks like a pineapple with a dangling bouquet of leaves and flower buds. Some siphonophore species occur in the shallows, such as the Portuguese man-of-war, with its purple balloon floating at the surface, but many live in the deep and are exceptionally delicate and difficult to catch whole. Their fragile bodies are constructed in a very different way from those of the other jellies. As Haeckel well knew, siphonophores challenge the notion of what it means to be an individual.

Rather than separate polyp and medusa stages taking turns throughout the life cycle, siphonophores put the two together simultaneously in one body. The polyps and medusae, collectively known as zooids, join into long chains that can stretch for dozens of yards or more. A siphonophore of the genus *Apolemia* was filmed in 2020 in a deep canyon off Ningaloo in Western Australia; arranged in a giant spiral and measuring an estimated 150 feet long, it was a strong contender for the longest animal on record.

Those great long bodies consist, curiously, of zooids that don't all look the same. Other colonial animals, like corals, are built from multiple, identical polyps that are semi-autonomous, each one able to feed itself and reproduce. In siphonophores, some zooids feed, others make eggs or sperm, some are balloons filled with gas and help the colony float, and rows of zooids pulse their medusa bells in synchrony, propelling and steering the colony through the water.

The zooids have become so specialized for their particular task, they can't survive on their own. Siphonophores are a team effort, blurring the lines between one animal and many.

Haeckel's *Kunstformen der Natur* also contains one final tableau of jellies that commonly live in the deep but are quite different and distantly related to the others. Known as ctenophores (with a silent *c*), they are covered in eight strips of minute hairs, like tiny eyelashes, called cilia, which gleam like iridescent rainbows when light falls on them.* These hairs beat in coordinated waves, propelling ctenophores gently and smoothly around like ambling, transparent gooseberries, or alien spacecraft, gliding through the water.

∽

For page after page in *Kunstformen der Natur*, Ernst Haeckel showed the miscellany of animals with delicate jelly bodies that live in the deep sea, but he never saw one alive. In the decades following his studies, these animals also slipped out of sight for the people who studied life in the open seas. Ships became faster, and ocean scientists used bigger, more mechanized equipment, making it harder to catch fragile animals and keep them from falling apart.

Not until the second half of the twentieth century did individual, living animals begin to come back into view, when researchers put themselves in the water to witness life well below the surface. In the early 1970s, William Hamner, of the University of California at Davis, realized the potential for scuba diving, then a relatively recent invention, to study animals in midwater. He lamented the costly, ship-based research cruises and rigid timetables planned years in advance. "It is not surprising," he wrote in 1975, "that research vessels do not regularly stop while someone swims around the ship looking at jellyfish."

---

* These have their own phylum, Ctenophora, and they compete with sponges for being the oldest branch on the animal evolutionary tree. The name means "comb bearer" in Greek, and they are also commonly known as comb jellies.

Hamner and colleagues worked out how to dive safely when the bottom of the sea is nowhere in sight, pioneering what came to be known as blue-water diving. "When you're floating in the open ocean, you lose any feeling of where you are," Alice Alldredge recalls of her days as a PhD student in Hamner's lab. "The light can be diffuse, and you're not always certain where the surface is." A spider web of ropes connects divers to a downline from the surface, making sure nobody gets disoriented or lost. "It's clear blue everywhere," says Alldredge. "It's quite a lovely experience just to be part of that world."

The blue-water divers found themselves surrounded by scyphozoans, siphonophores, and ctenophores; they recorded their findings with waterproof tape recorders and microphones pressed to their throats, keeping their hands free to carefully collect individual animals in glass jars and plastic bags. "We didn't realize how abundant these gelatinous plankton were until we started going down with scuba and looking at them with our own eyes," says Alldredge.

Despite being restricted by their air supplies and pressure to the upper 100 feet or so of the ocean, blue-water divers paved the way toward important studies of the deep. Alldredge focused on larvaceans, varieties of sea squirts that look like tadpoles and live inside giant balloons of slime.* Referred to as houses, these intricate mucous structures vary in shape by species—those of giant larvaceans (*Bathochordaeus mcnutti*) look like fluted, inflatable angel wings—and function as feeding filters, trapping tiny particles from the water. When the houses get clogged, larvaceans cast them off and make new ones, five or six a day. Diving in blue waters off the Bahamas, Alldredge deduced that abandoned larvacean houses sink swiftly, creating flurries of marine snow and sending nutritious pulses of carbon-rich food into the deep.

★ Being sea squirts (also known as tunicates), larvaceans are chordates, members of Chordata, the phylum of animals that includes mammals, reptiles, birds, fish, and amphibians.

Blue-water divers also showed that it was well worth the effort to directly observe midwaters that teem with jelly-based life-forms, not only in the upper ocean but much deeper too. Essentially the same technique—watching and carefully collecting animals—has been transferred into the deep using submersibles, leading to a new appreciation of how abundant and important the gelatinous animals truly are, all through the deep.

ᴄ๏

Until not so long ago, it was generally thought the animals of deep midwater gained food and energy via one simple route: marine snow falls and gets caught and eaten by zooplankton (mostly tiny crustaceans, like krill and copepods, plus larval stages of various animals), which in turn get eaten by trillions of lanternfish, small silver fish schooling though the midnight and twilight zones. Delicate jelly creatures of all different kinds were considered something of a sideshow, playing no major role in the food web. They catch their share of marine snow, but few other animals were thought to eat these watery bags of jelly, making them a trophic dead end—creatures that don't pass their energy on to other animals at a higher level, and when they die, their decomposing remains tumble back down to the bottom of the food web. In fact, the deep sea is a tangled web of jelly.

A classic way to construct a food web—to learn who eats whom and draw connections through an ecosystem—involves opening up animals' stomachs to examine their last meals. The problem is that a gut full of gelatinous plankton quickly turns to unidentifiable mush. An alternative approach is to watch acts of predation in real time. Such encounters are rare but not impossible to see in the deep sea, especially with enough time spent in the water. Since the Monterey Bay Aquarium Research Institute (MBARI) was founded on the California coast in the 1980s, staff have been exploring the deep waters of the bay on a regular basis and compiling a huge archive of video footage from remote-operated submersibles. In 2017, Anela

Choy, then a postdoctoral researcher at MBARI, led a study that searched through the archive for those serendipitous moments when animals were eating or being eaten right in front of the camera. Among the predators filmed mid-hunt were squid with fish wrapped in their arms and a narcomedusa with a paralyzed siphonophore snagged in its tentacles. Even if the hunt is over, it can be easy to discern what a gelatinous animal has recently eaten because the prey is visible through its transparent body. Like a set of glass Russian dolls, there could be a krill inside a ctenophore or a fish inside a scyphozoan. In one scene from the archive, a seven-arm octopus★ was cradling the half-eaten remains of a large yellow scyphozoan. The octopus had eaten the most nutritious parts, the stomach and gonads, but held onto the remaining stinging tentacles, perhaps to use as a weapon or a tool for catching more food, a behavior never seen before.

Choy and her collaborators pored over the archive and found hundreds of shots of predation in action, and gradually, link by link, a complex web of feasting unfurled. The paper publishing their findings depicts these connections in a diagram, which the scientists call the "birthday party figure" because it's so colorful, with bright streamers looping between different deep-sea animal groups. It shows something that doesn't normally happen at birthday parties: all the guests are eating each other. "Each line is an intricately intimate story of feeding," says Choy. With the help of decades of underwater footage, she peered into the deep and observed how animals make their living.

The greatest surprise Choy and her colleagues uncovered in the deep feeding frenzy lay among the fragile, gelatinous animals that don't fit the standard model of predators. Jelly animals don't have huge teeth or eyes, and yet there they were, tangled up at the heart

---

★ Named for the males, which coil their sperm-bearing arm in a sac under their right eye for safekeeping (fighting octopuses will try to tear off each other's vital limbs), leaving only seven arms visible.

of the deep-sea food web. In the video archive, dinner plate jellies—*Solmissus*, a type of narcomedusa that can indeed grow to the size of a dinner plate—were spotted catching dozens of different prey types, including other jellies, worms, siphonophores, and krill, and forming links throughout the food web. Bring one to the surface, however, and a dinner plate jelly bears no resemblance to a voracious predator. "It's just this clear gelatinous stuff that falls through your fingers," says Choy.

This new view of midwater feeding reveals a jelly web as intricate as some of the animals' bodies themselves. Species that variously go by the name jellyfish can no longer be shuffled aside as an irrelevance or stuffed into a single box on a food web diagram. They are far more important than anyone imagined they could be, as both prey and predators, channeling energy from sinking particles of marine snow and passing it on through ecosystems. And their influence is not confined to the deep. Animals known from shallower seas are connected into this jelly web, including ones that directly matter to people. Major commercial fisheries worth billions of dollars draw on this deep gelatinous energy. Yellowfin, bluefin, and albacore tuna dive into the twilight zone and hunt for squid, which in turn feed on scyphozoans and trachymedusae. Midwater fish such as lancetfish and opah eat gelatinous plankton, and while they're not targeted by fisheries, they form important prey for other animals that are, including tuna and sharks. Tentacles of the jelly web reach into the lives of all manner of ocean wildlife. Penguins around Antarctica and migrating leatherback turtles are regular gelativores. Great white sharks, fur seals, sea lions, sperm whales, and many other marine species depend on food that, one way or another, is connected to the abundant gelatinous animals of the deep.

～

Exploring with submersibles, deep-sea scientists are adding many new and notable members to the cast of jelly-based creatures living in midwater. A gossamer worm looks like a centipede doing a dragon dance at Chinese New Year. As one swims, rippling waves pass along its dozens of legs (or parapodia) and a pair of long tentacles trails back from its head. "They're supercool, superfast animals," says Karen Osborn, curator of marine invertebrates at the Smithsonian's National Museum of Natural History in Washington, DC. Their acrobatics make them difficult to catch—they could easily swim out of a net— and explain why so little was known about gossamer worms for so long. Those that do end up getting caught in nets don't tend to fare well. Their bodies are essentially water balloons and are easily burst. If they're not too badly hurt, muscles on the outside will squeeze out the liquid, and shrink and seal off the damaged part; then, slowly, the rest of the body reinflates. Such self-repair is unlikely, though, for a gossamer worm caught and battered in a trawl net. Before scientists had a chance to watch these animals alive in their native habitat, descriptions typically depicted them as a finger's length, when in fact they can grow to several feet long.

The best way to catch a gossamer worm is from a deep-diving submersible, after chasing and tiring it out so it has to stop and rest. "Being just a bag of water, they don't have a whole lot of reserves," Osborn says. Then, the sub's slurp gun attachment can gently suck up the weary worm, or it can be delicately trapped in a clear acrylic canister. "Those are the pristine, beautiful ones," Osborn adds.

As well as discovering more than a dozen species of gossamers, Osborn has been the first to encounter many other worms swimming in the deep. "Every single time we take the submersible out into the water, we find something we haven't seen before." She admits those discoveries are rarely eureka moments. When something new and strange comes into view, a standard response from scientists is more likely "What the heck is that? That doesn't make any sense!"

Scientists might watch and film the new creature for a while and perhaps catch a specimen to bring back to help describe a new spe-cies. Even then, preserved bodies can sit untouched on laboratory shelves for years because of the scarcity of deep-sea scientists and funding. Deciding what to study can be a challenge. Osborn tries to pick animals that seem likely to play a key role in the ecosystem, the abundant and diverse groups, or ones that will help her understand how the oceans work. In the case of worms, she wants to know how so many of them abandoned the seabed and swam off, never to touch a hard surface again, leaving behind their creeping ancestors.

This dramatic departure is matched by equally dramatic evolutionary changes in the worms' bodies that allowed them to cope with this new environment. In 2007, in the Celebes Sea between Indonesia and the Philippines, Osborn and colleagues found almost 10,000 feet down worms that look like squid. She placed the species within its own new genus, *Teuthidodrilus*, the squidworm. It has tentacles longer than its body with sensitive tendrils at the ends. Living in midwater, animals need to expand their sensory realm and know what's going on all around them, which is exactly what squidworms do with their tentacles. They're like cats with long whiskers all over their heads, not just under their noses.

Swimming worms join the ranks of deep midwater animals that evolved gelatinous bodies. Osborn discovered a species of polychaete worm that is known by the name *Chaetopterus pugaporcinus*, the pig's-rump worm. One of its body segments has swelled into a fluid-filled bubble, like a pair of buttocks, that helps it to float.

Swima bombiviridis, another worm Osborn discovered in the deep, also lives up to its name: *Swima* signifies that these worms are good at swimming, rowing through the water with fans of bristles all along their bodies, moving forward and backward with equal ease; *bombiviridis*★ indicates that, when disturbed, they hurl glowing green bombs, fluid-filled orbs attached to their bodies that burst into light for a few seconds.

★ *Bombi* comes from the Latin *bombus*, meaning "humming" or "buzzing," from which the English word *bomb* is derived. *Viridis* stems from the Latin for green.

The green bombers are one of many glowing worms in the deep sea. A pig's-rump worm, gently prodded, glows bright blue for a few seconds and squirts a shower of green glowing particles.* Disturb a gossamer worm, and it may toss puffs of yellow light into the water. Such dazzling displays are quite normal in the deep sea.

༄

Squid and octopuses can be bioluminescent, as can sharks and bony fish, shrimp and krill; they squeeze glowing slime and particles into the water or illuminate parts of their bodies. Most of the delicate, gelatinous animals Ernst Haeckel drew can make their own light too: some scyphozoans, almost all the ctenophores and siphonophores, the narcomedusae and trachymedusae. Larvaceans glow too, their houses filling with luminescent particles of marine snow.

The long-standing hunch that the deep sea is full of glowing animals is corroborated by more data extracted from MBARI's video archive. The videos shot in open water show more than 350,000 identifiable animals, which are divided into two groups: those that are known to be light makers and those that are not. Of all the animals caught on MBARI's cameras in midwater, 76 percent were bioluminescent.

Different light-making animals dominate at different depths; siphonophores are common in the upper 1,600 feet; then narcomedusae and trachymedusae take over for the next 3,300 feet; the midnight zone, down to around 7,400 feet, is the domain of the polychaete worms, the green bombers, pig's-rumps, gossamers, and many more besides; below them, in the deepest waters, larvaceans predominate. Bioluminescence is clearly common from the surface all the way down into the abyss. But the question that doesn't yet have a full, satisfying answer is, *why*?

---

* The particles are emitted from the crack between the worm's buttocks, or more correctly, the middorsal ciliated groove.

༃

Making light is evidently an important skill that animals have evolved to survive in the vast, hungry space of deep midwater, by mixing cocktails of luminescent chemicals or by keeping glowing bacteria inside their bodies. Researchers have presented theories for how those lights are used: deep-sea anglerfish lure prey into their mouths with a dangling, glowing lure; *Erenna* siphonophores have red lights on twitching side branches of their tentacles that lure in fish; shrimp spew confusing clouds of glowing goo in the face of a predator. However, these behaviors have rarely been recorded in the sea.

"I call them 'Just So Stories,'" Steven Haddock from MBARI says, "like 'How did the tiger get its stripes?' It's so hard to get beyond that."

Capturing images of bioluminescence in action in the deep is fiendishly difficult. Bright lights of a submersible tend to drown out nature's lights. With the sub's lights switched off, the animals' lights can be brief flashes too dim for a camera to detect, even if it happens to be pointing in the right direction.

The majority of glowing sea creatures that have been photographed and filmed were recorded switching on their lights in laboratories. There, they are prodded or bathed in chemicals that coax them to make light. Flash a light at bioluminescent species, and some will wink back. But these are just individual animals revealing their ability to glow. They're not illuminating at will, throwing lights at each other or sending flashing messages through the dark toward mates, predators, or prey. To confirm how animals use their bioluminescence requires allowing them to behave normally in the wild.

People have witnessed bioluminescence through the portholes of diving submersibles, their eyes able to quickly accommodate to detect faint flashes of light, but there's no way to record, replay, and analyze what a human eye perceives. Back in 1994, Haddock was diving in a submersible at about 2,500 feet in the Bahamas, when he saw an arrow worm darting off into the distance, leaving behind a plume of blue luminescence. It had been assumed these slender, transparent animals can't make light, and only Haddock's memory of that fleeting sparkle provided proof to the contrary. More recently, using a new supersensitive camera mounted on a submersible with red lights so as not to spook the animals, Haddock filmed an arrow worm releasing glowing, spinning donut rings into the water. Having proven the camera system works, Haddock has a wish list of behaviors he hopes to film one day, from lantern sharks hiding themselves in the twilight zone with a cloak of blue light on their bellies, to squid reeling out two long tentacles like fishing rods covered in alluring, twinkling lights.

৵

Animal illuminations have led to some surprising adaptations among life in the deep. Fish living in freshwater pools and streams in deep caves on land have commonly lost their vision, and even their eyes, as these complex organs have no use in the constant dark. Conversely, fish living in the dark of the deep sea have done the opposite and evolved extremely good vision—all so they can detect biolumi-nescence. Their eyes have become supersensitive, with dozens of photopigments packed into their retinas that are tuned to different wavelengths of light, so they can not only see the faint flashes of other animals but make out different colors. Most other vertebrates become color-blind when it gets dark, humans included; rods in their retinas, the structures responsible for low-light vision, contain only a single type of pigment. In contrast, one fish species, the spiny silverfin, was revealed in a recent study to have thirty-eight types of rod pigments. Scientists sequenced the genes and reproduced the pigments in the laboratory and then, by shining lights on them, worked out which wavelengths they are most sensitive to. As these little fish swim through the twilight zone, they can distinguish many more subtle shades of blues and greens—the most common color for bioluminescent lights—than a human eye.

The fireworks displays in the deep have also led midwater animals to evolve ways not to be seen. Many predators hunt with searchlights, and even moving in the deep can create light, disturbing plankton and marine snow particles that spontaneously glow when they're touched. Skin that reflects as little ambient illumination as possible offers a competitive edge, meaning animals are less likely to get noticed. As a consequence, swimming through the oceans are a lot of ultra-black fish.

Teaming up with collaborators, Karen Osborn set about collecting samples of black fish skin. Measurements of their reflectance showed that various deep-sea fish are among the blackest animals on the planet, matching the birds of paradise that use ultra-black feathers to offset the colorful plumes and enhance their vibrant mating displays. Examining the fish skin under a microscope, the team saw it was packed full of melanin, the same pigment found in the skin of humans and many other animals. The key to the fish skins' extreme blackness is the size and arrangement of those melanin granules. When photons of light fall on the skin, they bounce sideways between granules (like the ball ricocheting between flippers and bumpers inside a pinball machine) and essentially get trapped, with very little light escaping.*

The study, published in 2020, revealed that melanin-packed skin is frequently found in deep-sea fish. Osborn and colleagues identified

---

* A sheet of black construction paper reflects roughly 10 percent of the light falling on it. A new car tire reflects just over 1 percent of the ambient light. All the fish Osborn and colleagues measured had a reflectance of less than 1 percent. The blackest fish they studied had around the same reflectance as the blackest human engineered material, called Vantablack, constructed from carbon nanotubes.

seven cases of ultra-black fish evolving independently among sixteen distantly related species. Some use their blackness to avoid falling prey to other glowing animals; some prevent their own bioluminescent lures from reflecting off their bodies and giving the game away. Together, they show that living in a sunless realm of the deep, it pays not only to evolve a way of making light but also to hide as shadows that are darker than the deep sea itself.

In a Chemical World

When Yeti crabs were discovered, it would have been poetic if they were found to eat marine snow. In fact, they do something even stranger. These abominable crustaceans were seen first in 2005 during a deep-sea research cruise in the eastern Pacific south of Easter Island. They are pale colored, with a thumb-size body and long front claws covered in luxuriant, bristly extensions of their shells, called seta. Tipped with a pair of goofy-looking, rounded pincers, these pelts of blond fur give the animal the look of a deep-sea crab that might appear on *The Muppet Show*.

One of these newly seen crabs was plucked from the deep and officially named *Kiwa hirsuta*, after Kiwa, a Polynesian god of the sea, and *hirsuta*, meaning "hairy" or "shaggy" in Latin. But everyone still knows them as Yeti crabs.★

Growing on the body of that first Yeti specimen were stringy colonies of bacteria, which sparked the idea that the species has a rather unusual way of feeding, by farming microbes in its furry sleeves and then eating them. And these are no ordinary bacteria, but ones capable of doing something that, until a few decades ago, nobody

---

★ In a quirk of taxonomy, Yeti crabs are not what crustacean experts consider to be true crabs (of the infraorder Brachyura); rather, they are technically squat lobsters (infraorder Anomura), ranked alongside hermit crabs, king crabs, and coconut crabs. Many animals are called "crab" for convenience.

thought possible. The unconventional microbial feat allows Yetis, plus swarms of other animals, to thrive at hydrothermal vents—some of the most dramatic, forbidding, and downright dangerous places in the deep.

_ల_

In 1977, in another part of the eastern Pacific, north of the Galápagos Islands, scientists diving inside the submersible *Alvin* laid eyes for the first time on a hydrothermal vent.

"Isn't the deep ocean supposed to be like a desert?" geologist Jack Corliss asked from inside *Alvin* via the telephone link to the ship a mile and a half above. "Well, there's all these animals down here."

Through *Alvin*'s viewing port, Corliss saw tall chimneys with shimmering fluids pouring out, and surrounding them were thousands of animals. He saw nine-foot-long worms with scarlet feathery plumes and clams the size of dinner plates. He didn't know it at the time, but Corliss was looking at an ecosystem cut off from the sun that would revolutionize the view of life on earth.

Since then, more than 650 hydrothermal vent fields have been located throughout the deep, each field a cluster of dozens or even hundreds of individual vent chimneys. Close to three hundred fields have been visually confirmed, the rest inferred based on chemical and geological tests. Vents form along mid-ocean ridges, the underwater mountain chains that weave across the planet at the edges of tectonic plates. They also form mid-plate, on the flanks and tops of seamounts, as well as at subduction zones, where chains of submerged volcanoes are arranged in arcs alongside oceanic trenches. In all these volcanic regions, chambers of molten magma push up from the mantle and into the oceanic crust. Seawater percolates down through cracks in the seabed, as far as three miles down, depending on the depth of the magma chamber. Once it reaches the scorching molten rock, the water becomes superheated and buoyant, flowing upward through cracks deep within the crust; en route, the rising seawater reacts with the surrounding rocks, picking up dissolved minerals and metals. With its chemical composition substantially altered, the circulating seawater becomes what's known as hydrothermal fluid, which continues to gush upward and eventually bursts back through the seabed, like the deep-sea equivalent of hot springs and geysers on land—only much hotter and more toxic. Commonly, the hydrothermal vents emit fluids at hundreds of degrees; only the tremendous pressure in the deep sea prevents the hydrothermal fluids from boiling and turning to gas.

It has been calculated that the entire volume of the ocean cycles through hydrothermal vents every ten to twenty million years. This so-called hydrothermal circulation acts as a giant reactor, balancing the ocean's chemistry and drawing heat from the earth's interior.

As the venting fluids collide with the cold seawater, some of the dissolved minerals and metals precipitate out and solidify, over time building spires and chimneys, some as fast as a foot per day. The chimneys are made of different types of metallic rocks, often iron sulfides, and they can reach over 100 feet tall. One of the tallest, which scientists named Godzilla, was located in the Endeavour vent field, on the Juan de Fuca Ridge off the west coast of Vancouver Island. This monster of a vent chimney reached fifteen stories high (150 feet) and 33 feet wide until in the 1990s it became unstable and toppled over. Vent chimneys have flues running through the middle, and typically, searing, metal-rich, cloudy fluids pour out of the top and spurt through culverts in the side. Commonly, they're known as black smokers, although this isn't smoke, and nothing is actually on fire.

Every ocean has hydrothermal vents. Many are known along the Mid-Atlantic Ridge, which bisects the Atlantic roughly north–south, and the East Pacific Rise, which runs between the Gulf of California and Antarctica. The Mediterranean has vents at the Hellenic Arc, where the African Plate dives beneath the smaller Aegean Sea Plate. Vents were more recently discovered on ridges in the Indian

Ocean and near Antarctica on the edges of the minor Scotia Plate, off the tip of South America. In 2008, vents were found for the first time in the Arctic Ocean, on the Gakkel Ridge, which slices across the top of the planet. One, Loki's Castle, was named after the trickster god of Norse mythology, partly because the cluster of five vent chimneys look like the kind of fantastical citadel where Loki might reside and also because these most northerly known vents were especially tricky to find in the wild, inaccessible seas between Norway and Greenland. Undoubtedly, more vents remain to be discovered, especially in remote seas where nobody has gone to check, including in the far south along the Southeast Indian Ridge and the Pacific-Antarctic Ridge.

Wherever they may lie, vents are never easy to find, being between one and three miles down and surrounded by a haze of particles that interfere with remote-mapping equipment, like ship-based sonar. And these are rare, small habitats. Most individual vent fields would fit inside an auditorium, and all the world's hydrothermal vents are estimated to collectively cover a total area of less than twenty square miles, somewhat smaller than Manhattan.

Even the easiest to reach and best-studied vent fields keep providing new surprises. Since the 1980s, scientists have been studying the Endeavour vent field, where Godzilla once towered, along with forty-six other named vents lying in five distinct fields. In 2020, results from a new study of the region were unveiled, in which an autonomous underwater vehicle—an untethered, self-steering, deep-diving submersible—mapped the Endeavour seabed using sonar at a resolution of four feet. The map shows dozens of vents, all sticking their turrets skyward along a narrow valley eight miles long. In all, researchers from the Monterey Bay Aquarium Research Institute have identified 572 vent chimneys at Endeavour, standing between ten and eighty-nine feet high, including many that had gone undetected but stand right next to vents that had been studied for decades.

The chimney rocks, and the fluids they emit, vary in composition from vent to vent. The hottest and deepest is the Beebe vent field, near the Cayman Islands, named after pioneering deep-sea explorer William Beebe. The narrow chimneys of rock composed of metal sulfides are close to 16,400 feet down and spew hydrothermal fluids of 757 degrees Fahrenheit.* In the Pacific, the deepest known vents lie in the Pescadero Basin, off the coast of Mexico's Baja California peninsula, at over 12,500 feet deep. These ones are not the common black smokers but a rarer kind, white smokers, which have clear fluids venting at somewhat lower temperatures, shimmering like the air above hot tarmac, and forming chimneys from various pale minerals, including silica and barium sulfate. The Pescadero Basin vents, spewing fluids at 554 degrees Fahrenheit, have been depositing white and brown carbonate minerals, making spiky chimneys and overhanging caverns, where puddles of hydrothermal fluids collect before cascading upward, in silver curtains, like waterfalls in reverse.

Spectacular as they can be, hydrothermal vents appear to be places that animals would naturally avoid. As the fluids flow through the earth's crust, they get not only unbearably hot but also lose their dissolved oxygen and become highly acidic, with a pH usually between two and three (around the acidity of lemon juice or stomach acid; seawater is normally slightly alkaline, with a pH around eight). Vent fluids also get loaded with toxic chemicals, such as methane and hydrogen sulfide. Combined with the extreme pressure and permanent darkness, this conjures a vision of a suffocating, sulfurous purgatory, and yet, as Jack Corliss and many other scientists have seen, hydrothermal vents are thriving with life.

∽

---

* These fluids are supercritical, acting simultaneously like a gas and a liquid, which is a rarity in hydrothermal vents.

Viewed through the portholes or cameras of a submersible, some hydrothermal vent chimneys appear at first to be covered in white rice, but closer inspection reveals the grains are moving and twitching. Each one is a thumb-size shrimp with a fan-shaped tail, like a little lobster. Scoop a gallon of seawater from around one of these vents, and it would contain around eleven thousand shrimp.

Other vents are covered in piles of snails with shining black shells made of iron—the only animals known to make body coverings from iron—and a distinctly un-snaillike foot sticking out, covered in overlapping scales; other snails cling together in long chains, perhaps mating with the next snail in the stack, which hangs down like a living, molluscan stalactite.

Elsewhere, the view might resemble the hunched form of a giant, napping sea monster with a coat of long, luxuriant fur. In fact, this covering comprises thickets of worms, all living inside white tubes, their pink tips poking out like artists' paintbrushes.

Watch closely, and you might see pairs of shining worms picking fights with each other. The size of a young mouse, each has two rows of what look like large, iridescent blue sequins fixed along its back and a shock of golden fur sticking out from underneath.* No one yet knows the cause of the glittering scale worms' conflict, but each bounces angrily on the spot for a while, before throwing punches with its long proboscis and biting chunks out of its opponent.

Just as you would expect to encounter particular species in different mountain ranges on land—mountain lions or mountain gorillas, snow leopards or alpacas—so there are regional differences in the species to be found across mid-ocean ridges and hydrothermal vent fields. Northeastern Pacific vents are dominated by skinny tube worms of the genus *Ridgeia*. Western Pacific vents are home to

---

* They belong to the genus *Peinaleopolynoe*, a name derived from the Greek word *peinaleos*, meaning "hungry" or "famished." One species has been named *P. elvisi*, the hungry Elvis worm, because of its golden-pink scales, reminiscent of the sparkly costumes favored later in life by the King of Rock and Roll.

barnacles, limpets, and hairy snails. On the Mid-Atlantic Ridge, mussels and shrimp dominate.

In all, more than seven hundred species have been catalogued living around hydrothermal vents, including fish, octopuses, crabs, worms, starfish, and anemones; around eight out of ten of these species are endemic, living in no other habitat. Previously unknown species are frequently discovered, including puzzling new life-forms. In 2015, at the Pescadero Basin vent in the Gulf of California, a mysterious animal was encountered that looks like a purple sock. "Think of a sock that you've taken off and thrown on the floor," worm expert Greg Rouse told *BBC News*. "They literally look like that." Originally discovered sixty years ago but never seen alive, the animal had baffled experts as to what kind of creature it was. Genetic tests suggested it could be a mollusk, but in fact traces of DNA had come from clams these sock animals ate, although how exactly is another unanswered mystery: the purple sock has no gut, no teeth—it's just a hollow bag. Tests from the 2015 specimen confirmed these animals belong to their own, very early branch of the animal tree of life. Rouse and colleagues named it *Xenoturbella*.★

The sprawling mass of creatures living on vents can rival that on the same area of tropical coral reef, except with a smaller selection of species, and some prospering in immense abundance. Just as on a coral reef, there can be so many animals that they cover every inch of available space around a vent, sometimes piling up in multiple layers of animal life. And yet videos and photographs of vents with abundant animals filling the frame are somewhat deceptive. Exploring the deep, it's always important to wonder what's behind you. Pan the camera around, and just a few yards away, vent ecosystems quickly taper out. Some vent chimneys are surrounded by areas of diffuse venting, where cooler fluids bubble out through mounded

---

★ The name stems from Greek words meaning "strange turbulence."

domes of sediment and rubble. In these spots, with temperatures in the tens rather than hundreds of degrees, animals have learned to use the gentle warmth they offer in the otherwise frigid deep. Near the Galápagos Islands, scientists spotted a great pile of egg cases left close to a hydrothermal vent. They're thought to belong to deep-water skates, flattened relatives of sharks, using the warm water as an incubator to quicken gestation of their unhatched eggs.

∽

Until hydrothermal vents were discovered, and their living inhabitants studied, in the late 1970s and '80s, they had been hiding one of the deep sea's greatest secrets: chemosynthesis, a dark alternative to photosynthesis.

Generally, it had been assumed that life on Earth depends entirely on the sun. The only known source of energy for biological systems was the radiation beaming in from Earth's nearest star—energy that drives the photosynthetic machinery inside plants, algae, and some bacteria, generating food on which all living things rely. Then, suddenly, scientists came across an ecosystem flourishing in the dark, powered not by sunlight but by chemicals.

Chemosynthesis is carried out by various types of microbes that survive on the methane and hydrogen sulfide pouring from vents. By oxidizing these compounds, microbes release energy, some of which they use to grow and divide, and some to convert carbon dioxide into sugars. Plants do a similar thing with sunlight, but chemosynthetic microbes do it in the dark. All they need from the illuminated world is oxygen, which is released by algae and plants, dissolves in the ocean, and sinks on cold, deep-flowing currents.

The crowded ecosystems at hydrothermal vents are based on the food provided by chemosynthesis. Shrimp and crabs pick and chew on tangled mats of microbes growing over vent chimneys, while many animals don't go to the bother of hunting around for bacteria to eat, instead inviting microbes to live inside their bodies.

The giant tube worm, *Riftia pachyptila*,* which Corliss saw through *Alvin*'s window, was the animal that first revealed the truth about chemosynthesis. The notion of an alternative energy pathway had been proposed without evidence in the late nineteenth century by Sergei Winogradsky, a Russian scientist, and by Wilhelm Pfeffer, a German scientist, but nobody had yet found any chemosynthetic organisms. Not long after the discovery of hydrothermal vents in 1977, Colleen Cavanaugh, a first-year graduate student at Harvard University, attended a lecture about the mouthless, gutless tube worm. Hearing that the worm has a spongy organ, the trophosome, that takes up half of its nine-foot-long body and is filled with sulfur crystals, she examined a sample under a microscope and discovered it is packed with sulfur-oxidizing bacteria—one hundred billion of them in a teaspoon of tissue. The feathers sticking out of the worm's tube are its gills, flush with red blood that absorbs everything the bacteria need from the seawater: carbon dioxide, oxygen, and hydrogen sulfide. These are delivered via the worm's bloodstream to the trophosome, where the bacteria chemosynthesize, feeding the worm from the inside. The setup is a clear win-win situation, a symbiosis from which both partners stand to benefit.

Subsequent discoveries of vent animals revealed they have evolved various ways to pamper their own personal microbial colonies. The scaly-foot snail, a gastropod with a shiny, iron-based shell and a foot covered in hundreds of scales, has evolved a microbe-carrying pouch in its throat. The rest of the snail's body has adapted to keep the microbes content. Its relatively enormous heart takes up 4 percent of its body volume. (If your heart were in the same proportion, it would be nearly as big as your head.)† The heart pumps a large blood supply through a giant gill, which absorbs oxygen and sulfides from

---

* The species name stems from Greek words meaning "thick feather."

† Chong Chen, now at the Japan Agency for Marine-Earth Science and Technology, describes this as "the heart of a dragon" in his 2015 paper on the internal anatomy of these peculiar snails.

the vent fluids, thus serving the needs of the bacteria on which the snails have come to depend.

The unique iron shell and scale-covered foot offer further hints as to how these snails survive on a chemical, microbial diet. When people saw the snails for the first time, in 2000, they reasonably assumed the metallic exoskeleton had evolved as some form of protection from an outside danger; perhaps the scales prevented vent-dwelling predators from chewing the soft flesh underneath. The real story is the exact opposite: the snails are defending themselves from an internal threat, because while the chemosynthetic bacteria provide food, in the process they also release sulfur, which is toxic to snails. Close examination of the snails' scales reveals them to be made up of thousands of nanoscopic tubes, which act as tiny tailpipes expelling sulfurous toxins from the snails' bodies. When the sulfur reaches the surface of the scales, it reacts with iron in the water and forms nanoparticles of iron sulfide, some in the form of iron pyrite, or fool's gold, making the scales black and shiny.* And so, these snails in shining armor have evolved an antidote to protect themselves from poisons that come from within.

In contrast to the scaly-foot snail, the vent shrimp, *Rimicaris exoculata*, doesn't have a special organ where bacteria grow; instead, it has diverse communities of microbes growing all over its gills and the inside of its mouth. To give the microbes all they need, this shrimp has evolved a giant eye on its back, packed with the visual pigment rhodopsin. This simple eyespot can't form clear images but allows the shrimp to sense the thermal radiation emanating from vents, a dim glow that's undetectable to human eyes. Thus, the shrimp can stay close to the chimneys and the hot venting fluids, prime locations for providing a constant supply of chemicals to their microbial

---

* Not all scaly-foot snails are black. Those living in a vent field that happens to have less iron pouring through the chimneys are white; scientists plucked a few white scales from one of those snails and placed it on a vent field where black snails live, and after two weeks in iron-rich water, the white scales turned black.

companions, in turn providing food for the shrimp, which either eat the microbes or absorb their waste products.

In addition to domesticating microbes, animals living in and around vents also have to survive the scorching, toxic conditions. Among the toughest species is a worm that builds sticky tubes directly on the sides of chimneys. The Pompeii worm, as it's known, in honor of the ancient Roman city destroyed by a volcano, has a gray, fleecy coat of stringy bacteria—which, it has been suggested, detoxifies heavy metals and poisonous hydrogen sulfide in the vent fluids. The five-inch worm produces an antibiotic that seems to kill off unwanted microbes and leave only the right kind of bacteria that create the protective overcoat. As for the searing heat, it's not clear exactly how hot the water gets inside the Pompeii worms' tubes. Temperature probes poked in the tail end have read as high as 140 degrees Fahrenheit, with spikes to 170 degrees or more. When deep-sea biologists brought Pompeii worms carefully to the surface in pressurized containers, most died when the water inside was heated to 120 or 130 degrees Fahrenheit. Even so, these worms are some of the most heatproof animals on the planet. Their only close contenders are Saharan silver ants, which dash from their burrows to forage in short bursts on the carcasses of animals that have perished on the desert sands, in temperatures reaching 158 degrees Fahrenheit.

Clues as to the Pompeii worm's resistance to its fiery world lie hidden among the molecular tweaks inscribed in its genes. It produces heat-shock proteins that allow its cells to keep functioning and prevent their vital molecules from unraveling in the heat; it makes super-tough collagen molecules that don't collapse under the immense pressure; and it produces an extra-efficient form of hemoglobin that absorbs oxygen even at very low levels.

Even tougher are the microbes that live not inside animals but directly on the vent chimneys. Among them are hyperthermophiles—lovers of extra-high temperatures—that grow best at 175 degrees Fahrenheit or more. In 2003, Derek Lovley and Kazem Kashefi, from the University of Massachusetts at Amherst, identified a vent-chimney microbe known as Strain 121. It carried on dividing and growing when placed in an oven at 250 degrees Fahrenheit (121 degrees Celsius).

∽

Life exists on hydrothermal vents by virtue of many intimate adaptations to the heat and the toxins and the unusual chemosynthetic diet, but there is a downside. With their specializations, vent-dwelling animals are unable to move more than a few feet away from the life-giving chemicals and heat. This is a volatile, volcanic realm, and these ecosystems are by their very nature ephemeral. Sooner or later an eruption will strike, and lava will break through the oceanic crust and wipe out a vent ecosystem, or a tectonic shift will close off a conduit to the surface, and the vent will sputter out and go cold.

Hydrothermal vents are especially erratic and short-lived in the Pacific, the world's oldest ocean. For tens of millions of years, rivers have swept mud and sediments onto the edges of the tectonic plates. The huge weight of this influx pushes down the plates at subduction zones and drags seafloor with it, tearing the mid-ocean ridges ferociously apart. Each year, between four and six inches of new seafloor are made at the East Pacific Rise. That may not sound like much, a hand span at most, but it's a greater amount of new seafloor than is being made anywhere else on the planet. The Atlantic is relatively young and calm, expanding by two inches per year. The Indian Ocean expands the slowest of all, only a fingernail's width a year, and thus contains the longest-lasting known vents.

Vent-dwelling animals won't survive in the long term if they simply stay put and endure the heat and toxins. Successful species need to hedge their bets and disperse to other vents. The adults can't travel between vent fields; they would starve en route, and besides, most of them are not highly mobile, and many of them, like the tube worms and clams, don't move at all. Instead, they send their larvae, the minute transparent versions of themselves that hatch from eggs and often look entirely different from the adult form, with extra spines or giant eyes or long, hairy appendages to aid their nascent survival.

The young wanderers venture along the ridges, exploring this uniquely linear realm. It's possible to draw most mid-ocean ridges on a world map in one long line without lifting the pen from the page. Dotted along this winding line are the hydrothermal vents, which larvae float between, often riding currents entrained along the ridges. On slower-spreading ridges, wide rift valleys act as giant gutters, transporting larvae and preventing them from drifting off into the cold, vent-free abyss.

Over time, individual species slide along the ridges, like beads on a string, colonizing new vents or joining existing subpopulations. The distance larvae can travel is influenced in part by their diet. Unlike their parents, some larvae can feed themselves and set off on long, meandering journeys. Vent shrimp living along the Mid-Atlantic Ridge exist as larvae for weeks and months, rising up to eat plankton in shallower seas; then, with their energy reserves built up, they sink back down and seek a vent to settle on. Throughout their 4,000-mile range, subpopulations of vent shrimp on distant vent fields are well connected, with a constant flow of larvae moving between them.

Other animals, such as the scaly-foot snail, have larvae that are far less intrepid. Rather than feeding themselves, the young snails drift off, carrying with them a food parcel in the form of a large yolk, which is all they have to sustain them until they find another vent. Genetic studies indicate there's very little mixing between the snail's three known populations spaced out across the Southwest Indian Ridge. From one population of snails on the Longqi vent field, south of Madagascar, only a few hundred larvae, out of hundreds of thousands each generation, reach the Kairei field, the nearest known populated vents, 1,400 miles to the northeast; so far, no one has discovered any additional scaly-foot snails in between.

Local conditions also influence the arrangement of vent species across the deep. In 2015, an expedition explored the vents of the Gulf of California, where the team saw just how different nearby vents can be. They found the white smokers of Pescadero Basin are covered in tube worms of the genus *Oasisia*, which grow in white tubes like crooked pencils, with fluffy tufts of red gills poking out, and live so densely that up to eighty would sprout from a single page of this book. Living among those tube worms are iridescent scale worms, yellow polychaetes, and anemones blooming like flowers, some red, some white. On these vents, *Riftia* tube worms are a rare sight, with their longer tubes and lipstick-like gills, and there are not many crabs or fish. At another vent field, a cluster of black smokers only forty-five miles away, the animal life is very different. Heatproof Pompeii worms are everywhere, as are *Riftia* tube worms, while little pale limpets nestled in between are hunted by slender pink fish called eelpouts.

All in all, the research team spotted a total of sixty-one distinct animal species in the area, dozens of them new to science, but only seven lived at both the black and white smokers. The scientists also studied the waters around the vents, searching for DNA fragments that identified which species of minute larvae were drifting through. A great mixing was revealed. Floating larvae from black and white smokers were everywhere, not just in waters near vents where they were born or where others like them live; the black smoker species showed up near white smokers and vice versa. Evidently, larvae sometimes arrive at vents and find the local geology and the chemistry not to their liking and for one reason or another they don't settle.

✺

Discovering chemosynthetic life at hydrothermal vents led to a revolution in thinking about life not only on Earth but elsewhere too.

It showed that life is not confined to a mild, sunny surface world, and it raised expectations over the possibility that living things could evolve on other planets. If creatures can thrive in the toxic dark of vents, then perhaps other life-forms are out there, somewhere in this galaxy or another.

After chemosynthesis was found at vents, scientists began to find chemical-harnessing microbes all through the seas; in the sediments around coral reefs, mangroves, and seagrass meadows; on sunken logs and sunken whales; around sewage outfalls. Wherever decomposition takes place and dissolved gases are made, chemosynthetic organisms can move in. Tube worms have been found growing on sacks of beans rotting in the hold of a ship that sank in 1979 in over 3,000 feet of water off the coast of Spain. The mail steamer SS *Persia*, sunk in the Mediterranean by a German submarine in 1915, was located in 2003, at 9,000 feet, with tube worms growing on piles of decomposing paper in the mailroom.

In the early 1980s, another ecosystem powered entirely by chemicals was discovered. In the Gulf of Mexico, at the base of a giant underwater cliff, at a depth of 10,500 feet, a team of deep-sea biologists diving in the submersible *Alvin* saw the seabed covered in mussels and thickets of giant tube worms, with snails, limpets, octopuses, fish, starfish, and shrimp. This was not a vent with scorching hydrothermal fluids but a much milder chemosynthetic ecosystem, where animals depend on cool bubbles of methane and hydrogen sulfide that seep up through the seabed from the same deposits of hydrocarbons for which people drill.

Since they were first spotted in the Gulf of Mexico, thousands more of these so-called cold seeps have been found scattered through the deep, from the Arctic to the Southern Ocean, the Red Sea to Australia, anywhere with cracks in the seabed above buried deposits of oil and gas. Animals that flock to cold seeps include many that resemble species from hydrothermal vents—including a white crab with furry arms—strongly suggesting that the two ecosystems are linked.

A year after the first species of Yeti crab was found, a second one was spotted during a geological expedition off the Pacific coast of Costa Rica. At a cold seep on the top of a seamount, dozens of odd-looking crabs were nestled among the methane bubbles, and, most unusually, they were rhythmically swinging their gangly claws from side to side, all of them dancing to different silent beats.

Geologists inside the deep-submersible *Alvin* scooped up two dancing crabs and brought them back to the ship's lab, together with a note for the onboard biologist, Andrew Thurber, reading:

This is a new species. You should describe it.

Thurber called the crab *Kiwa puravida*, its species name a common Spanish saying in Costa Rica meaning "pure life." Studying the specimens helped him confirm the original theory about the crab's unconventional diet. Chemical analysis of their muscles revealed a distinctive type of fatty acid made by chemosynthetic bacteria. More specimens brought up to the ship, these ones live, proceeded to groom their furry arms with fine bristles on their claws, combing out the stringy bacteria and then swiping them into their mouths and swallowing.

The Yeti dance may also play a crucial part in the crab's dining habits. On a cold seep, it's possible the chemosynthetic bacteria exhaust the chemicals in the water immediately surrounding their host crab.★ Like all good farmers, Yetis know how to keep their livestock content and well fed. By waving their claws, they stir the water and bring in fresh chemicals. Hydrothermal vents, in contrast to gentler cold seeps, have turbulent fluids actively pouring out of them, making it less likely that pockets of depleted water will cling

---

★ In a similar way, all the colored syrup gets sucked through a straw from one spot of a Slush Puppie, or the tequila from a frozen margarita.

to a crab's claws. The flow of chemical food is continually replenished at vents, so there's no need for those Yetis to dance.

༄

In 2010, a research expedition to the freezing waters surrounding Antarctica found hydrothermal vents covered in thousands of crabs. This was an unlikely place to find crustaceans, which usually avoid very cold water, because most species are unable to remove magnesium from their blood in such temperatures and so become paralyzed. And yet, there were masses of crabs that looked similar to the Yetis found elsewhere, only stockier and stouter and with soft gingery hairs all over their bodies, most densely packed on their ventral surface—which is to say, they are crabs with hairy chests. A member of that expedition, Christopher Nicolai Roterman, then a PhD student at Oxford University, came up with the nickname for these crabs. Thinking of actors renowned for showing off their hirsute chests, he considered Sean Connery as a possibility, as well as Lee Majors.* But in the end, David Hasselhoff, from the television series *Baywatch*, won out, and the Hoff crab was born.†

Watching images relayed to the surface from the submersible, the team of biologists soon realized these were not just piles of crabs scrabbling over each other to get to the chimney peaks, but that the crab crowds were highly segregated. At the top of the chimneys, closest to the vent fluids, were the biggest male crabs, some as big as a human fist. Daring to go closer to the vent chimneys, the male Hoff crabs grow bigger because they become smothered in dense bacterial colonies proliferating in the hydrothermal chemicals and as a consequence have plenty to eat. But these crabs also take more

---

* In an episode of the 1970s TV series *The Six Million Dollar Man*, Majors's character even went searching for Bigfoot, a close cryptozoological cousin of the Yeti.

† The scientific name for this species is *Kiwa tyleri*, in honor of the British deep-sea biologist Paul Tyler. The paper describing this new species makes no reference to Tyler ever showing off a hairy chest.

risks. Yeti crabs have no eyes—they find their way around solely by their sense of touch, feeling differences in temperature and chemicals in the water. Watching the submersible's video feed, the scientists saw one particular crab dip a claw into the shimmering fluid pouring from a chimney, only to immediately flinch and pull back. The submersible pilot reached in and collected that very crab. Later, in the ship's lab (with the windows wide open to let out the Hoff's natural stench of rotten eggs from its sulfurous bacteria), they discovered the muscle in that crab's claw was pink and opaque, rather than the more usual transparent, watery tissue. The crab had got too close and boiled its claw.

On the flanks of the chimneys, away from scorching fluids, were mixed gatherings of Hoff crabs. There, in water around fifty degrees Fahrenheit, were smaller males and females, presumably mating with each other, although surprisingly, given the surveillance, none were caught in the act. Farther out was a safer zone, where females were rearing their eggs, which are stuck to the underside of their bodies. The water away from the vents holds more oxygen, vital for the developing eggs, and there's less chance of being turned into crab bisque. But it means the brooding females have little to eat, because they're not bathed in vent fluids and chemosynthetic bacteria don't grow in their fur. The females make a trade-off, retreating to the edges of the Hoff's Goldilocks zone and into cooler waters, where their eggs survive, but it's so cold they can't move; slowly, the brooding crabs starve.

It's the kind of sacrifice that various animal mothers make for their offspring. Most female octopuses will lay a single clutch of eggs on the seabed, then stand guard, never moving away and not eating for weeks, or for several years in the case of deep-sea octopuses. Hoff crabs may do something similar. Exactly how long a female Hoff watches over her unhatched eggs or whether she dies at the end is unknown, but it seems likely. When the original Hoff-watching team returned to the Antarctic vents, they recognized a few females that were still sitting in the same spots after a year. Their shells were yellow and brown from layers of oxidizing metal sulfides, suggesting they weren't feeding and growing and hadn't molted in a long time. The starving, paralyzed female crabs were starting to go rusty.

When the Hoff crab larvae eventually hatch, the frigid waters of the Southern Ocean may help them disperse in a rather unusual way. As the larvae stray from the warmth of a vent, their development likely comes to an abrupt halt. This hasn't been tested in Hoffs but has been observed in Pompeii worms. In a laboratory, cooled to just below thirty-six degrees Fahrenheit, Pompeii worm eggs stopped dividing—but they didn't die. The temperature was raised again several days later, and the eggs continued developing. In the deep, cold sea, Hoff crab eggs in a state of suspended animation may drift until they eventually reach another vent, where they warm up, wake up, and start to grow. Like a form of cryopreservation, this could allow chilled eggs and larvae to eventually join existing populations or colonize new distant vents.

Such occasional long-distance dispersal helps to explain the rather puzzling distribution of Hoffs and other species of Yeti crabs around the world. Hoff crabs especially pose a geographic enigma, stuck out on their own in the Atlantic sector of the Southern Ocean, cut off from all the other known Yetis, including their closest cousins, a fourth species that has been found thousands of miles away in the Indian Ocean.★

In order to work out how Hoff crabs got where they are today, Christopher Nicolai Roterman and colleagues traced their evolutionary tale and the changing patterns of their habitat. Currently, no mid-ocean ridges directly connect the realm of the Hoff crab to the Pacific. However, studies of past tectonic arrangements indicate that twenty million years ago, a saw-toothed chain of ridges ran

---

★ At the time of this writing, the Indian Ocean Yeti crabs, similar to the original Hoff only even stouter, are waiting for scientists to officially describe them as a separate species, which they appear to be.

through the Drake Passage and around Cape Horn, offering a likely route for the Hoff's ancestors. An ancient Pacific population could have dispersed as cryopreserved larvae drifting from vent to vent— sliding like beads along the ridges—all the way into the Atlantic. Subsequently, around twelve million years ago, that pathway closed behind them as those connecting ridges disappeared, leaving the Hoffs isolated from their ancestors and primed to become a separate species. The timing fits with Roterman's estimates of when the species split from its relatives, based on differences in their DNA.

Yeti crab genetics also allowed Roterman to draw an evolutionary family tree, showing how the known species are related to each other. Initially, with four Yeti species to consider, the arrangement suggested that the Yeti family first evolved on cold seeps. According to that version of the story, Yetis later moved from seeps to vents, taking their bacteria-eating habits with them.

As well as Yetis, various other seep and vent species are closely related, such as the giant tube worms that belong to the same family (the Siboglinidae) as the bone-eating worms *Osedax*. Experts have not yet fully decided, but it could be that seeps, vents, and whale falls provide chemical oases dotted across the deep seabed, which the animals and their ancestors have been jumping between, like stepping-stones.

დ

Emerging from the story of the Yeti crabs is evidence that contradicts an old idea about hydrothermal vents. Soon after the vents' discovery in the late 1970s, a theory emerged among deep-sea biologists that vent ecosystems may have offered a safe refuge from global mass extinctions. While ecosystems elsewhere were being periodically demolished by colliding asteroids, massive volcanic eruptions, and runaway climate change, vent species could have been buffered from the chaos above and sustained by geochemical energy bubbling through the seafloor.

However, studies have subsequently shown that most groups of animals living on vents today evolved relatively recently (geologically speaking), perhaps only in the last few tens of millions of years. The same is true of Yeti crabs. A glimpse of what they used to look like comes from a fossil crab called *Pristinaspina gelasina* with a dimpled shell and forward-facing spines, dating back to the mid-Cretaceous (around a hundred million years ago), which was found in Alaska and looks to be a kind of proto-Yeti. Molecular clocks from living species suggest Yeti crabs first evolved on vents around thirty or forty million years ago, timing that Roterman thinks is no coincidence—it came after the end of a period of intense global heating known as the Paleocene-Eocene Thermal Maximum, when the earth was a steaming hothouse. During that time, around fifty-five million years ago, vents were unsuitable territories for crabs, partly because of the heat but more importantly the lack of oxygen. (Yetis have relatively small gills and rely on a good supply of oxygen in the water to survive.) Soaring shallow sea temperatures stemmed the flow of sinking oxygen-rich water, and the deep sea became suffocated, like a stagnant pond. In the Pacific, throughout this hothouse period, there was almost no oxygen at all in deep waters. That particular climate crisis lasted around one hundred thousand years, but only after millions of years did oxygen flow back down and ventilate the Pacific again, and the ancestors of Yeti crabs had a chance to move into the deep and onto hydrothermal vents.

Other parts of the Yeti crabs' story are proving less easy to explain, especially now that two additional species are being added to the family. In 2013, researchers from Korea were on an icebreaker near Antarctica, thousands of miles south of New Zealand, when they dredged up the crushed bodies of several pale crabs. Piecing together the broken bits, they had enough to describe a new Yeti species, *Kiwa araonae* (named after the icebreaker *Araon*). A sixth, as yet unnamed Yeti, showed up much farther north in the Pacific—close to where Charles Darwin drew inspiration for his theory of natural selection. When Darwin set sail from the Galápagos Islands in 1835, heading for Australia aboard HMS *Beagle*, he had no idea he was passing above smoking mountain ranges, or that clinging to their peaks were white crabs surviving on the microbes growing in their fur.

Nearly two centuries later, these Pacific Yeti crabs have been brought to the surface and are throwing new light on the evolution of Yetis. In order to accommodate them on the family tree, Roterman added another branch, which rearranged things and shifted the most likely origins of Yetis. Now it seems the family may have first evolved on vents, and then some moved to cold seeps, or at least that one site in Costa Rica, which remains the only known seep where Yetis live.

The two newest Yeti species are also raising more questions. DNA sequences revealed them to be most closely related to each other, despite now living thousands of miles apart—one off Antarctica, the other near the Galápagos Islands. Even more challenging, the first Yeti species glimpsed by humans, *Kiwa hirsuta*, lives in between the two. That particular part of the puzzle remains unsolved, but Roterman thinks many more Yetis have yet to be found, which could help decipher their distribution and evolution. The Pacific-Antarctic Ridge is a strip of prime Yeti-spotting territory in the southern Pacific between the locations of the two new species, but it remains almost entirely unexplored because the remote, freezing, stormy seas keep research vessels away. If Roterman is right, there are undiscovered Yetis all the way along it.

There could also be vents where Yetis used to live but were wiped out by volcanic eruptions on the volatile Pacific ridges. The perplexing family tree and patchy ranges across the globe are strong hints of the Yetis' turbulent past and present. "We're just looking at a snapshot in time," says Roterman. "Populations on vents maintain themselves in a *Whac-A-Mole* kind of way," he says. "They keep appearing and disappearing." Some populations will hang on, while others go extinct and blink out, and others slide up and down the lines of ridges, spreading to other vents within reach. The hunt for Yetis will continue, and there's a good chance that the next species discovered will change the story again.

Highs and Lows

From a short way away, it looked as though a cluster of giant, balled-up spiders were lying scattered across the lower flanks of a mountain, one located close to two miles underwater. A deep-diving submersible was transmitting real-time images of the scene along a cable up to the ship at the surface, then via satellite link to YouTube. Onlookers around the world leaned in and saw that these were in fact octopuses, a thousand or more. Such a large congregation had never been seen before—octopuses are habitually solitary, even sociopathic animals. Evidently, these ones weren't troubled by one another's presence. It was a peaceful scene. The pale violet animals had their arms folded over their bodies, suckers outermost. Here and there a siphon tube huffed as one of them took a breath, and a coiled arm stretched then tucked back in, showing glimpses underneath of clutches of lozenge-shaped eggs. They were all females brooding their unhatched young.

The streaming view switched to the auxiliary camera looking down from above onto the submersible, which shone a puddle of light onto the underwater mountainside that stretched away into the darkness. This was Davidson Seamount, off the coast of central California, one of the biggest seamounts in US waters. Roughly oblong-shaped, it is twenty-six miles long, eight miles wide, and more than a mile tall, its peak lying far beneath the waves.

When scientists first spotted the cephalopods on the Davidson's lower flanks during that dive in October 2018, they had an idea as to why the brooding females were gathering there. They could be speeding up the development of their eggs. Previously, a single female octopus had been found nearby, brooding her eggs on the steep wall of Monterey Canyon. Scientists from the Monterey Bay Aquarium Research Institute (MBARI) went back eighteen times with a submersible and saw her again and again, still sitting there, identifiable from her scratches and scars. They sent down morsels of food to offer her, but she paid no attention. She just sat there, apparently without moving from that spot, protecting her eggs from predators and replenishing the oxygen with water squirted through her siphon. Eventually, almost five years after they first saw the solo brooding octopus, the MBARI scientists went back and she was gone. Presumably, her eggs had hatched, and the young had drifted away, by which time the starved mother octopus would have died, as most do after they breed just once in their lifetime. The octopus crowd at Davidson Seamount could be attempting to avoid such a long wait by incubating their eggs in warm water percolating from a shallow magma chamber inside the mountain. The following year the science team went back to the same spot—this time with a temperature probe fixed to the submersible—and found the brooding octopuses still there, basking in water that was fifty degrees Fahrenheit, much warmer than the ambient temperature, which typically hovers just above freezing. These conditions were warm enough to speed the growth of the unhatched young and potentially reduce their five-year brooding time. It would explain the ribbons of octopuses nestled along fractures in the mountainside where balmy water trickles out.

These warm springs are valuable territory for brooding female octopuses as well as other animals that have something to gain. Indeed, the returning scientists spied an egg hatching and a tiny octopus emerging, only to be immediately grabbed by a waiting shrimp. For a few minutes, the shrimp and the baby octopus wrestled in front of the camera. "I feel like maybe the octopus could take him," said one of the scientists commentating on the live video stream. Eventually, the hatchling broke free and swam off, and the shrimp returned to the egg clutch to wait for another miniature octopus to appear.

Being within a day's reach of the California coast, Davidson Seamount is well known compared to most other underwater mountains, which are far more remote and difficult to get to. Scientists have been to Davidson dozens of times and sent autonomous submersibles to map the details of its contours, and yet big discoveries are still being made, like octopus nurseries. It's one of fewer than three hundred seamounts that have been visited and studied in any detail. The majority of these ubiquitous features scattered through the deep sea have yet to be explored.

◦◦

Scientists have known of seamounts since the mid-nineteenth century, when underwater peaks were found one by one, essentially by touch. The first to be given a name, in 1869, lies midway between the Azores and mainland Europe. A team of Swedish scientists had lowered a dredging net over the side of their ship, expecting it to take an hour or more to reach the seabed, but after a few minutes the line went slack. The dredge had landed on the peak of a giant underwater mountain, only 600 feet beneath the surface. They named the seamount Josephine, after their ship. It was around this time that the depth of the oceans became a matter of great international importance, when telegraph cables were for the first time being stretched across the seabed between Europe and North America. Surveying expeditions were dispatched to lower sounding wires, measure depths, and find the best routes to lay the cables; in the process, they occasionally stumbled across seamounts.

"To our surprise and delight, the sinker brought up at sixty-six fathoms!" wrote Herbert Laws Webb in 1890, recalling his time aboard the cable ship *Dacia* a few years earlier while surveying the route for a telegraphic cable between the Canary Islands and Spain. "It was obvious we had pitched upon a bank, or rather a mountain, of startling proportions, perhaps the lost island of Atlantis itself."

The abundance of seamounts began to come to light only when other methods were invented for finding them. The newest techniques involve spotting them from space. Seamounts can be so big and dense they exert a gravitational pull on the seawater around them, essentially drawing more water toward their center of mass, in the same way the moon tugs at the oceans and generates the global tides; being incompressible, seawater doesn't squeeze in around seamounts but piles up above them. Satellites precisely measure the height of the ocean surface, locating slight bulges created by massive, basaltic peaks below the waterline. Various estimates from satellite studies indicate that the biggest seamounts—5,000 feet or higher—number between thirty thousand and more than one hundred thousand worldwide and occur in the Indian and Atlantic Oceans, around Antarctica, in the Mediterranean, and in highest concentration in the central Pacific. All are underwater volcanoes, skirting mid-ocean ridges and subduction zones, and scattered across forty or fifty oceanic hot spots where the earth's crust thins and magma billows up from the mantle.

As the resolution of satellite sensors improves, they'll be able to detect smaller seamounts, and the global count will doubtless rise. Still, though, the only technique currently available to detect lower peaks employs sonar. First developed during World War II for detecting submarines and warships, the technology has been repurposed by scientists to survey the seabed. Shipborne devices direct beams of sound downward, and sensors listen for the echoes bouncing off solid surfaces, which are then interpreted as three-dimensional topographical maps identifying raised features on the seabed.

Whether many of these are sea hills or seamounts has been a matter of much debate. On land, no universal definition exists of the height a mountain must reach; historically, minimum heights for terrestrial mountains have ranged from 1,000 to 2,000 feet, making one person's tall hill another's small mountain. Meanwhile underwater, 3,300 feet has been considered the minimum height for a seamount. However, as more seamounts have been surveyed and studied, little geological or ecological justification has come to light to impose such a height limit. Smaller seamounts, 330 feet or higher, can host important deep-sea ecosystems similar to those seen on more imposing underwater peaks.

Detailed acoustic maps have yet to be made for the entire deep sea, so a precise tally of these smaller seamounts is unavailable. Nevertheless, a high-end estimate for the number of underwater volcanic peaks, made by extrapolating the known to the unknown, reaches a speculative twenty-five million. Together, all these seamounts, big and small, create a vast, fragmented habitat, a living biome far bigger than all the world's rain forests put together and home to a comparably dazzling array of species.

✍

Danish fabulist Hans Christian Andersen could easily have set his fairy tale "The Little Mermaid" on a seamount. His protagonist could wander through forests made not of plants but ancient animals that grow in so many shapes and colors. She could hide among the folds of a giant sponge and never be seen or sit in tall treelike structures that sprout from the mountainside. She could press her chewed bubblegum onto the branches, adding to the pink, knobbly sculptures. Getting ready for a party, she might make a dress from golden lace, pluck an iridescent spiral to drape across her shoulders, and grab a sea cucumber, shake it until it glowed red, and use it as lipstick.

Umbrella-shaped sea lilies could be twirled overhead to deflect the falling marine snow; sea pens could be used to write in her diary; and basket stars with coiling, branching arms could be worn as an elaborate hat. The problem is, readers might assume that Andersen had made up all these details, whereas many of them are true.

~

Among the seamounts that scientists have visited, they've seen great diversity of habitats and species. Not all seamounts are the same; some are continuations of the muddy abyss and not obviously distinct from their surroundings; many, though, attract species that need a hard surface to settle on—in particular, corals.

In shallow tropical seas, reef-building corals hog not only the sunlight but the limelight. These are the corals most people know about, the ones that sculpt atolls and build edifices like the Great Barrier Reef. However, more types of coral live in deep, cold seas than in the warm shallows. Out of roughly five thousand known coral species, well over half—some thirty-three hundred—live in the deep.

Corals are a wide assortment of animals, all close relatives of sea anemones and jellyfish and other soft-bodied creatures with tentacles and stingers. Corals are discernible by their bodies, which are made up of minute polyps, each with a stalk and a ring of tentacles that look like a flower's petals, only these ones twitch and fidget. Some corals are solitary and live one by one; most live in colonies, splitting to form more polyps and sticking together in their hundreds and thousands. Corals may shed eggs and sperm into the water, or they hold onto fertilized eggs and brood them within their polyps. The eggs hatch into larvae, which drift off until landing on a piece of suitable seabed, and there they set up their own colony and begin to divide and grow.

A major difference between the corals that live in shallow seas and those in deep seas is the way they eat. Inside the polyps of most tropical corals are zooxanthellae, single-celled, sun-supping microbes that turn carbon dioxide into sugars and feed their coral hosts. (These zooxanthellae are lost during outbreaks of coral bleaching, when corals get overheated and stressed.) Corals can grow at least five miles underwater, and down deep, there's no sunshine to be had. Instead of soaking up the sun, they rely on their skills as stationary hunters, snagging plankton with their tiny stinging tentacles and feeding on particles of marine snow. This is one reason corals like to grow on seamounts as well as the steep walls of underwater canyons; when deep, slow currents meet the sheer flanks of a seamount or escarpment, the seawater has a tendency to swirl upward, like winds buffeting a cliff face and generating updrafts on which birds like to hover. The accelerating water sweeps away silt from seamounts and keeps the lava slopes clear and ready for coral larvae that need a hard landing place. And once corals have established, the seamount currents bring streams of particles and planktonic prey to feed these mountain climbers. In the deep sea, corals like a sturdy breeze.

Common on seamounts are octocorals, so called for the eight tentacles in their polyps (many corals have just six). This big group includes plumed sea pens standing more than six feet tall and spiraling shiny bottlebrushes of the genus *Iridogorgia*;★ bamboo corals have treelike skeletons divided into knuckles, resembling their plant namesake; sea fans look like lungs squashed flat, complete with branching filigrees of air sacs. Some of these octocorals occupy shallow seas, but 75 percent of the species in this group live in the deep. A similar portion of black corals are deep dwellers; while these can look like frizzy white shrubs or orange ostrich feathers or tall yellow corkscrews, all are black on the inside, with skeletons made of chitin (the same hard material that forms shrimp shells and beetle wings).

★ *Irido* is from the Greek for "rainbow," and *gorgia* derives from "gorgonian"; this group of corals, including octocorals, is named after the snake-haired Gorgons of Greek mythology because of their complex, branching shapes.

Octocorals and black corals are joined in the deep by various stony corals, the scleractinians, which have limestone skeletons. Among these is the cosmopolitan species *Lophelia pertusa*, which grows in white thickets all through the deep. A 2012 study revealed *Lophelia pertusa* contain mitochondria that are genetically almost identical to another coral genus, *Desmophyllum*, leading to calls for its renaming as *Desmophyllum pertusa*, the convention being that the older genus (named in 1834) beats the more recent one (from 1849). However, not all experts agree with the ruling, which may change again pending further genetic tests. "We write *Desmophyllum* but we say *Lophelia*," says deep-sea biologist Nils Piechaud. Whichever name they should go by, these corals are prominent on seamounts and canyons and grow in great mounds in the abyss. In 2018, scientists discovered them growing off the coast of South Carolina in a mound at least 330 feet tall and stretching for eighty miles. In the Mediterranean as well as along the northwestern coast of Africa and on the Mid-Atlantic Ridge, these stony corals have been growing continuously in the same places for fifty thousand years.

Lace corals, in particular, have a special association with the deep.★ Another group with limestone skeletons, they are generally small and delicate, pigmented red, pink, blue, brown, or purple, colors that go unseen in the dark deep and may serve some other purpose; perhaps they are the by-product of a bad-tasting compound that puts off chewing predators. Around 90 percent of the several hundred known species of lace corals are deep dwellers. What's more, lace corals are originally from the deep. Fossils indicate they first evolved in the deep sea during the Paleocene, around sixty-five million years ago. Genetic studies reveal they flourished and diversified into numerous deep species, then some made a break for the surface. On four separate occasions over the last forty million years, lace corals

---

★ Within the Cnidaria, the lace corals, officially known as stylasterids, are hydrozoans, placing them among the narcomedusae, hydromedusae, and siphonophores.

dispatched larvae skyward and gave rise to species that now live in tropical and temperate surface seas. This goes against a long-held idea that presumes the recent living history of the oceans is a story of the deep receiving species from above. While that's true for many groups of animals that migrated downward from the more hospitable shallows, the lace corals and others have shown that marine species can also go in the opposite direction.

Alongside corals are various animals that likewise look a lot like plants and take similar advantage of the deep, craggy mountainsides and streams of waterborne food. Stalked crinoids, also known as sea lilies, live only in the deep. These relatives of sea cucumbers and sea urchins stand tall and hold out five feathery arms to sift food from the water.

Seamounts are also often covered in sponges, the organ-free, mouthless creatures that could have been the first animals to evolve, at least six hundred million years ago.★ Throughout the eons, daily life for sponges has mainly involved interminably drawing water through the sides of their porous bodies and extracting particles of food. (There are also some carnivorous sponges that snag small fish and crustaceans.) Until recently, sponges were generally assumed to be motionless, but thirty years' worth of time-lapse photography from cameras at Station M, a long-term study site on the abyssal plain off the California coast, have spotted sponges behaving in unexpected ways. Some roll around the abyss, like tumbleweed, riding the slow, deep currents; and some perform what appear to be slow-motion sneezes, which can take weeks to complete, perhaps to expel irritating particles from their bodies.

Their lives may be simple, and their sneezes long and drawn out, but deep-sea sponges can be stunning to look at; some are ear shaped, others pom-poms on stalks, and one looks like a glass of milk frozen

---

★ Sponges are placed in their own phylum, Porifera, from the Latin for pore-bearing; their bodies are indeed full of holes.

in mid-spill. The carnivorous sponge nicknamed Sputnik resembles a miniature Soviet-era satellite, with long, plankton-catching spines. Hexactinellid sponges build their skeletons from fine threads of silicon dioxide, the same material as sand and glass. Some hexactinellids hold themselves aloft on long stalks and look like shocked sock puppets, mouths agape. One species of hexactinellid, the Venus' flower-basket sponge (*Euplectella aspergillum*), grows as hollow tubes, sealed at each end, which look like they've been knitted from strands of glass; trapped inside each tube, male-and-female pairs of shrimp pick at the scraps of food wafting through the porous sponge walls and release their larvae, which escape the glassy cage and drift off to find a sponge of their own.

On the flanks and tops of seamounts and the steep walls of underwater canyons, animal-made forests flourish with "trees" of corals, sponges, and sea lilies. In 2017, diving on a seamount near Johnston Atoll in the North Pacific, 800 miles southwest of Hawaii, scientists encountered a scene that looked to them like it had come straight out of a Dr. Seuss book. They nicknamed it "The Forest of the Weird." A dense community of sponges and corals stood tall on stalks and their bodies, yellow, white and pink, were all oriented in the same direction as if their attention had been caught by something in the distance. In truth, their wide fluted funnels and alien-like heads with hollow "eyes" were all growing in such a way to catch particles in the prevailing current.

Besides sharing a similar sedentary, water-sifting lifestyle, many of the animals that form these deep forests also happen to have exceptionally long life spans.

Bamboo corals can live between thirty-five and close to two hundred years; colonies growing on seamounts today were already a decade or so old by the time Charles Darwin set sail in 1831 on his global voyage of discovery on HMS *Beagle*. Individual sea lilies can live for 340 years. It's possible to find living specimens on seamounts that would have arrived as larvae in the late seventeenth century and started to grow around the time of the Salem witch trials. Had William Shakespeare the means and inclination to explore one of the world's forested seamounts, he would have seen hexactinellid sponges that are still alive today, four hundred years later.

Even longer-lived are gold corals (another type of cnidarian), which can survive for several millennia. Gold corals on seamounts today began growing twenty-seven hundred years ago during the early days of ancient Rome. The oldest seamount dwellers are black corals, with living colonies that settled and began growing during the Bronze Age, when pharaohs of the Old Kingdom of Egypt were building their great pyramids, around forty-two hundred years ago.

Many organisms in the deep live to a great age, but why depth and longevity tend to go together is not entirely clear. Most likely the effect stems from the combined influence of temperature, light, and food all decreasing with depth. Rather than living fast, consuming fast, and dying young, deep-sea animals take their time, growing slowly, waiting for the next meager meal to come along and for the next opportunity to mate.

We know about the ancient lives of corals thanks to radioisotope dating and studies of how much these colonial animals grow each year. Seen through a microscope and illuminated in ultraviolet light, a slice of coral looks like a tree stump, with concentric circular growth rings. Although the deep is dark all year, still the seasons reach into it; pulses of food fall down when the shallower seas above are warmer and more productive, and so corals grow faster or slower depending on the time of year. The growth rings not only allow researchers to work out a coral's age but also to look into the past and use the coral as a time capsule.

Etched into the skeletons of deep-sea corals is a global archive of how the oceans used to be. Scientists have worked out how to measure minute traces of chemicals, which tell them what the temperature, nutrients, and pH were in the surrounding seawater when that particular part of the coral was growing, tens, hundreds, or thousands of years previously. For instance, corals collected off Nova Scotia in Canada showed a distinct change in nitrogen isotopes when they were growing in the 1970s. This coincides with the acceleration of anthropogenic climate change and suggests that major currents in the Atlantic were beginning to shift. Long-lived corals provide a record stretching far back into the past; they're helping us build a picture of how the oceans have been changing, with and without human influence, and they're helping us improve forecasts of what lies ahead.

⁓

Over the centuries and millennia, as the corals, sponges, and sea lilies have formed old-growth forests on seamounts, they've provided habitats, shelter, and food for other animals, which have moved in around them. Perching on coral branches are squat lobsters nipping food from the water and Venus flytrap anemones, which catch prey by folding themselves in half just like the carnivorous plants do; more sea urchin relatives, the brittle stars and snake stars, wrap themselves in knots around coral fans; cat sharks lay their egg cases among thickets of octocorals, leaving them hanging from the branches like Christmas decorations; octopuses arrive not only to brood their eggs but to prowl and hunt among the sponge groves.

Seamount residents are joined by a carnival of migrants. Tuna and swordfish, sea turtles and elephant seals, hammerhead, blue, and whale sharks, dolphins and seabirds all spend time swimming around or soaring in the air above seamounts, where they feed, find mates, or just find their way.

The hungry ones come for a feast stirred up by the shapes of some seamounts that act as a zooplankton trap. Every night, great swarms of these minute animals rise up from the twilight zone to feed at the sea surface while it's darker and they're safer from predators that hunt by sight. Before sunrise, the zooplankton swim back down. However, if during the night they happen to drift over a seamount, there may be no clear path to the deep, and thus swarms of zooplankton get stuck at the summit. This phenomenon, called topographic blockage, may help to explain how life flourishes above many seamounts. Smaller fish come to feed on the zooplankton, which in turn get eaten by bigger fish, cetaceans, and seabirds.

Migrating animals have various ways of finding seamounts. Albatrosses and petrels may smell their way from mount to mount, following a trail of dimethyl sulfide, the chemical that wafts into the air from dense shoals of grazing zooplankton. Sharks and turtles may sense the geomagnetic anomalies associated with seamounts and mark them as waypoints on the maps in their minds. This could be how Japanese eels find their way each year to Suruga Seamount, 1,500 miles south of Japan. When the moon is new, mature eels swim toward this spot in the Pacific, which serves them well as a marker for spawning. Their eggs hatch into leaf-shaped larvae, which ride the North Equatorial Current westward, then join the Kuroshio Current, sweeping north toward the rivers of Asia, where the young eels will grow and mature in fresh water. If spawning happened any farther south than Suruga, there's a risk the larvae would miss the west-flowing current and travel south instead, finding themselves adrift with no freshwater habitat within reach.

Humpback whales may also follow magnetic maps to find their way to seamounts, although exactly why they go there and take time to pause remains something of a mystery. Near the South Pacific island of New Caledonia, satellite tags and sensors fixed to migrating humpbacks have revealed that many of them linger at seamounts, sometimes for a week or longer. The whales seem to prefer tall mountains, with peaks submerged not far below the surface, around 260 feet at most. They could be resting, feeding, or perhaps breeding; the seamounts offer obvious features where whales can meet up and find partners. It's possible that male humpbacks come to seamounts to sing their long, complex songs. The mountainsides could act as musical arenas, with acoustic properties that help to broadcast their melodies into the wide, open ocean.

❧

Seamounts lie in the deep, out of sight, but they make their presence felt above the waves and on land. On November 11, 2018, for about a half hour, a strange rumble rolled across the earth. Seismographs located the source of the low-frequency tremor near the Indian Ocean island of Mayotte, between Madagascar and Mozambique. But for some time, geologists were mystified, unable to work out why the globe had resonated for so long, like an enormous bell.

Six months later, scientists on board the French research ship *Marion Dufresne* surveyed the region and found not a prehistoric sea serpent slithering across the abyss, as some people had imagined, but a brand-new seamount. The huge underwater volcano hadn't been there in seabed maps drawn three years earlier. The seamount was made by what was quite possibly the largest underwater eruption ever detected. The grumbling, humming sound may have emanated from the vast magma chamber, miles beneath the seafloor, collapsing in on itself. Why the seamount formed in that particular place remains unclear. Some geologists think it might be a hot spot, like the one forming the Hawaiian seamounts in the Pacific; others think it could be linked to the ancient rift where Madagascar split from mainland Africa 135 million years ago; or it could be an extension of the active East African Rift, which is slowly tearing the continent apart.

As well as triggering earthquakes when they form, seamounts can at times make earthquakes worse. At subduction zones, where one tectonic plate dives under another, seamounts generate a rough surface that sticks the plates together, like a strip of Velcro, building up stress, which is eventually released as a more explosive quake.

Conversely, geologists have discovered, in some circumstances seamounts actually lessen the severity of earthquakes. In April 2014, a major quake struck the northern coast of Chile with a moment magnitude of 8.2, but it wasn't as big as geologists had been expecting. Chile is frequently hit by earthquakes because just offshore, the Nazca tectonic plate is sinking beneath the South American Plate. A long stretch of the subduction zone hadn't experienced a major quake since 1877, and one was definitely due. When it finally did strike in 2014, it seems a cluster of seamounts blocked the spread of the seismic rupture, dampening the quake.

The ultimate fate for all seamounts is to be drawn to the edges of tectonic plates, as if they're standing on a very slow moving walkway, traveling at a speed of a couple of inches per year. Instead of stepping off at the end of the walkway, the mountains get dragged down into a deep trench at the subduction zone and hauled back toward the earth's mantle.

Currently, some seamounts are in the throes of falling into trenches, shifting from being the highest points in the abyss to the lowest. Christmas Seamount in the Indian Ocean is nearing the Java Trench, and to the north of New Zealand, Osbourn and Bougainville Seamounts are tipping over by a few degrees as they slip into the Tonga and Kermadec Trenches. There are also traces of seamounts that were subducted long ago. In the western Pacific lie the remains of at least four giant seamounts that got jammed as they fell into the Mariana Trench. By the time they have plunged into trenches, seamounts have largely been stripped of their coral and sponge forests—these depths are too great for them to flourish—but other animals can survive this far down and make themselves at home at the oceans' deepest points.

⁊

In a tide pool on the coast of Kodiak Island, off Alaska, or anywhere else along North America's Pacific coast as far south as Santa Barbara, lives a small fish, shaped like a tadpole and orange or purplish in color. If you try to pick one up, it clings to a rock with its pelvic fins, which are shaped into a sucker and act rather like a snail's foot, giving these fish their molluscan name. The tide pool snailfish, as this one is known, belongs to a curious family, the Liparidae. It has relatives in the Arctic and Antarctica that make antifreeze to stop themselves from turning into blocks of ice. Offshore in the Pacific, snailfish lay their eggs inside the gill chambers of king crabs (how they do this without getting mortally pinched remains a mystery). And there are species of snailfish living in oceanic trenches all the way down in the hadal zone, deeper than any other vertebrates.

"If you hold one in your hand you can see through the skull and look at the brain," says Mackenzie Gerringer, assistant professor at the State University of New York at Geneseo and hadal snailfish specialist, who aims to understand how these pudgy, pale pink fish came to thrive at depths below 20,000 feet. Snailfish are a far cry from archetypal deep-sea fish, such as anglerfish and viperfish with their inky-black skin and yawning jaws decked in glassy fangs. And yet, as Gerringer and her colleagues are finding out, snailfish are brilliantly adapted for living at extreme depths within the steep walls of oceanic trenches.

So far, at least fifteen snailfish species have been found living in ten trenches, one or two species per trench, including one eponymously named the Mariana snailfish. It's officially the deepest-documented vertebrate, seen alive and well at 26,503 feet, more than five miles down.

The Mariana snailfish pushes right up against the predicted depth limit for ocean-dwelling fish. Once they reach 26,900 feet, snailfish may be physiologically barred from going any deeper. The reason for this has to do with the way fish adapt their bodies to cope with the mounting pressure. Reaching 26,000 feet, the pressure is eight hundred times the surface pressure, or the equivalent of an elephant standing on every square inch of your body. Pressure in the hadal zone is so high, it's enough to bend biological molecules out of shape and block their vital functions. One way deep-sea animals cope is by loading their tissues with trimethylamine oxide (or TMAO), a chemical that affords protection for enzymes by preventing water from pressing into their active sites, regions that bind to substrate molecules and promote chemical reactions needed for healthy living cells and bodies. TMAO also protects molecular connections within other proteins around the body. The deeper animals dwell, the more pressure they experience and the more TMAO they need. As a result, the concentration of TMAO increases linearly with a fish's depth range. TMAO also happens to be the molecule that makes fish smell fishy, so presumably the deep-sea snailfish smell the worst of all.

However, a fish can contain only so much TMAO, and 26,900 feet is calculated as the point below which fish would need so much of the pressure-protective chemical that it would fundamentally mess with their biology. Living in the ocean, fish must adapt their bodies to survive in seawater, which is considerably saltier than their bodies and hence a more concentrated solution; in general, ocean salinity is around 3 to 4 percent, while marine fish usually have body fluids with the salt content equivalent to around 0.9 percent.* That being so, oceangoing fish spontaneously lose a lot of water across the membranes in their gills and skin by the process of osmosis, whereby water molecules diffuse from regions of lower to higher concentration (and thus tending toward equalizing the concentration on both sides of a biological membrane). To make up for this water loss, marine fish drink a lot of seawater and pump excess salts out of their gills.†

The osmotic balance shifts as TMAO builds up in the tissues of deep-sea fish, increasing the effective concentration of their tissues. Below 26,900 feet, there would be so much TMAO that their bodies total salt content would shift from being less concentrated than

---

* Put another way, ocean salinity is thirty to forty parts per thousand or roughly four to five ounces of dissolved salts per gallon (predominantly sodium chloride); all the dissolved ions inside a marine fish make up a concentration of around nine parts per thousand.

† Humans don't have this ability, which is why it's a bad idea to drink seawater, because your body will use more water to expel the salts.

seawater to more concentrated; then osmosis would begin to run in the opposite direction, with water absorbed through the skin and gills. Salmon, eels, and other migrating fish face a similar complication when they move into fresh waters. To cope, they stop drinking and begin to urinate a lot more, producing copious streams of dilute urine while their kidneys work overtime pumping vital salts back into the bloodstream. Adapting to the saltwater/freshwater transition takes time and energy, but for salmon and eels it's worth the effort, because their goal is to complete a vital part of their life cycle, to reach spawning and feeding grounds inland. Snailfish likely have little incentive to endure the radical remodeling required of their physiology if they were to dive down below 26,900 feet. As far as anyone knows, they don't descend to the bottom of trenches to breed. "To get to that tiny little percent of the bottom of the martini glass," says Gerringer, "might not be worth it on an evolutionary scale."

Snailfish have several other pressure adaptations written into their genes, as revealed when scientists in China sequenced the entire genome of the Mariana snailfish. They found it has multiple copies of genes that adjust the chemical makeup of its cell membranes, adding more unsaturated fatty acids, which keeps them pliant and less likely to crack—more like a layer of olive oil than butter—so cells don't burst under pressure. A mutation in a gene that normally regulates how developing bones are hardened and mineralized leaves Mariana snailfish with bendable skeletons made of cartilage (like sharks), which seem to be more pressure-tolerant than hard, fragile bones.

∽

Living in trenches, besides the immense pressure, snailfish face the same issue as all deep-sea animals: they have to find something to eat. With their V-shaped structure, like giant collecting devices, trenches funnel marine snow to the bottom; earthquakes frequently shake the sides, triggering underwater avalanches that bring in yet more snow and organic debris from the abyss. Thus, trenches are less hungry places than they could be, but snailfish don't eat snow.

The most common inhabitants of trenches are scavenging crustaceans called amphipods.* They are supremely unfussy eaters and will devour anything that falls into a trench. Amphipods have been seen at the very bottom of the Mariana Trench, where the pressure is so high it should in theory dissolve the calcium carbonate in their exoskeletons. In 2019, researchers at the Japan Agency for Marine-Earth Science and Technology discovered that amphipods cover themselves in aluminum gel (they consume metallic compounds from deep-sea muds to create this gel), which prevents their shells from melting away. Snailfish take advantage of the crustacean abundance in trenches and have adapted to a diet made up almost entirely of amphipods.

With small dark dots for eyes, snailfish have very poor vision and instead they hunt using their heightened sense of touch. Their lips appear puckered, with a row along each jaw of fluid-filled dimples capable of detecting ripples in the water made by wriggling, twitching amphipods. This helps a snailfish decide in which direction to lunge and snap.

Another of the snailfishes' secrets lies within their jaws, as revealed when Gerringer took a rare specimen of a Mariana snailfish and put it in a CT scanner. The intricate, three-dimensional view of the snailfish's skeleton revealed a second set of jaws at the back of the throat, known as pharyngeal jaws, which look like a pair of small, spiky toothbrushes. These, Gerringer thinks, help snailfish grab and crunch amphipods that they have sucked and slurped into their mouths.

---

* Amphipods have a series of legs that take on different forms, hence their name, derived from Greek words *amphi*, meaning "both," and *poda*, meaning "foot." Isopods, like the giant isopods in the Gulf of Mexico, generally have legs that all look the same—hence *iso*, meaning "equal."

Even though trench-dwelling snailfish have their staple diet reasonably well provided for, like other deep-sea organisms they are not replete with food and still need to save energy and operate as efficiently as possible. To investigate the biomechanics of these fish, Gerringer took a rather unusual approach. Snailfish caught in baited traps don't survive the journey to the surface, because of the combined stress of the rise in temperature and drop in pressure. To collect live snailfish would require an expensive pressurized, refrigerated capsule that could somehow be operated remotely from many miles above. Gerringer instead decided to make a replica snailfish. "It turns out that it's easier, cheaper, and faster to build a hadal snailfish than it is to go get one," she says.

She designed a robotic model to test an idea she had about the jelly that real snailfish have under their skin. Many fish have slime on the outside of their bodies. Snailfish have slime on the inside. "If you look at snailfishes, and especially if you hold one when they're first caught," she says, "they're full of goo."

The reason for this could be to help them swim more efficiently. A fish with a big round head and a tail stuck straight on—the basics of a snailfish's anatomy—suffers from drag vortices. Tadpoles are this shape, and they overcome the hydrodynamic drag by rapidly beating their tails, which is all very well in a shallow pond where there's plenty of food to fuel such energetic movements, but it's not so good for a fish living in the hungry deep sea.

Gerringer pieced together a sixteen-inch robot, slightly bigger than a real snailfish, using a 3D-printed body and fins, together with plastic bottle caps, electrical tape, a small battery and motor, and a cast silicon-rubber tail with a spring and two lengths of piano wire that made it beat from side to side. An important part of the robot was the volume-adjustable skin placed over its tail, ingeniously fashioned from a latex condom; when the condom was empty, the robot fish had a tadpole's profile; filled with water, the condom mimicked a layer of jelly, giving the robot a fatter base to its tail, like a snailfish has.

When the robotic fish set off around its aquarium tank in Gerringer's lab, it swam more than three times faster with its tail padded out with imitation jelly than without. The jelly that lines a snailfish's body makes it more streamlined, like the fairing on aircraft, giving it a smoother outline and reducing drag. As well as helping the fish swim, the gelatinous tissues have the added advantage of boosting buoyancy, making snailfish less likely to sink down into those forbidden depths of the trench where their physiology would not cope.

There is still a lot that Gerringer and colleagues don't yet know about the remarkably remote and unreachable hadal snailfish. Juveniles have been seen in trenches at depths slightly lower than adults, but for now no one knows why. No one knows whether snailfish spend their whole life in trenches or if there are times when they emerge or particular places they go to spawn and feed. There are trenches Gerringer would love to visit, like the remote Aleutian Trench off Alaska, which likely contains undiscovered snailfish species. But as her and other's studies are showing, at the heart of deep-sea biology lies the ambition to understand how life is possible, how species survive and ecosystems flourish under extreme conditions. Naming new and ever-stranger life-forms is just the beginning of the story.

∽

"February in the Gulf is the worst," said Jason Tripp. "Not January. Not March. February."

Tripp, a seasoned submersible pilot, had worked for years in the Gulf of Mexico, and he told me this on board the *Pelican*, back on the day when we motored south from the Louisiana coast—February twelfth. Then he rolled up his sleeves and showed me the pale blue anti-nausea bands on his wrists, placed there like talismans. "I don't get seasick," he said, "but I've got these."

I remembered this gloomy declaration when, midway through the expedition, high winds and nine-foot waves brought the science to a halt. The sea became too rough for the crew to safely lift the submersible off the back deck and into the water; it could spin and twist its cable or swing through the air and slam into the ship.

Deprived of our vital workhorse, we were stranded more than a mile above the study site, with no way of touching or seeing it, waiting for the sea to ease. At nighttime, down in my stateroom below the waterline, the waves roared against the outside of the hull, and I learned to fly, ever so briefly, as my whole body got left behind at the top of a wave, then sharply reconnected with the falling ship. In the daytime, I sat in the galley with others from the science team trying to read and write while holding our laptops firmly in place to stop them sliding across the table. Members of the crew took turns to monitor the sea state and the ship's position, letting the vessel drift a short way and then motoring back toward the study site. Our path, drawn loop after loop on the GPS map, looked like a crumpled flower.

Eventually the waves calmed, and to everyone's relief the submersible was deployed. I was in the galley watching the underwater view streaming from below when the screen went blank. This had happened several times before, and usually the connection quickly restored itself, so at first I thought nothing of it. However, this blackout was caused by something more worrying. At the worst possible moment, a rogue wave had hit the ship side on. The cable slipped and jammed tight on the pulley, leaving the submersible stuck around 100 feet down with no obvious way of being freed. The sub was hanging powerless below the ship, like a child's toy car on a string.

With no hint of panic or drama, the *Pelican*'s crew and the submersible engineers donned their safety gear and gradually and painstakingly fixed the problem, figuring how to secure and reel in the cable. Hours later, we all looked on at the yellow submersible sitting innocently back on the deck as if nothing had happened. Then, just when the sub was ready to go back in the water, another weather front bowled in to greet us, the waves got unfeasibly big, and the expedition was called off.

The *Pelican* steamed north until flying pelicans came into view, gliding by like small pterosaurs, welcoming us back to shore. For one last night I slept on the ship, as it sat still, moored in the harbor, but in my bunk I continued to rise and fall, waking every hour, convinced we were underway and heading back out to float above the deep. Whenever I return to shore, it always takes time for the sea to let me go. This time my landsickness was worse than I'd ever experienced. I had been out in the Gulf for almost two weeks, in constantly rough conditions; for two further weeks, my body thought I was still there, and when I closed my eyes, my mind rocked with the memory of waves.

⁓

Seven weeks later, the team took the *Pelican* back into the Gulf and, with fair weather and more time for science, explored a cold seep and its neighboring brine pool.

Dotted across the bottom of the Gulf of Mexico are pools with rippling, silvery surfaces. Cold seep habitats often fringe these pools, with dense beds of mussels and clams feeding their chemosynthetic microbes on the methane and hydrogen sulfide that comes bubbling through the seabed. Fish, shrimp, and crabs successfully hunt for prey in the cold seeps, unless they touch the silvery pools. The dead bodies of those unfortunates lie scattered around. In the pools are the entombed and preserved corpses of crabs and giant isopods (like the ones we saw eating the alligator) that fell into the water, which is five times saltier than regular seawater. The pools have no oxygen either, making them even more deadly.

The brine forming these pools has seeped up through the seafloor from buried layers of salt laid down around 160 million years ago, during the Jurassic period, when the Gulf of Mexico was cut off from the Atlantic. The isolated water body evaporated and dried up, leaving solid blankets of salts lining the bottom, in places close to five miles thick. Eventually the Gulf flooded again, around the time the Rocky Mountains were forming; sediments eroded from the new mountain range and washed into the Gulf, burying the salted crust. With a massive weight of sediments pressing down, the salt layers have bent and deformed, a process known as salt tectonics. Seawater percolates down through cracks, dissolving the salts and forming the concentrated brines, which then get squeezed upward. Being so much saltier and therefore denser than the surrounding seawater, the brine doesn't mix but accumulates in pools. Besides the Gulf of Mexico, brine pools are also known to form in the Red Sea, the Mediterranean, and near Antarctica; some are puddles, others are huge salty lakes, many miles wide.

The *Pelican*'s submersible set off to explore a modest-size pool, 100 feet or so across. But soon the brine pool started to shrink, and before long it was completely empty. Presumably the hypersaline water had seeped back into a crack in the seabed—something that is likely to happen regularly at the thousands of other brine pools but had never previously been documented.

Even more startling, at the bottom of the toxic puddle were small mounds of mud, and on them sat living animals—clusters of large, spiky sea urchins and acorn worms*—all apparently alive and doing well. The worms were a new species, lurid green and purple, and looked like partially inflated modeling balloons covered in pimples.

These green worms and sea urchins were the first animals known to survive at the bottom of a toxic brine pool. No one yet knows how they tolerate such hostile conditions, but uncovering their very existence was the kind of discovery in the deep that comes when scientists happen to be looking in the right place at the right time.

---

* Also called spoon worms, these are types of polychaete worms officially known as echiurans.

PART TWO

DEPEND

Deep Matters

As soon as you stop thinking about it, the deep can so easily vanish out of mind—more so than that other great distant realm, outer space. The deep has no stars at night to remind us it is there, and no moon shining down. And yet, this hidden place reaches into our daily lives and makes vital things happen without our knowing. The deep, quite simply, makes this planet habitable.

By its vast volume and restless motion—and the superior heat-soaking nature of water*—the ocean brings into balance Earth's interactions with the sun. Solar radiation beaming down would soon make conditions here unbearably hot were there not so much water to absorb it, especially now that the atmosphere is gaining a thickening layer of greenhouse gases. More than 90 percent of the extra heat trapped by human-emitted carbon dioxide has been taken up by the oceans. Without all the oceans' water, global temperatures on land would already be over 96 degrees Fahrenheit higher than during preindustrial times; across the United States, average summer temperatures would exceed 160 degrees Fahrenheit.

---

* Water has a far higher heat capacity than air, meaning it takes more energy to heat the same amount; it's why swimmers get colder in water than walkers in air of the same temperature, because the water draws more heat from the body; it also means water has a far greater capacity for trapping and storing heat than air.

As a consequence of all this sequestered heat, the ocean is the warmest it has ever been in recorded human history. Some regions are warming faster than others, but across the ocean as a whole, a 2020 study confirmed the average global temperature between the surface and 6,600 feet has been relentlessly rising year after year. In 2019, this upper layer of the ocean, deeper than a mile, was 0.135 degrees Fahrenheit warmer than the average between 1981 and 2010. That might seem an insignificant amount, in and of itself, except the heat required to elevate the ocean's top 6,600 feet by this much is equivalent to the explosion of 3.6 billion atomic bombs of the type detonated over Hiroshima. This mounting temperature is incontrovertible proof that human emissions of heat-trapping gases are driving the climate crisis; no other reasonable explanation exists for the warming ocean.

Since 2000, the ocean's temperature has been accurately monitored by a flotilla of robotic instruments called Argo floats. Research institutes around the world have collectively released around four thousand of these three-foot-long tubes, leaving them to drift by themselves for four or five years before the batteries die. Each probe is preprogrammed to sink and park itself at 3,300 feet, then periodically double its depth and gradually rise upward, measuring salinity, water speed, and temperature as it goes. At the surface, the Argo floats deliver their data back to base via satellite. The autonomous probes now provide nearly global coverage, with data extrapolated to fill in the horizontal gaps between measurements, but most are limited to the upper 6,600 feet, just the beginning of the deep.

Ship-based measurements are showing that heat from the atmosphere is also flowing much deeper down. Close to a fifth of the ocean's heat is stored below 6,600 feet, from the midnight zone reaching down into the abyss. Most of that is in the Southern Ocean, in the deep basins surrounding Antarctica; a lot of heat is also stashed in the deep on the western flank of the Mid-Atlantic Ridge and off the Atlantic coast of South America, in the Brazil Basin. And as the climate crisis worsens, more heat is sinking deeper, and abyssal waters are warming at an accelerating pace. Cold waters, deeper than 13,000 feet, in the South Pacific Ocean have been warming twice as fast in the 2010s as in the 1990s.

Warmer water makes its way into the deep via dense sinking currents, part of a planetary circulation system that plays another vital role in ameliorating the climate and making life on Earth possible. The strongest solar radiation beats down at the equator, the planet's midriff, which lies closest to the sun. If the ocean stood still, the equator would get hotter and hotter, while the polar regions became ever colder. As it is, much of the equatorial heat is absorbed into surface seas that continually slide away, sending warmth to northerly and southerly regions.

The driving force for this circulation, known as the global conveyor belt, is a combination of winds that ruffle and snag the sea surface and the sinking of cold, salty waters into the deep. In the Arctic, when sea ice forms at the surface, the surrounding seawater becomes more saline because most of the salt is squeezed out of the frozen ice crystals. The saltier seawater also cools, losing its heat to the polar atmosphere, and the resulting dense water sinks thousands of feet and begins a slow abyssal flow in a series of loops weaving around the planet.* The underwater current creeps across the deep seafloor, past Greenland and into the Labrador Sea, where more cold, dense water is added into the mix, and then it flows due south through the middle of the Atlantic, all the way to Antarctica. There the deep current gets supercharged with another vital injection of sinking water—known as Antarctic bottom water—the ocean's

---

* It takes on average 1,000 years for individual water molecules to complete a single loop of the conveyor belt.

densest, coldest water, which then seeps into the abyss of every major ocean basin.* Waters of the deep conveyor belt continue: some swirls into the Atlantic and the western Indian Ocean; some circles Antarctica, south of New Zealand, and heads northward into the Pacific. Eventually the tributaries approach the equator, where they warm and rise before joining a spiraling route, westward through Southeast Asia and across the Indian Ocean, then northward through the Atlantic and eventually to the portion of the conveyor belt known as the Gulf Stream, which swings from the Caribbean Sea along North America's eastern coast. Along the way, this draft of warm water releases heat to the atmosphere and is responsible for the relatively mild climate of western Europe; it's what keeps winters warmer in Portugal than in New York, France warmer than Nova Scotia.

Many important components keep the conveyor belt running—the formation of sea ice; the earth's spinning, which bends currents different ways in the Northern and Southern Hemispheres—but if the ocean were shallow everywhere, without the density-driven tumble of water to great depths tugging in surface water to replace it, the global currents would grind to a halt. As things stand, the ocean takes deep breaths, constantly inhaling and slowly exhaling over decades and centuries, mixing its contents and in the process not just regulating heat but also distributing nutrients, oxygen, and carbon throughout the ocean.

There are signs, however, in the past few decades, to suggest that parts of this circulation have begun to falter due to global heating. Antarctic bottom water has been getting measurably warmer, fresher, and less dense since the 1990s, due to a complex mix of changes involving sea ice and glaciers calving off the continental ice shelves. Increased fresh water pouring into the North Atlantic, including

---

* Known to form in the Ross Sea, the Weddell Sea, the Adélie coast, and Cape Darnley in East Antarctica (a source detected by sensors fixed to diving elephant seals), Antarctic bottom water can be as cold as thirty degrees Fahrenheit, its salt content high enough to prevent it from freezing.

from Greenland's melting ice caps, is reducing the salinity of the seawater that sinks into the deep, making it less dense and weakening the force of this essential part of the global conveyor belt. As a consequence, since the mid-twentieth century, equatorial waters that normally flow northward across the Atlantic have slowed by 15 percent, and there is a one in six chance of a temporary shutdown of this part of the conveyor belt in the next hundred years, triggering a big chill across Europe. Atlantic circulation has significantly weakened before, at the end of the last ice age when enormous continental ice sheets melted, so it could quite possibly happen again. More worrying still, the collapse of the Atlantic circulation system is one of the tipping points that could knock the earth into an irreversible climate catastrophe, leaving no room for any doubt that what happens to seawater as it flows through the deep is of great consequence.

⁓

Along many coasts, especially those on the easterly continental margins, winds push surface waters offshore and deep waters are drawn upward to replace them. Upwelling waters bring a stream of dissolved nutrients from the deep into the sunlit shallows, stimulating blooms of phytoplankton that inject food into the ecosystem. Just like plants on land, the minute photosynthesizing plankton grow best when fertilized with key elements and compounds, which can otherwise run low in the crowded surface seas. The most fertile coastal ecosystems and the world's most productive fisheries occur in regions of intense upwelling. Twenty percent of all the seafood caught globally comes from the four biggest upwelling systems, the California Current off western North America, the Humboldt Current along South America's Pacific coast, and the Canary and Benguela Currents off western and southwestern Africa, which together cover only 1 percent of the ocean surface. These waters supply much of the favorite seafood in North American and European diets; tuna caught in the eastern Atlantic off African coasts and packed into cans and Peruvian anchovies ground into fish meal and fed to farmed salmon and shrimp are all nourished directly by nutrients from the deep.

Carbon flowing in the opposite direction to the upwelling nutrients has its own crucial impact on the rest of the living planet. Phytoplankton harness the sun's energy, using it to convert carbon dioxide into carbohydrates. Some of the carbon in those organic molecules gets consumed by grazing zooplankton and breathed out as carbon dioxide, which swiftly returns to the atmosphere. And some of that carbon stays in the ocean; uneaten phytoplankton die and sink as particles of marine snow, together with dead zooplankton, their feces, abandoned larvacean houses, and other clumps of biological debris. As it falls, the blizzard is intercepted by all sorts of snow catchers, from narcomedusae to vampire squid; particles reaching the abyss stay down deep and get passed on around the food web or drop to the seabed, adding to layers of organic-rich ooze in the sediments. For thousands of years this abyssal carbon is banished to the deep and kept far out of reach of the atmosphere.

Snowfall in the deep—formally known as the biological carbon pump—varies across space and time. Spring blooms of phytoplankton in the North Atlantic are triggered by warming seas and create great pulses of sinking carbon. Snowdrifts build up on seamounts and abyssal hills. Flurries of snow are funneled downward by underwater canyons. In 2014 and 2015, two massive phytoplankton blooms were detected in the Southern Ocean, in a remote region that is normally a planktonic desert, deprived of the vital nutrient iron. (Continental shelves and atmospheric dust blowing off land are typical sources of iron for the oceans.) Analysis of water samples revealed the iron had upwelled from nearby deep-sea vents, revealing for the first time the role that hydrothermalism can play in boosting the carbon pump;★ scorching plumes spew iron from

---

★ The marker was a form of primordial helium, with a particular isotope, which comes from the earth's mantle and gets picked up and emitted by hydrothermal fluids.

the earth's mantle toward the ocean's surface, where it stimulates plankton blooms and the resulting avalanches of marine snow, fortifying stores of carbon in the deep.

Sperm whales offer a similar service of fertilizing the surface by bringing up iron from down below. While diving in the twilight and midnight zones, all the whales' nonessential bodily functions shut down; there's no digestion, and they defecate only at the sea surface. When they do come up to breathe and void their bowels, what comes out is a floating, iron-rich slick of liquid feces, an ideal phytoplankton fertilizer. Every year, sperm whales around Antarctica bring up approximately fifty tons of iron from the deep, triggering phytoplankton blooms. The resulting export of carbon from the atmosphere, annually around 440,000 tons, offsets the carbon dioxide the whales exhale, making them a net carbon sink, although now on a much smaller scale than they once were. Before industrial whaling, abundant Antarctic sperm whales fertilized enough phytoplankton to remove more than 2 million tons of carbon from the atmosphere every year, equivalent to the annual carbon emissions from the city of Washington, DC.

Accurately gauging how much carbon is swept into the deep by the snowy particles falling through the entire global ocean is a monumental task, given the scale, fluctuations, and intricacies involved. Estimates range from approximately 5 to 16 gigatons of carbon per year. Besides the carbon in marine snow particles sinking under gravity, more carbon is actively pulled into deep waters by a daily mass migration to and from the surface. Every day, as the sun sets around the world, a tremendous living wave races upward, as billions of zooplankton, fish, krill, squid, and jellies rise to hunt in the relative safety of the darkening shallows; when the sun reappears, they return to the darkness below, where they digest and defecate, releasing carbon consumed above. The strength of these so-called particle injection pumps has yet to be fully studied, but they may sequester as much carbon as the particles of marine snow that drift down under the force of gravity.

Increasingly, it's becoming obvious that ocean ecosystems are fundamental for the global climate. In total, a third of humanity's carbon emissions make their way into the ocean, saving the earth from an unthinkably swift and catastrophic version of the climate crisis. What lies ahead will depend crucially on what happens in the deep. Small changes in marine snowfall can significantly alter carbon sequestration in the ocean and hence carbon dioxide levels in the atmosphere. The full scale of the biological pump is still being resolved. In 2020, researchers at the Woods Hole Oceanographic Institution discovered that the efficiency of the biological pump has been drastically underrated. Traditionally, climate models assume there's a fixed depth (429 feet or 150 meters) above which there's enough sunlight to power photosynthesis. A huge data set of chlorophyll measurements, identifying where phytoplankton actually grow, revealed how much the sun's penetration differs in depth around the globe and through the seasons. By taking into account the variable sunlit zone, the Woods Hole team gauged that twice as much carbon sinks into the ocean every year than previous estimates, showing that the biological pump is even more powerful and critical for the climate.

∾

Our appreciation of the deep, and all it provides, should also stretch much further back in time, to the origins of life itself around four billion years ago. A leading theory proposes that living cells first emerged in the deep sea, specifically within hydrothermal vents. It was an idea first fleshed out in the early 1990s by NASA chemist Michael Russell. He postulated that tiny pores inside vent chimney walls could have provided templates for living cells, creating the necessary conditions for life-giving reactions to take place. This would have required vent temperatures to be low enough to not immediately boil the first signs of life into an overcooked primordial soup. And in 2000, researchers found just the kind of cool vent to fit Russell's theory. They were visiting the Atlantis Massif, a huge seamount south of the Azores, nine miles from the Mid-Atlantic Ridge, and saw a giant forest of sculpted, white carbonate spires that formed from chemical reactions in seabed rocks. The largest was 100 feet across and 200 feet tall. The Lost City, as the white smokers have been named, form the oldest known vent field in the world, thought to have been continually active for at least 120,000 years. Conditions like these would have been more prevalent in a much younger planet, when the earth's core was more hotly radioactive. As long as there has been an ocean, there have been hydrothermal vents, setting the stage for the first living cells to assemble.

In laboratories far from these vent systems, scientists have been re-creating conditions of the primeval deep sea and hunting for sparks of life. At NASA's Jet Propulsion Laboratory in California, Laurie Barge and Erika Flores have grown miniature hydrothermal vents, a few inches tall, which have successfully generated amino acids. Their next step will be to see whether these small molecules can accumulate in chimneys and join together into peptides and then proteins.

A major breakthrough took place in 2019, at University College London (UCL), when simple protocells assembled themselves inside a reactor built to simulate a hydrothermal vent. A mixture of fatty acids and fatty alcohols spontaneously formed these basic cells, with a membrane wrapped around a droplet of liquid. In previous studies, similar protocells had fallen apart in the presence of even low concentrations of sodium chloride, leading some researchers to suggest it was time to call off the search for origins of life in the salty ocean. But the UCL researchers showed that with the right recipe of ingredients, these simple cells were in fact more likely to form and be more stable with the addition of heat and salt, keeping the vent-origin theory of life well and truly alive.

Another strand of evidence came to light in 2017 in northern Canada, from a rare fragment of the earth's primitive oceanic crust preserved on the continental plate. Scientists found microscopic tubes and filaments, half the width of a human hair and made of the iron-rich mineral hematite, which have the same characteristic branching shape as microbes that live on hydrothermal vents today, hinting that they grew on ancient vents. The rocks embedded with these minute structures are at a minimum 3.77 billion years old, making them by far the world's oldest known fossils and the remains of the very earliest living cells;★ some experts in the field think they could be as much as 4.28 billion years old.

Life began on Earth such a mind-bendingly long time ago that we will probably never know for sure how it started. There are clues to be found and studies to be done to simulate the past and watch for vital signs of self-replicating biology, and not just here on Earth but elsewhere in the universe. Hydrothermal vents have been detected beneath the icy crusts on Saturn's moon Enceladus and Jupiter's moon Europa, possibly even in an ancient ocean on Mars, offering up the tantalizing possibility that living cells could have sparked into existence there too.

The deep sea also offers clues as to what happened after early cells first arose and inoculated the rest of the earth with life. For the subsequent two billion years, there were only simple, single-celled creatures, the bacteria and archaea. The next seminal step in the evolution of life—the growth of complex cells, the eukaryotes—likely took place in the deep. You and I are eukaryotes, along with all the other animals, plants, algae, and fungi, and we all have structures inside our cells, such as the mitochondria that generate energy and the nucleus where DNA is stored. It's thought eukaryotes may have emerged when one microbe absorbed another; those cellular

---

★ Prior to their discovery, the oldest known fossils were three hundred million years younger.

structures could have formed from swallowed microbes. But exactly how that happened has long remained one of life's greatest mysteries.

In 2019, researchers from Japan announced they had successfully grown in their lab a strange type of microbe that could be the closest living relative to early eukaryotes. More than a decade earlier, scientists diving inside the submersible *Shinkai 6500* collected mud samples from more than a mile deep, hoping to find microbes that could help clean up oil spills. In the laboratory, the researchers found traces of a rare type of cell known as Asgard archaea. These cells appear to have a mix of microbial and eukaryotic genes and had previously been known only from fragments of DNA also found in the deep sea. This was the first time anyone had found intact Asgard cells, and the team waited patiently for more than ten years while the cells multiplied at a sedate pace. While more familiar microbes like *E. coli* divide once every twenty minutes, an Asgard cell takes twenty-five days to split in two. They're also quite particular, growing only in conditions that mimic the cold, oxygen-poor deep and only in the company of other microbes. As the Japanese team saw among the slowly dividing cells, Asgard archaea have long appendages—they look like confused octopuses—and caught up in their arms are bacteria. Perhaps billions of years ago, Asgard-like cells got even more intimately entangled in other bacteria, engulfing them entirely and leading to the first eukaryotic cells. Now the search is on for more Asgard cells, to uncover more of this secret from the past that lies hidden in the present, down there in the deep.

Deep Cures

In 1986, half a ton of black, amorphous sponge, *Halichondria*, was hauled up from the shallow seas off the coast of Japan. Extracts of it were subsequently found to contain a powerful chemical that showed promise as a new tumor-killing medicine. In 1995, a different, bright yellow sponge, *Lissodendoryx*, collected from deeper waters off the Kaikoura Peninsula in New Zealand, yielded the same chemical, only in much higher concentrations. More than one ton of the sponge was needed to produce a half-gram droplet of what researchers by then knew as a compound called halichondrin B, which is remarkably toxic toward a variety of cancer cells. A molecular tweak led to the simpler but still effective molecule called eribulin.

The upshot, almost twenty-five years after its discovery, was the release in 2010 of eribulin as a chemotherapy drug for use in the late stages of metastatic breast cancer. It remains the only drug available that clinical trials have shown can prolong the lives of people whose cancer has spread to other parts of their body and who have already been through several rounds of chemotherapy. The molecule stops tumors from growing by binding to microtubules, the structures inside cells that play a key role in pulling chromosomes apart during cell division. With its microtubules blocked, a cell can't divide, and a tumor is halted in its tracks.

Searching for new drugs in the oceans has so far yielded a catalogue of some thirty thousand bioactive molecules, known as marine natural products, all of them with useful chemical properties of some kind. Out of those, hundreds have reached the stage of preclinical trials, dozens are in clinical trials with human patients, and six have been approved and released to the pharmaceuticals market. Eribulin is derived from the deepest-dwelling species of the six, but the yellow sponge, *Lissodendoryx*, lives not that far down, only 330 feet. However, the lack of drugs based on truly deep species is likely to change soon.

People have long been turning to the natural world for new therapies and medicines, and now they're paying more attention to the deep ocean and finding it's well worth the effort. As the hunt for cures goes deeper, an untapped reservoir of new chemicals is opening up, and a compelling reason is emerging for why the deep sea matters to us all.

∽

The Marine Institute in Galway has produced what it calls "The Real Map of Ireland." It's a map with no water, showing the rugged seabed topography that extends the country's maritime territory to ten times its land area. The island sits on a wide, shallow continental shelf, no more than 1,000 feet below the water surface. This natural extension of the land has allowed Ireland to claim sovereign rights to explore the natural resources across this huge area of seabed.

To the west, plunging into the Rockall Trough and the Porcupine Abyssal Plain, is a long, rocky escarpment etched with steep valleys and canyons. This is where Louise Allcock goes to look for ideas for new medicines. To collect specimens, her team sends a remote-operated submersible over the edge of Ireland's continental shelf, down to between 3,000 and 8,000 feet. There they use robotic arms and grippers to carefully snip small pieces of sponges and corals, as if they were pruning a flower garden; new laboratory techniques mean it's no longer necessary to take tons of living material—and along the continental edge, there are plenty of these plantlike animals to choose from.

"I've never seen this level of abundance anywhere else," says All-cock, a biologist who has explored many other parts of the deep sea. Similar to seamounts adorned in animal-made forests, the canyons and escarpments at the sunken edges of continents offer ideal rocky conditions, with strong currents sweeping in food particles for deep-sea corals and sponges to settle and thrive, including those that live for hundreds and thousands of years.

Allcock is hunting for corals and sponges because most of the time these animals don't move, which makes them easy for scientists to collect. More importantly, they can't scuttle or swim away from predators, and as a consequence, corals and sponges have evolved an armory of complex chemical weapons that stop other creatures from eating them. These secondary metabolites are made by cells but aren't essential for growth; instead, they have evolved important secondary roles in the organism, often with novel functions.

Similar bioactive by-products are common in plants, which face the same challenge as corals and sponges of being rooted to the spot. Tannins in tea, nicotine in tobacco, and caffeine in coffee are all secondary metabolites that evolved to prevent fungal infections and ward off munching insects.

Humans have harnessed the medicinal power of plant metabolites for millennia, in traditional herbal remedies as well as many modern, plant-based medicines, including codeine, morphine, aspirin, and the motion-sickness drug scopolamine. And we aren't the only animals to do it. Other species self-prescribe plants too: for instance, white-nosed coatis kill fleas and ticks by vigorously rubbing tree bark on their fur; Anubis baboons seem to treat schistosomiasis (also known as bilharzia, a disease caused by parasitic worms) by chewing on certain fruits and leaves. Not yet widely featured as medicinal ingredients, corals and sponges are likely to catch up with plants in their contributions to modern medicine cabinets.

Relative to their terrestrial counterparts, molecules from marine species are generally more potent and are deadlier to tumor cells and pathogens. Marine natural products also contain far greater chemical novelty than those from any land-based life-forms. The shape of a biological molecule determines how it works; novel shapes make for novel effects. At their core, the majority of marine molecules have large, elaborate structures seen nowhere else, which gives them tremendous potential for developing into groundbreaking new drugs. This is especially true for species living in the deep, which have evolved to survive in a unique mix of extreme conditions of immense pressure and low temperature, no light and little food. The ways their bodies work, even the way they construct their cells and their metabolites, are all wildly different from the workings of other living things. As a result, creatures of the deep hold a formidable chemical cache all of their own.

Most of the marine natural products discovered so far have come from corals and sponges, which have proven to have an astonishingly high hit rate in the deep; a survey in the twilight zone around the Pacific island of Guam found 75 percent of coral and sponge samples contained biologically active molecules.

After specimens have been brought up from the deep, microbiologists take mashed extracts and test them to see whether they might halt cancers or neurodegenerative diseases, or to see if they kill specific pathogens, such as those that cause malaria and tuberculosis. Samples also go to chemists, who begin the task of isolating unusual molecules and elucidating their structure. Finding the compounds that show the most promise and working out whether they are something new that hasn't been seen before are the first steps toward deciding which ones will get fed into the pipeline of drug development. These select compounds will have their molecular formulas tweaked in subtle ways to try to make them even more effective.

Pharmaceutical companies will get involved only when they know a compound can be synthesized in large quantities; new drugs won't be harvested from wild animals in the ocean. Besides new drugs, other potent biological molecules are being discovered in the deep sea. In laboratories around the world, researchers use enzymes called taq polymerases, originally isolated from hydrothermal vent microbes, to make millions of accurate copies of DNA fragments, a key step in all sorts of genetic tests, from DNA fingerprinting at crime scenes to identifying the presence of viruses, like the one that causes Covid-19.

Already many deep-sea compounds are showing great potential as the basis for lifesaving drugs of the future. A sponge called *Xestospongia*, taken from a deep seamount off the Pacific island of New Caledonia, contains compounds effective against malaria-causing parasites, including the most dangerous form, *Plasmodium falciparum*. A species of crinoid that looks like a tiny, gray balled-up fist, collected at 1,150 feet off the Caribbean island of Curaçao, contains compounds that inhibit proliferation in multi-drug-resistant ovarian cancer cell lines and another that inhibits leukemia cells. From the Ross Sea in Antarctica, a sea squirt called *Aplidium* has been found that contains compounds with antileukemic, anti-inflammatory, and antiviral properties. Possible anticancer agents have been discovered inside chemosynthetic mussels from hydrothermal vents on the Mid-Atlantic Ridge. At the bottom of the South China Sea, mud-dwelling fungi produce a substance that inhibits a key enzyme of the human immunodeficiency virus (HIV). Deepest of all, at the bottom of the Mariana Trench, 35,755 feet down, a new strain of bacteria was discovered, *Dermacoccus abyssi*, which contains a variety of compounds that kill cancerous cells.

The deep is also providing plenty of ideas for a particular group of medicines that are especially sought after. What the human world urgently needs are new types of antibiotics.

∽

On a bright September morning, I went to the sea, as I try to do every day when I'm in France, and this time I found something new on the beach. On the sand, near the high tide mark, five metal guardrails had been set up with yellow-and-red-striped tape laced between them, along with a signboard, which read:

Accès interdit pour raisons sanitaires (Germes pathogènes)

There was no obvious indication of anything pathogenic lying behind the rails, just a few pockmarks in the sand, as if someone had been digging with a large spade. *Ne pas toucher*, the striped tape repeatedly declared, but whatever I was supposed to not touch had already gone.

A large decaying whale had floated into the bay and stranded on the sand as the tide fell. Earlier that morning, the whale had been taken away by local officers for *l'équarrissage* (rendering down).

I left the beach feeling unsettled about the *germes pathogènes*. It's a good idea not to get too close to live whales because they breathe out bacteria in their spouts, and I can imagine that quite a microbial soup soon stirs inside a whale's carcass. At the time, I happened to have a small cut on my foot, and if I had stepped on the sand where that dead whale had lain—or even pushed my foot into its carcass—there's no knowing whether I would have contracted a nasty bacterial infection, but it was discomforting to see my local beach cordoned off to ensure public safety following this brief visit from a dead animal.

The following week, a study hit the news that crystallized my vague worries. On the other side of the Atlantic, in the warm waters of Indian River Lagoon in Florida, researchers had found that wild bottlenose dolphins were infected with multiple strains of drug-resistant, pathogenic bacteria—and over time that resistance had been rising, in ways that closely mirror what is happening in hospitals. Between 2003 and 2015, bacteria isolated from swabs taken from the dolphins' blowholes, stomachs, and feces were found to have doubled their resistance to a variety of antibiotics commonly used in modern human medicine. It was one of a handful of studies showing how dolphins and other marine animals that spend their lives swimming in the dilute effluents of human lives are being increasingly exposed to drug-resistant bacteria.★ Microbial resistance is proliferating because of a deluge of antibiotics entering the environment from the traces of medicines that pass undigested through a human body into sewage systems and waterways, and from the antibiotics liberally and routinely administered to livestock so they grow faster and survive in poor living conditions.

Antibiotics normally work by killing bacteria that cause infections, but they don't always kill off 100 percent of the offending microbes. Tougher bacterial strains will survive and thrive, especially in the absence of competing bacteria that the antibiotics do manage to dispatch. These durable strains can ultimately give rise to so-called superbugs, the bacteria that are resistant to one or more major antibiotics and cause stubborn infections that are difficult to treat.

Antibiotic resistance is nothing new. In 1915, a young World War I soldier named Ernest Cable died of dysentery from a strain of the bacteria *Shigella flexneri* that was already resistant to penicillin—even though it was more than a decade before Alexander Fleming would discover the world's first antibiotic drug. Cable also wouldn't have been saved by a shot of erythromycin (an antibiotic not discovered until 1949), because the bacteria was resistant to that too. Even further back, thousand-year-old mummies from the Incan Empire have inside them preserved remains of gut bacteria with genes for antibiotic resistance. And soil samples containing bacteria with drug-resistance genes have been found in thirty-thousand-year-old frozen tundra where woolly mammoths once ambled.

The fact that resistance predates modern drugs shouldn't come as a big surprise, given that most existing antibiotics are derived

---

★ Some of these resistant bacterial strains are known to cause infections in marine mammals, although it would become a potential problem only if a sick dolphin were to be treated by a veterinarian, who may struggle to find a drug that works.

from naturally occurring toxins made by bacteria themselves or by microscopic fungi; *Penicillium chrysogenum* is the species of blue-green mold-forming fungus that Fleming originally found growing on his unwashed Petri dishes.

In order to survive and compete for space and resources, microbes constantly engage in chemical warfare. They kill each other by producing lethal secondary metabolites. Nature's antibiotics existed for billions of years before humans started using them. It follows that microbes are constantly evolving ways to survive chemical attacks from their neighbors. Thus, microbial genes for producing antibiotics evolve, followed closely by genes for resistance. It's an arms race with enemies evolving weapons and opponents responding with new ways to divert or block their effects. Genes that encode resistance can even jump between bacterial cells, on small loops of DNA called plasmids, and that way rapidly spread. Then, as resistance rises, microbes evolve new toxins to inflict a new wave of attack, and the process of resistance and toxicity cycles on.

Superbugs are the result of that natural process being enormously accelerated by modern medicine and farming. Antibiotics are made in laboratories and administered to humans and livestock in far bigger quantities than ever occur naturally. By exposing bacteria to such huge doses of their own medicine, humans are causing what used to be rare genetic mutations to swiftly become commonplace. A recent example is colistin, an antibiotic that has been available since the 1950s but is not often used in human patients because it causes kidney damage; it has, though, been widely adopted as a growth-promoter in livestock. In 2015, a gene called *mcr-1*, which confers resistance to colistin, was found in bacteria infecting pigs in China. Within eighteen months, the *mcr-1* gene had jumped between bacteria and was found across five continents, in some places infecting 100 percent of animals on farms; colistin-resistant bacteria have also been found in a growing number of people. Despite its nasty side effects, colistin is still used as an antibiotic of last resort to treat stubborn infections, but with the spread of the *mcr-1* gene, it could soon be tossed onto the pile of obsolete drugs.

The rise of antibiotic resistance has become a global epidemic that's widely regarded as one of the biggest threats to the future of human health. The drugs we have—like vancomycin, methicillin, and penicillin—are not working like they used to, and new antibiotics are needed to take their place. Without them, even routine operations could become life-threatening. It's forecast that by 2050, drug-resistant infections will cause an annual death toll of at least ten million people.

One reason superbugs are now proliferating is that no new class of antibiotic has been introduced for thirty years. Antibiotics within the same class share a common mode of action and kill bacteria in a similar way. Beta-lactams, for example, the class including penicillin, work by inhibiting cross-links from forming properly in bacterial cell walls, weakening them and causing them to burst; tetracyclines work by blocking protein synthesis in bacteria so they can't reproduce and grow; quinolones interfere with the replication of bacterial DNA.

Most available antibiotics are variations of existing drugs. They pound away at the same old targets within bacteria cells, which are becoming increasingly wise to their game. To sidestep that problem and produce antibiotics to which bacteria haven't yet built up resistance will require the discovery of brand-new killing mechanisms. It could be a toxin that punches holes in cell walls by targeting different molecules or by interfering somehow with key enzymes; ideally it is something that nobody has even thought of. The hunt for those kinds of innovations is drawing scientists toward the bacteria found living inside deep-sea corals and sponges. The ultimate goal is to find chemicals produced by bacteria to kill each other in unusual ways.

∽

At Plymouth University, on Britain's south coast, deep-sea biologist Kerry Howell is a specialist in coral and sponge ecosystems and the complex communities of microbes that live inside them. Some microbes serve no productive purpose, whereas symbiotic microbes provide benefits to corals and sponges; they're not thought to be chemosynthetic, like vent microbes, but they may help their hosts obtain food or key nutrients, similar to the way bacteria do inside bone-eating worms.

Mat Upton, also at Plymouth University, tests Howell's sponges and corals, mashing up a sample and spreading the resulting slurry onto Petri dishes and incubating them to see what grows. If expanding colonies of microbes emerge, Upton's team picks out and isolates pure strains, which can then be tested to see which other microbes they kill.

A key step is to persuade those microbes to start making toxic compounds—not something that goes on all the time, as bacteria switch on their chemical defenses only when they need them. One approach is to give microbes a chemical nudge, bathing them in substances known to switch on genes for antibiotic production. When growing microbes in the lab, the conditions are so artificial, at most two or three different compounds will be produced. "I have to remind myself that we're probably looking at a tiny fraction of what's there," says Upton. Try as he may to keep the bacteria comfortable, a laboratory in Plymouth is a long way from the deep sea.

Upton is also taking an alternative strategy and searching not just for the toxins themselves but for the genetic instructions for making them. Sequencing bacterial DNA can reveal maybe twenty or thirty gene systems linked to antibiotic production. This way it's possible to identify compounds bacteria have the capacity to make, whether or not they actually switch those genes on.

This will work only for the varieties of deep-sea bacteria that are piezotolerant—they tolerate the high pressure of the deep but also function when grown in a lab. Much trickier are the obligate piezophiles, which actually grow better and faster under the crushing pressures of the deep; they are so well adapted to these conditions, they don't survive at the surface. To study such microbes, researchers have developed pressurized sampling containers and lab equipment. Researchers at the Japan Agency for Marine-Earth Science and Technology have even built a synthetic hydrothermal vent in the lab, replicating the conditions that some especially choosy microbes require. These ones refuse to grow unless they're convinced they are still more than a mile underwater, on a toxic, scorching, high-pressure vent. Once colonies are established in labs, researchers can set about investigating how these extremophiles function and what unusual chemistry comes into play when their growing conditions are just right.

Already, the Plymouth team has made what could be a major breakthrough. Among the microbes extracted from a deep-sea hex-actinellid sponge, they have found strains capable of killing one of the most common superbugs, methicillin-resistant *Staphylococcus aureus*, or MRSA. The crucial and difficult question is whether the compound they've isolated is a new class of antibiotic, or if it works the same way as one we already know about.

It will take time—maybe a decade or longer—for compounds discovered in the deep sea to progress through the drugs pipeline. There's no guarantee any of them will emerge from the other end as new drugs. And even if some deep-sea antibiotics do make it all the way through, they may not immediately emerge onto the market. Rather than rush new antibiotics into mass production, and risk losing their potency all too quickly, companies are beginning to lock them up in a pharmacological war chest. Instead of making money by selling as much of the drug as possible, a pharmaceutical company might be given a billion-dollar finder's fee, and the new drug held back until it's really needed.

The possibility of finding lifesaving molecules will endure and provide a lasting incentive to protect deep-sea species and ecosystems from harm. Nobody knows how many more thousands or millions of new species and microbes will be discovered, as more people probe and explore the deep. Countless potent molecules will come to light only when upcoming generations of scientists pioneer new ways of exploring the chemistry of the deep to find solutions for future problems that nobody can predict. Those are reasons enough to do whatever we can to keep these deep species alive and these ecosystems intact and healthy.

PART THREE

EXPLOIT

Fishing Deep

At the bottom of the sea lives a particular type of brick-red fish whose name was changed so people would eat it. Who on earth would choose slimehead for dinner? Never mind that its slimy head provides a marvelous way of sensing the surroundings while living in the dark deep. The goo flowing through channels in its skin and oozing from its pores is an excellent conducting medium to detect vibrations and ripples in the water, a predator to avoid or prey to be eaten. The slimehead has a big, rounded head with huge, forlorn eyes and downturned mouth—a sad-looking frown, even for a fish—and a body covered in coarse scales. Usually, when these fish are seen, they're already dead, and their color has faded to tangerine orange. So, instead of slimehead, they came to be known as orange roughy.★

The story of orange roughy is often told in numbers. The number of years roughies must wait before breeding for the first time: between twenty and forty. The number of years they can live (given a chance): 250, a figure known from counting layers of material laid down in their otoliths (ear bones), like tree rings. The depths they inhabit: between 600 and 6,000 feet. The number of tons of orange roughies that were captured within a few minutes, in a single trawl shot, at the height of a late-twentieth-century fishing spree: more than fifty, in one giant

---

★ The species, *Hoplostethus atlanticus*, is a member of the Trachichthyidae family, the name of which is derived from Latin words *trachy*, meaning "rough," and *ichthys*, meaning "fish."

net holding an animal weight equal to twenty-five rhinoceroses or one hundred polar bears, so many foot-long fish the individuals got blurred and lost in the crowd. Another number remained unresolved for too long: the weight of orange roughies that were in the deep to begin with, before the trawlers arrived.

Concerned conservationists often hold the orange roughy aloft as a warning of what happens when deep-sea life is regarded as an industrial resource, and a stark reminder of the perils of not knowing. Orange roughies haven't gone extinct; even so, given the species' huge range through the Atlantic, Pacific, and Indian Oceans, the fact that humans have dented its global population is an astonishing and saddening achievement, and one that has happened because a concerted effort has been made to turn the roughy's natural abundance into profit.

The assault began in the late 1970s and early '80s, roughly a century after the species was named and at around the time several key discoveries were made. Crucially, orange roughy was found to be the kind of fish a lot of people like to eat. Unlike other deep fish, which tend to have unpalatable, watery tissues, orange roughy has firm, freezable, and unfishy flesh. Even people who aren't avid seafood fans might accept an orange roughy fillet.

Orange roughies also proved easy to catch. The fish have the convenient habit of gathering together in enormous shoals to feed and mate, not in blank open waters but often clustered around seamounts, giving fishers something large to aim at. Equipped with new sonar devices and satellite-based GPS, fishers can find and precisely target seamounts, even when the peaks are a mile or more below the surface. Fishing capacity also leapt forward in the twentieth century, with the arrival of a new generation of factory trawlers that can range far from shore and are equipped with gigantic trawl nets, with five-ton doors holding them open, capable of swallowing entire shoals in a single gulp. And so, after beating their tails against dark waters for countless long lifetimes, the orange roughies found their

Above: Giant isopods (around 12 inches long) eating an alligator carcass deployed from the research vessel *Pelican*, Gulf of Mexico (7,155 feet).

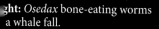

Above: Giant larvacean (1-inch, blue-edged body) and fluted mucus house.

Right: *Osedax* bone-eating worms on a whale fall.

Below: Ruby the Whale, in Monterey Canyon off California (9,842 feet), being consumed by bone-eating worms and surrounded by pink sea cucumbers, known as sea pigs.

From top left, clockwise: Pig's-rump worm; gossamer worm; hungry scale worm; gossamer worm; shining bomber worm. Not to scale.

From top left, clockwise: Siphonophore *Marrus orthocanna*; larvacean *Bathochordaeus stygius*; trachymedusa *Liriope* sp.; siphonophore *Chuniphyes* sp.; bioluminescent cyphozoan *Periphylla periphylla*; scyphozoan *Crossota norvegica*; narcomedusa *Aegina citrea*. Not to scale.

Below: Armhook squid (10 inches) eating an owlfish.

Above: Amphipod, *Eurythenes plasticus* (2 inches), from the Mariana Trench.

Below: Snailfish eating amphipods at a mackerel-baited trap in the Mariana Trench (23,087 feet).

Below: Vampire squid (12 inches) surrounded by marine snow, Monterey Bay (2,480 feet)

Above: Ctenophore with its feeding tentacles fully extended, Gulf of Mexico (4,790 feet).

Below: Hoff crabs (2 to 3 inches) on a hydrothermal vent chimney, East Scotia Ridge, Southern Ocean (around 7,900 feet).

Top left: Yellow glass sponge, Sibelius Seamount, North Pacific (8,133 feet).
Bottom left: Squat lobster residing on an *Acanthogorgia* octocoral, Gulf of Mexico.
Right: *Iridogorgia* octocoral with pink squat lobsters, Gulf of Mexico.

Below: Corals and glass sponges in the Forest of the Weird on a seamount near Johnston Atoll in the North Pacific (7,740 feet).

bove: Thorny tinselfish and *Lophelia* scleractinian coral, Gulf of Mexico (1,627 feet).

low: Seamount corals, including brittle star on the red coral in the foreground, bussy Seamount, North Pacific (7,200 feet).

Scaly-foot snail (1 inch) from Kairei hydrothermal
vent field, Indian Ocean.

world suddenly interrupted by humans, who came to take them away, ton by faceless ton.

This was part of a new wave of fishing that moved into more distant and deeper waters. Fishers were lured to the high seas by a lack of rules and regulations and by the promise of untouched waters to fill their nets, leaving behind the increasingly overcrowded fishing grounds and dwindling inshore stocks. Initial catches of orange roughies were tremendously high. "A Deep-Sea Fishery with a Rosy Future" was a headline in an article in *New Scientist* magazine from February 1989, cheerfully describing the thriving New Zealand fishery that took over 44,000 tons of orange roughies a year. The article extolled the virtues of the waxy oil that fills the species' swim bladders and bones. Orange roughy oil is ideal for use in cosmetics and high-grade lubricants, the article explained, with similar chemical properties to sperm whale oil, which had only recently become difficult to procure following the moratorium on commercial whaling in 1986.

Hauls of orange roughies were at first so massive, a lot went to waste. At St. Helen's Hill, a seamount off eastern Tasmania, reports emerged of the fish, already dead, tumbling back down into the deep when bulging nets burst, abraded by the roughies' skin. Catches that did make it back to the dock were often too much for local processing plants to handle, and tons of stinking, spoiled fish were heaved by the truckload into landfills.

Even with lost fish, fortunes were made. In 1990, over the course of just three weeks, the orange roughy catch from St. Helen's Hill was sold for AUD$24 million. People very quickly got used to the bounty. When a cap on quotas was announced for this fishing ground, the industry raged over the potential loss of dozens of jobs among trawlermen and fish factory workers, even though the fishery had been operating for less than six months.

As more people around the world caught wind of this untapped species, a gold rush mentality set in, and more orange roughies were dragged up from the deep. But these were catches that could not and would not last.

⤳

The early days of the booming orange roughy fisheries left scientists scrambling to keep up. This was a brand-new type and scale of fishing, and a species about which almost nothing was known. Fishing was already well underway by the time vital information was gathered on its biology.

In the 1990s, studies pushed the orange roughy's estimated average life span well over a hundred years and revealed its meager fecundity. After decades of abstinence, an orange roughy spawns only once every two years or so. During its lifetime, each female produces a modest thirty thousand to fifty thousand eggs, not a lot for a fish; a female Atlantic cod lays five million eggs in a single spawning. Fewer spawnings and fewer eggs make for a species that will only slowly replace its population numbers. The orange roughy turns out to be precisely the wrong type of fish to cope with intense levels of hunting.

Another major problem scientists faced was trying to count the number of orange roughies around the flanks of seamounts a mile or more underwater. Standard techniques of trawl surveys didn't work well for this shoaling species. For other fish, as the population declines, the numbers caught in nets will drop, allowing scientists to estimate how many there are in total and work out how many constitute a sustainable catch. Orange roughies, however, bunch together, and catch rates remain steady even as the population is shrinking. It meant that fish counts were inaccurate and highly inflated. In Australian waters, estimates of orange roughy populations commonly ranged over several orders of magnitude, from tens of thousands of tons to millions of tons. As an expert from Australia's Commonwealth Scientific and Industrial Research Organisation (CSIRO) said in the late 1980s, "The first objective of our work is to get the number of zeros correct." The problem of counting orange roughies also meant there were no obvious warning signs as the populations approached the brink of collapse.

All these uncertainties, combined with the orange roughy's sedate pace of life, led to fishing quotas being set far too high for the true numbers of the ancient, slow-growing fish. In many places, fisheries were opening without any regulation at all. Either way, the outcome was catastrophic and swift.

In 1992, French trawlers went to the Rockall Trough in the northeastern Atlantic and caught over 5,000 tons of roughies; after three years, they could find only 1,000 tons. A free-for-all Irish fishery began in 2001; catches peaked a year later, then slumped, and by 2005 the fishery had closed. Slice the data by seamount or fishery, even a whole region or the entire globe, and a bleak, repetitive pattern emerges. Graphs plotting the tonnage caught year by year have come to resemble the seamounts where the orange roughies congregate: a high peak and on either side a steep precipice. The fisheries boomed, and then all too soon they went bust.

～

Precisely how many orange roughies have been caught since trawl fisheries began is hard to know, because a lot have gone under the radar. Recent analysis, piecing together evidence of unreported and illegal catches, suggests the total global catch of orange roughies is double that shown in official records. Some of the missing fish may have been genuine mistakes in data handling, and some were deliberate false reports, made to dodge income taxes and fines imposed when trawlers overshot their quotas. As ancient fish slipped out of the deep and into cooked books, trawlers kept filling their nets by moving from one seamount to the next. The New Zealand fleet swept through national waters, then out into the high seas of the Pacific; the New Zealand fishing industry then helped start up fisheries farther afield, in the Indian Ocean, off the coast of Namibia, and in the North Atlantic.

Matthew Gianni was once a deep-sea fisherman off the California coast, at around the time orange roughy fishing was booming elsewhere. "It was like dropping a stone in the water and seeing the ripples going out all the way across the rest of the pond," he says, of the global propagation of orange roughy fisheries. He now campaigns tirelessly for the protection of ocean ecosystems and good governance of fisheries worldwide, especially in the high seas, and considers the behavior of the deep-sea trawlers that have depleted the orange roughy from seamounts closer to that of mining corporations than fisheries. They extract resources in a single hit, then move on.

Gianni was shocked on a visit a few years ago to his hometown of Pittsburgh, Pennsylvania, when he saw orange roughies stacked high on supermarket counters. "I remember thinking, what a waste, what a sad thing to do. Aside from everything else, what struck me was how grossly we undervalue nature. Here were fish that were a hundred years old or more from some of the deepest, remotest, most biologically diverse areas in the ocean, being sold by the pound for not much more than the price of farm-raised tilapia."

Gianni campaigns against deep-sea trawling for reasons beyond the plundering of orange roughies: "It was the collateral damage to biodiversity that really sparked my interest, and to be perfectly frank, outrage about trawling seamounts for orange roughy, way back in the late nineties." At the time, studies were beginning to reveal the indisputable truth that trawling destroys not only fish populations but entire ecosystems. "Ecologically, it's a ridiculous way to fish," says Gianni.

∽

When industrial trawlers began targeting seamounts, it became apparent that these underwater peaks were covered in rich and fragile ecosystems containing animals that were even more ancient than the orange roughies themselves.

Trawl nets were hauled up with fish crammed together with the smashed remnants of deep coral reefs. The first few times each new seamount was trawled, catches of fish could easily be equaled or outweighed by the tons of deepwater corals taken as bycatch, among them colonies that had been growing for hundreds, even thousands, of years. At the height of the orange roughy fisheries, trawlermen contemplated keeping the most valuable corals to sell, especially the gem-quality gold and black corals. Mostly, though, the huge, branching coral colonies were disentangled from the nets and pitched overboard, with little chance they would land back on a seamount, reattach, and carry on growing. For the fish-hunters, they were a passing inconvenience. The corals soon dwindled, until there were no more to bring up, as trawlers felled the millennia-old, animal-grown forests.

Despite the obvious physical impact of trawling on deepwater corals, proving what damage has been done a long way underwater is not a straightforward task, and such proof is often demanded before action is taken to do anything about it. Researchers can send submersibles or lower down cameras, but rarely has anyone looked at seamounts before the fishing started. Trawling industries repeatedly stand by the claim that seabed ecosystems could have been in a poor state before fishing began.

The best way to assess the full effect of trawling would be to do a detailed before-and-after study, but that almost never happens. One of the longest-running studies is focused on seamounts at Chatham Rise, to the east of New Zealand, the country's most important fishing grounds. To run an experiment testing the impacts of trawling, researchers picked out six mounts with differing fishing histories: Graveyard was heavily trawled all through the study; Zombie and Diabolical were sporadically trawled; Gothic had only low levels of trawling; and Ghoul has never been trawled.★ Most important for the study is Morgue, a seamount that was heavily trawled until 2001, then closed to fishing. If the cessation of trawling and the passage of time allow a healthy ecosystem to return, Morgue is the seamount where recovery should take place.

Four times, between 2001 and 2015, a research team visited the seamounts and used drop-down cameras to photograph the summits and flanks. They compared the seamounts with one another in each survey year, looking for any evidence that corals were growing back on Morgue, where trawling had stopped. Even though healthier seamounts not far away could have supplied a stream of coral larvae, the ecosystem at Morgue showed no inkling of regrowth or recovery. After fifteen years, it still looked a lot like the Graveyard seamount, which was still being trawled.

The persistent, depleted state of New Zealand's Morgue seamount aligns with other studies that track the vanishing of seamount species and find no hints of recovery. These same findings are used in two ways by groups of people with sharply conflicting intentions. Conservationists use the data to validate their calls for halting deep-sea trawling and greater protection for seamounts. The fishing industry commonly uses the same findings as an excuse to keep on with business as usual. If the reefs are never coming back, it doesn't matter if the same seamounts are trawled over and again.

However, a study from farther north in the Pacific tells a different story. In the late 1960s, trawlers from the Soviet Union began visiting the Hawaiian-Emperor seamount chain in the Pacific. Soviet fishers, joined by a couple of Japanese trawlers, were targeting not orange roughy but chiefly another, little-known species that also spawns at seamounts, slender armorhead, a silver-bodied fish with a sloping snout and a spiky Mohawk of spines along its back. The

---

★ The trend for giving the New Zealand's seamounts macabre names was started by fishers who lost gear to the craggy, underwater peaks; other seamounts in the area are called Mount Doom, Soul Destroyer, and Crypt.

armorhead fishery was colossal, taking more than 200,000 tons
of fish annually, but within little more than a decade was almost
entirely wiped out.★

Four decades later, a series of research expeditions returned to
see what had happened since. The team explored seven seamounts
in the Hawaiian-Emperor chain, four protected since the 1970s
and three that are still trawled. An autonomous underwater vehicle
floated over the seamounts at an altitude of about fifteen feet and,
moving at a speed of around a mile an hour, took more than half a
million photographs.

Many of the pictures showed barren seascapes etched with straight-
line trawl scars, reefs turned to rubble, broken stumps of coral colonies, massive doors ripped off the trawls, and abandoned nets still
filled with the smashed corals that had dragged them down.

And yet, among the bleak scenes were pictures showing something
else. On the seamounts where trawlers hadn't been for forty years,
healthy meadows of octocoral fans and bushy reefs of scleractinian
corals now grow. Corals have grown over the trawl scars. Fragments
of coral spilling from the lost nets weren't all dead, and some had
begun to sprout and regrow. The protected seamount ecosystems
are taking small but vital steps toward recovery.

The surveys revealed some even bigger surprises. Pictures from
three of the still-trawled seamounts—Kammu, Yuryaka, and Koko—
showed scenes nobody was expecting. In the fields of coral rubble
are glimmers of life holding on and growing back. Coral larvae have
drifted in, settled, and grown into new, young polyps. Here and
there are pockets of larger corals, pink, yellow, and white octocoral
fans and bushy black corals. Some may be recovering, and some
could be remnants the trawls missed. Among them, other animals
have returned, such as perching feather stars and wandering crabs.

★ By contrast, in 2017, the recovering population of cod in the whole of the North Sea
was estimated at around 165,000 tons.

Sadly, these findings can't be transferred to other trawled sea-mounts. New Zealand mounts are far too different, their summits deeper by more than a thousand feet and colonized by a distinctive entourage of corals that grow very slowly and can't recover in mere decades. Scleractinian corals there build a tangled matrix of hard skeletons, ten feet deep, with living coral only on the top four to eight inches. After trawlers come along and strip away that thin living veneer, there is only a slim chance that coral larvae will drift in from neighboring seamounts, because whenever these corals find good growing conditions they tend not to spawn. Instead of broadcasting larvae into the uncertain oceans, the corals make copies of themselves by budding, dropping fragments that grow into new colonies on the same seamounts, reducing their chance for long-distance recovery.

On the Hawaiian seamounts, the dominant corals are octocoral sea fans, which grow faster and are more likely to produce larvae than the hard corals. Missing, though, were ancient gold corals, suggesting that the ecosystems can grow back, but they may never be quite the same as they were before. Even so, these mounts in the northern reaches of the Pacific offer the hopeful message that all is not lost. Some seamount ecosystems, in one form or another, can begin to come back after trawl nets have passed by.

This strips away the delusion that continuing to trawl the same seamounts, over and over, is a pragmatic choice. The coral forests may not be gone for good; if trawling stops, they stand a chance of recovering. New coral colonies growing on the battered Hawaiian-Emperor seamounts must have come from somewhere, and the most likely sources are nearby mounts that have never been trawled. The more those untrawled places are left alone, the more intact corals will remain, and the greater the chances that life will once again thrive on these underwater mountains.

These ecosystems are unlike shallow tropical coral reefs, in that few people will dive among their deep animal forests and gaze at the wildlife that live there. Nonetheless, their existence holds important value for humanity and the planet as a whole in several ways. Future medicines wait to be found among the toxic chemicals lodged inside seamount corals and sponges. Dense gardens of deep-sea sponges soak up carbon and enrich waters with nutrients that upwell and feed fisheries in the shallows. Stories of the past are written inside ancient coral skeletons, which reveal how the climate has been changing and allow more accurate predictions of what will happen next. In their thousands, maybe millions, seamount ecosystems play their untold role in the healthy functioning of the entire global ocean, cycling nutrients and storing carbon, providing habitat for so many species besides the corals themselves, offering feeding and spawning grounds, and providing nurseries for young animals to grow up in before moving off elsewhere. Like the felling of ancient terrestrial forests that take centuries to mature, the destruction of deep-water corals leaves the planet in a diminished state, losing the magnificent life-forms that far outlive humans and invite us to contemplate the existence of something utterly different from ourselves.

Viewing these ecosystems only through a narrow lens of what can be taken and sold overlooks everything else that is lost in the process.

❧

In addition to orange roughy and slender armorhead, a menagerie of unusual fish has been extracted from the deep sea by industrial trawlers. Greenland halibut is a giant, three-foot-long flatfish with an eye on its forehead and an unusual habit of swimming upright, giving it forward-facing, cyclopean vision. Blue ling is a slender cousin of cod, and longnose velvet dogfish does indeed have a long nose and dark, velvety-looking skin, as well as elliptical eyes and a distrusting look. There are splendid alfonsinos and blackbelly rose-fish, longfin codling and Patagonian toothfish, whiptails and rattails, slickheads and oreos.

Not all are as long-lived or vulnerable to overfishing as orange roughy. In particular, species from the cod family are generally in better shape, having evolved first in shallower seas then moved deeper, bringing with them faster growth rates and greater resilience to fishing. Some, though, are doing far worse. Roundnose grenadier, with its firm, tasty flesh, has been a favorite on restaurant menus in France and is highly endangered. So too is the gulper shark, with its mesmerizing emerald eyes. This deep-sea shark species is targeted not for food but for the squalene in its oily liver, a chemical that goes into making cosmetics, vaccines, and hemorrhoid creams.

Over the decades, the expanding footprint of deep trawlers has gone truly global, extending to the shelf edges off every continent except Antarctica. In every ocean, seamounts are trawled.

Scouring so much of the deep with their enormous nets suggests trawlers must gather enough fish to feed the world. The most recent figures, including estimates of illegal and unreported catches, show that is far from true. In total, over the past sixty-five years, the global catch of deep-living fish has been just shy of 28 million tons. Compared to the volume of fish caught throughout the oceans in that time—closer to 6 billion tons—the deep has provided less than half of one percent.

The economic value of these deep fish is equally unimpressive, especially considering that many countries deliberately encourage deep-sea trawling with financial handouts. Fishing is one of the primary industries that many countries seem reluctant to let go of; jobs are at stake, and to some extent food security, but chiefly prevailing are powerful lobbies and a stubborn nostalgia for an activity that humankind has been doing in one form or another for millennia. As such, governments find ways of keeping fishing industries afloat. Government subsidies to keep deep-trawling fleets operating range from boatbuilding and buyback to port construction and renovations, tax exemptions, and most significantly, fuel subsidies. With their long ranges and powerful engines, deep-sea trawlers rack up massive fuel costs. Every deep-sea fishing country, with the notable exception of New Zealand, foots a portion of that bill by providing a discount on diesel fuel. The most generous is Japan, giving twenty-five US cents on the liter, followed by Australia (twenty cents) and then Russia, South Korea, and Iceland (all nineteen cents).

Each year, the global fleet of deep-water trawlers lands a catch worth an estimated US$601 million. Reported profits for trawlers are at most 10 percent, in this case roughly US$60 million. The same fleets also benefit from subsidies to the tune of US$152 million—two and a half times the overall profit. As these calculations intimate, if it weren't for governments propping them up, the bulk of deep-water trawlers working the high seas would be operating at a loss.

If it costs so much, provides so little food, and reaps such huge ecological damage, the glaring question is, why trawl for fish in the deep at all? "Because some boats can make money," Matthew Gianni suggests. "That's the bottom line. And the rules and regulations have been sufficiently lax or not well enforced that there's very little to stop them from doing it." In 2004, Gianni cofounded the Deep Sea Conservation Coalition and began campaigning to bring deepwater fishing under control. The coalition has had successes, such as a ban on trawling below 2,625 feet in seas of the European Union, which came into effect in 2017. If that ban can be successfully enforced, and if it leads the way to similar restrictions elsewhere, then it will be an important step toward curbing an industry that yields relatively trivial economic benefits but has a fearsome capacity to vandalize our living planet.

⁓

With an eagerness that borders on compulsion to hunt these animals, trawlers are again increasingly on the hunt for orange roughies off New Zealand, bringing with them promises that this time things will be different.

The trawling industry invested millions of dollars in orange roughy research, including a new technique for counting the fish. Using a combination of sonar and video, researchers can now work out with greater confidence the number of fish that are down there, and there are apparently enough orange roughies to declare the species recovered in some areas and ready to fish all over again. There are enough, even, to earn the fishery approval from the Marine Stewardship Council (MSC), an organization that positions itself as the gold standard for fisheries eco-labeling. The MSC logo is intended to signal to conscientious seafood consumers which fish are good choices to make, ethically and environmentally. In 2016, New Zealand orange roughy was put on the MSC's good fish list.

Granting orange roughy an eco-label was an ambitious feat of rebranding for a species that suffered such an epic eco-catastrophe. "It doesn't surprise me at all," observes Frédéric Le Manach, scientific director at the Paris-based nongovernmental organization (NGO) Bloom. "The MSC doesn't certify sustainable fisheries, it certifies managed fisheries." The two, as Le Manach points out, are not necessarily the same.

Fleets trawling for orange roughies on New Zealand's seamounts are certainly being better managed now than the original, freewheeling fisheries. Besides the improved fish-counting technology, catch quotas are extremely low compared to what they were, recently only hundreds of tons a year rather than tens of thousands.

However, it's unclear whether trawling for orange roughies at the new level turns even a slim profit, though the trawling companies are so huge they can easily absorb the losses. A more challenging issue is whether the MSC's claims to sustainability are well founded. A 2012 study estimated that of all the fisheries with MSC labels, more than a third were being overfished and depleted. Le Manach charges the organization with becoming obsessed with aggressive expansion and claims its certification process is shot through with conflicts of interest. The MSC is an independent, nonprofit organization based in London and is funded largely by royalties from sales of eco-labeled fish. To keep more money coming in, the organization needs to keep certifying fisheries. The MSC oversees a relatively small portion of global fishing, pinning its logos on an estimated 15 percent of the world's captured wild fish, but it aims for more.★ Le Manach thinks the MSC's hurry to certify a growing mass of seafood, to meet ravenous demand from giant supermarket and fast-food chains, means its environmental standards have been slipping.

The MSC doesn't conduct assessments itself. Fisheries that want an eco-label are invited to select a third-party certifier to do the job, interpreting the wordy criteria the MSC has laid down—in documents five hundred pages long—within which lies a lot of wiggle room. Nothing prevents a fishery from picking a certifier that has a good track record in giving favorable outcomes, which creates an incentive for certifying agencies to leniently interpret the MSC's standards. The certifier gets paid; the fishery gets its eco-label.

Concerned experts and public groups can lodge objections to any of the MSC's decisions, but that process is subject to the same nebulous documentation. A group of fisheries scientists and conservationists published a peer-reviewed paper in 2013 pointing out that of nineteen official objections to the MSC's proposed certifications, only one was upheld and resulted in a fishery not being certified. The authors wrote that the MSC's criteria for sustainable fishing are "too lenient and discretionary, and allow for overly generous interpretation."

More recently, in 2019, a UK parliamentary committee called on the MSC to address concerns raised during an inquiry into the organization's standards. Fierce criticism came from NGOs and scientists over a tuna fishery in the Pacific that incidentally catches sharks and sea turtles but nevertheless was given an MSC label. Other controversial MSC-approved fisheries include one targeting Antarctic krill, which are staple food for whales, and the New Zealand trawl fishery for hoki, which kills endangered Salvin's albatrosses when they dive

★ The remaining 85 percent of global fish catches either don't meet the MSC's standards or have not yet gone through the lengthy and expensive process of certification.

underwater. In 2020, the MSC granted the first ever certification for Atlantic bluefin tuna, a globally endangered species that fetches extortionate prices in the sushi trade. The certification went ahead despite objections raised by the World Wildlife Fund and the Pew Charitable Trusts that bluefins are only just beginning to recover from decades of overfishing.

Amid its tainted reputation, the MSC has declared the orange roughy a great comeback story, but the details offer no cause for celebration. The MSC allegedly excluded numerous scientific reports in its certification process, including a controversial report to the New Zealand government revealing massive dumping and underreporting of the orange roughy catch, just as in years past. In December 2016, an article posted on the MSC's website stated that orange roughy stocks had "increased to around 40 percent of the natural population size." Spin that the other way, and it means the species has undergone a 60 percent decline. For wild animals on land, equivalent trajectories are generally regarded as sorrowful signs of nature's demise. Between 1985 and 2015, the numbers of giraffes across the African continent fell by 40 percent. A similar proportion of lions disappeared in only twenty years. And in the rain forests of Borneo, since 1999, numbers of orangutans have dropped by at least half, as their habitat has been felled and replaced with palm oil plantations. In the world of industrial fishing, a 60 percent diminishment is considered a sign of success, of a wild population driven down to a point where money can still be made, year after year. But perhaps, instead, the orange roughy's recovery is the case of a dead cat bouncing, with a greenwashed eco-label tied to its collar.

Even with the new fish-finding technology and more accurate models to predict the effects of fishing, still there are important things nobody knows about orange roughy. Thousands and thousands of teenage or younger orange roughies should be out there, but such quantities have yet to be found.

In time, those missing teenagers will move into the spawning population, but until they show up, it's going to be difficult to know whether even reduced catch quotas can be sustainable in the short to medium term. Since they were born, these roughies have been slowly growing. As one-year-olds they were an inch long, at two a thumb's length, not quite reaching a hand span by the age of five. Where those young ones live and when they plan on joining the spawning shoals at seamounts are still not known. For fish that have a century or two of spawning ahead of them, there is no great rush to get started. As is so often the case, the slow pace of the deep is out of step with the timescale of impatient human demands.

⌀

Most fishing countries have given up trawling for orange roughies. New Zealand trawlers now bring in four of every five roughies caught worldwide, some from their own waters and some from the high seas, despite growing legal obligations to fish sustainably and protect vulnerable habitats like seamounts. It's especially shocking for a country that positions itself as a champion of environmentalism. "From New Zealand, you'd expect so much better," declares Matthew Gianni.

A convoluted system of United Nations resolutions aims to control fishing in the high seas, areas beyond national boundaries, which historically have been a free-for-all. These regulations are put into practice by a series of regional organizations, each with an unpronounceable acronym and its own way of doing things. At the South Pacific Regional Fisheries Management Organisation (SPRFMO), the issue is that most member states have no commercial interest in the orange roughy, and New Zealand has a powerful and litigious fishing lobby. For instance, in 2018, a change was proposed to the way orange roughies are trawled. The fishing lobby from New Zealand lodged an official objection, unwilling to let its self-proclaimed rights to trawl the high seas become "further eroded." To continue trawling as it wishes, the lobby openly signaled its intention to pursue legal action against the New Zealand government, which caved in to the ultimatum. The proposal was withdrawn.

However, since 2018, negotiations have been underway at the United Nations for a new global ocean treaty, which is expected to come into force sometime in the mid-2020s. The treaty likely will oversee all sorts of human activities in the high seas, from the search for new pharmaceuticals to the establishment and enforcement of marine reserves.

Gianni hopes the treaty will establish a single, global body with legally binding powers to make sure regulations are effectively enforced across the high seas. If the inevitable objections are overcome, the treaty might apply not only to deep-sea trawling but also to a new type of deep-sea fishing that could soon begin. Commercial interests are turning their attention to another source of potential profit that until now has been left alone in the deep.

∽

In 1789, explorers Alessandro Malaspina and José de Bustamante set sail from Cádiz, on Spain's first scientific expedition around the world, commanding two purpose-built frigates, *Descubierta* and *Atrevida*, named in honor of the vessels Captain James Cook commanded on his voyages a decade earlier, the *Discovery* and the *Resolution*. For five years, Malaspina and Bustamante studied and collected animals and plants across the Spanish kingdom, which stretched along the North, Central, and South American Pacific coasts, westward to the Philippines.

In 2010, marking the two hundredth anniversary of Malaspina's death, another Spanish expedition set off from Cádiz to circumnavigate the world, tracing much of the original route and studying what the oceans are like today. The team measured ubiquitous pollutants, plastics, and chemicals in the sea that weren't there in Malaspina and

Bustamante's time. They collected samples of seawater and plankton, which will be stored for the next three decades, kept for future marine scientists to study and ask questions of. And all the way through the 30,000-mile voyage, the ship's sonar was switched on, casting down beams of sound and listening for echoes bouncing up from below.

Chief targets were small silver fish that look like sardines or anchovies, only with bigger eyes and rows of spots along their bodies that glow in the dark. These are lanternfish, around 250 species of them, and they are not only the most common fish in the twilight zone but the most abundant vertebrates on the planet. Huge numbers of them were first noticed during the Second World War, when naval sonar operators saw echoes bouncing up from what appeared to be a solid seabed, one that rose to the surface at night and fell back down at daybreak. In fact, the pulses of sound were echoing off the swim bladders, the internal gas-filled bubbles, of billions of lanternfish, as they congregated in dense layers hiding in the deep, then at sunset swam up a mile or more to hunt at the surface. Together with other animals, such as the squid that chase after them, lanternfish perform on a nightly basis the greatest animal migration on the planet.

Prior to the 2010 Malaspina expedition, studies based on trawl surveys estimated that the twilight zone contains around a gigaton (a billion tons) of fish. But this was most likely an underestimate, because lanternfish, it turns out, actively avoid being caught and swim away from the open nets. The Malaspina acoustic survey didn't rely on nets and in 2014 its research led to new estimates of the abundance of twilight-zone fish, ranging between around 10 and 20 gigatons. The prospect of such a colossal quantity of fish sparked the revival of an old question: Could fish from the twilight zone help feed a growing human population?

Lanternfish are unlikely to appear directly on anybody's plate. They are far too oily and full of spiky bones for that. Nevertheless, their high oil content means they could be mashed down into fish meal for use as animal feed, mostly for fish farms. Following the Malaspina discovery, it has been suggested that if just half of the lower estimated mass of twilight-zone fish were caught—still around a massive 5 gigatons—it could theoretically be turned into enough fish meal to yield 1.25 gigatons of farmed seafood, which is considerably more than the annual 0.1 gigaton catch of wild fish today. Setting aside other environmental impacts of many types of fish farming, such as pollution from pharmaceuticals and feces, even if the lanternfish fishery were to open, it's questionable as to whether it would achieve the virtuous goal of securing food for everyone to eat. A lot of fish meal gets fed to salmon and shrimp that are destined for food-rich, developed countries, and a growing volume never gets eaten by humans at all: fish meal is increasingly being sold as a supplement in pet food.

Previous attempts to establish lanternfish fisheries, including by Russian and Icelandic fleets, have been a commercial flop. Fishing these deep waters has so far proven too expensive, and fish meal too cheap. Recently, though, prompted in part by the inflated estimates of lanternfish abundance, plans are underway to investigate how to make twilight fisheries profitable. The European Union has funded a five-year research project to investigate opportunities for twilight-zone fishing. In 2017, Norway issued forty-six exploratory fishing licenses for the twilight zone. It's likely that these fisheries will seek to become profitable not by producing low-cost fish meal but by supplying the more lucrative industry for so-called nutraceuticals. These include the omega-3 supplements added to yogurts and margarine, and the fish-oil pills more people are popping despite the lack of evidence that they do any good for the heart.*

Recent initiatives aimed at developing twilight fisheries reflect an overwhelming imperative to hunt for wild fish. Amid talk of sustainability, and always of the need to feed the world, is the

---

* A survey in 2018 of one hundred thousand people revealed little to no effect from taking omega-3 supplements in reducing any form of heart disease.

counter-assumption that to leave those fish unfished would some-how be a waste. The term *under*exploited is commonly used, as if the only purpose of those animals is for human benefit. The possibility of a thousand trillion shining fish cascading through the twilight zone is too tempting for many people to ignore.

To catch enough lanternfish and make it worth the effort, these fisheries will need to use colossal midwater trawl nets and most likely target the fish during the day, as they cluster together in deep layers that are easy to find with sonar. These nets won't touch the bottom and won't smash through thousand-year-old corals. But as they sieve and strain the open water, they will catch other animals—sharks, dolphins, turtles—that already have troubles enough.

In contrast to an ancient deep-sea species like orange roughy, lanternfish are more likely to withstand substantial hunting pres-sure; they're much faster growing, and their lives are measured not in centuries but in months, some living for less than two years. Nevertheless, fishing in the twilight zone could trigger a different kind of catastrophe by disrupting a system that is helping to keep the planet habitable.

Lanternfish and other twilight inhabitants play a key role in reg-ulating the climate. Going about their daily routine of swimming up and down, they form vital connections between the surface and the abyss, by which they boost the biological carbon pump (lan-ternfish are important components of the particle injection pumps, as defined by global climate modelers). The little fish feed in the shallows, then plunge downward, where they are hunted and eaten by bigger fish that stay down deep, adding to the abyssal stores of carbon kept away from the atmosphere for a long time to come. A study of part of the continental slope west of Ireland estimated that deep-dwelling fish capture and store the equivalent of more than 1 million tons of carbon dioxide each year.

Too little is known for anyone to be sure how quickly or critically the biological carbon pump might weaken if twilight-zone fisheries were to commence and damage that link between the surface and the deep. But there's a dangerous possibility the lanternfish could be a part of the inner workings of the global climate system that needs to be left alone, for all our sakes.

Alarmingly, not everyone agrees with the new elevated figure for the mass of twilight-zone fish. Even the original Malaspina study clearly states its uncertainty and the limitations of the methods used, but the headline news—that the twilight zone contains at least ten times the amount of fish as previously thought—is what grabbed people's attention.

Subsequent studies have looked more critically at those figures and the assumptions that lie behind them. Crucially, the Malaspina study assumed that the acoustic backscatter from the deep came entirely from fish. But they aren't the only animals in the twilight zone with reflective, gas-filled bubbles inside their bodies. Many siphonophores have them too, those intricate jellies that Ernst Haeckel identified and illustrated. And some twilight-zone fish don't have swim bladders, so they're not picked up on sonar studies.

A 2019 study reinterpreted the original acoustic data from the Malaspina expedition, taking these uncertainties into account. The resulting estimates of twilight-zone fish ranged from 2 to 16 gigatons. It's too soon to say where on this wide scale the true value lies, which means it is surely too soon to start catching lanternfish based on the risky premise that there are 10 or even 20 gigatons of them out there.

Recent history tells us that industrial fisheries repeatedly sweep into new regions to catch new species—always with devastating environmental effects. The big open question is whether those same mistakes can be avoided in the twilight zone, and whether regulations and controls will come soon enough.

The Eternal Junkyard

A lot goes missing in the deep. After it sank, RMS *Titanic* was lost for more than seventy years, even though searchers had a good idea of where she went down off the coast of Newfoundland. For decades, millionaires and dreamers concocted schemes for locating and salvaging the ship; they thought of finding it with giant magnets and of filling the hull with wax or freezing it into a block of ice so it would pop to the surface. Eventually, the wreck was located in September 1985, more than 12,500 feet down. The French-American team that found her had learned the trick of first searching for the debris field shed across the seabed, like the tail of a comet. Lying in its final resting place, the *Titanic*'s metal structure is being eaten away by bacteria that are forming fragile rusticles, making the ship look as though it were dripped all over in brown candle wax.* All plans to salvage the *Titanic* have now been abandoned, and sooner or later—maybe by 2030—the entire wreck will crumble into dust and gently blow away in the current.

The immense size of the deep ocean swallows debris from human lives. Two studies published in 2014 estimated the total amount of microplastics† floating on the surface of the world's oceans to

---

* In 2010, a new strain of bacteria was discovered on the wreck and named *Halomonas titanicae*.

† These are fragments smaller than five millimeters (just under a quarter inch).

be around 39,000 tons. That was far less than expected, given the amount thought to have been manufactured, thrown away, washed out to sea, and crumbled into pieces. These two surveys point toward there being tens of thousands of tons of missing plastic.

It has become a miserable truth that plastics are everywhere now: littering beaches on remote islands, trapped in Arctic sea ice, in soils, rivers, and lakes, and blowing in the wind. And a large portion of the oceans' missing plastic is ending up in the deep sea—how could it not?

Big pieces are easy enough to spot. In 2019, American multimillionaire adventurer Victor Vescovo descended almost seven miles into the Challenger Deep in the Mariana Trench. When he looked out the window of his submersible at the oceans' very deepest point, Vescovo saw a plastic bag and a bunch of candy wrappers.

Deep-sea sediments are also filled with microplastics. Until recently, the most heavily contaminated parts of the deep were thought to be submarine canyons, which act as garbage chutes, funneling plastics off the edges of continental shelves and into the abyss. Masses of microplastics also end up falling into oceanic trenches. Then, a 2020 study announced the highest concentrations of microplastics yet found in the deep—double previous estimates. The worst affected area researchers tested was in the Mediterranean, off the coast of Italy, where swirling currents blow like sandstorms across the deep seabed, collecting and concentrating microplastics. If the two open pages of this book were contaminated to the same extent, they would be covered in more than one hundred thousand plastic fragments.

A dusting of microplastics covers the abyssal seabed, and all sorts of bottom-dwelling animals have been found to eat or get tangled in plastic fibers, including sea cucumbers, sea pens, and hermit crabs. Amphipods living at the bottom of the deepest hadal trenches have been found with microplastics in their guts, including a newfound species, which was named, accordingly, *Eurythenes plasticus.* For decades already, deep-sea animals have been swallowing plastic fragments. Starfish and brittle stars from the Rockall Trough, 6,600 feet down off the northwestern coast of Ireland, which were collected in the 1970s, preserved and kept in storage, then recently brought out and examined, had microplastics picked out from their insides.

Plastics have also been found in the open midwater of the deep. Anela Choy and colleagues have been tracking microplastics in Monterey Bay using a submersible to collect seawater and catch marine snow at intervals down into the twilight zone. They've found a hidden garbage patch between 650 and 1,000 feet composed of flurries of plastic-contaminated marine snow. Plankton, sea butterflies, vampire squid, and other snow eaters are getting mouthfuls of this indigestible grit. Giant larvaceans have been found to filter microplastic particles from the water with their mucous bubble houses; either the plastic gets eaten by the larvacean and then excreted in its feces, or the larvacean abandons its plastic-flecked house—in either case adding to the fall of plasticized marine snow into the deep.

Impacts of microplastics have been traced throughout the bodies of individual organisms: a bellyful of plastic suppresses an animal's appetite so it stops feeding, and eventually it can starve and die; microplastics cause internal wounds and lesions; they pass into the bloodstream, even into cells, where they interfere with enzymes and gene expression. Among the animals affected, growth rates fall, and reproduction is interrupted. Harm comes not just from the plastics but also the toxic chemicals and coatings added during manufacturing, such as fire retardants and PCBs; ocean-borne microplastics get contaminated with other pollutants, pathogenic viruses, and bacteria picked up from seawater. Most challenging is untangling the effects of the ubiquitous microplastics on entire populations and ecosystems, including cryptic, sublethal impacts that are difficult to track but doubtless reach into the severely polluted deep.

Plastics have made a permanent mark on the planet. In 2019, scientists at Scripps Institution of Oceanography in San Diego analyzed a core of sediment taken from the seabed off Santa Barbara from 1,900 feet underwater. The thirty-inch cylindrical core consisted of neat sediment layers, each one presenting a year's worth of particles settling onto the seabed, stretching from 2010 back to the 1830s; these layers were so neat because there are no strong currents sweeping over this part of the seabed, and the sediments hold little oxygen, so not much lives there to burrow, trample, or otherwise stir things up. The team cut the muddy column into thin slices, then picked out and characterized every plastic scrap in each slice, be it fiber, film fragment, or misshapen globule. This time capsule revealed the arrival of plastics in the modern era, and it precisely tracked the growth of the plastics industry. Between 1945 and 2009, the number of plastic particles falling to the seabed increased exponentially, doubling every fifteen years, in direct proportion to the amount of plastics being manufactured worldwide. The plastic age has written an indelible message on the deep seafloor. The message reads: HUMANS WERE HERE.

⁓

When I was on board the *Pelican* in the Gulf of Mexico with Craig McClain and Clifton Nunnally, we had been hoping to visit the site of a disaster that had taken place nine years earlier and caused the worst ever deep-sea oil spill. But when the conditions in the Gulf stole away our days at sea, plans were abandoned to dive to the remains of the Macondo wellhead and the wreckage of the *Deepwater Horizon* drilling rig. On the surface, there would have been nothing to see, just the same circle of ocean surrounding us in all directions to the horizon. However, down on the seabed, things would have looked quite different where toxins and turmoil remain, as McClain and Nunnally had seen on a dive there two years earlier, in 2017. They sent down a remote-operated submersible, and when it reached the bottom, at around 5,000 feet, the first thing they saw on the camera feed was a single, steel-toed work boot lying on the seabed, no doubt worn by one of the workers from the stricken rig. "We all went silent," McClain said. "It was devastating." Eleven workers were killed when the *Deepwater Horizon* rig exploded on April 20, 2010.

Beyond the human tragedy, the submersible revealed the ecological catastrophe continuing on the seafloor. Over the course of eighty-seven days, approximately four million barrels of oil had poured from the blown-out Macondo wellhead into the Gulf, making it the biggest accidental oil spill in history. (The deliberate oil spill in waters of the Arabian Gulf in 1991 during the Gulf War may have been bigger.) A huge oil slick formed at the surface, polluting coastlines from Louisiana to Florida; salt marshes and beaches were oiled; thousands of dolphins and turtles were killed; a generation of fish larvae may have been poisoned and lost; toxins seem to have caused cardiac defects and triggered heart attacks in bluefin tuna and amberjack; and for a time, because of the contamination, a third of the Gulf of Mexico was closed to fishing.

The disaster was tragic enough at the surface, but a great deal of the spilled oil never left the deep. Around 3,300 feet down, a plume of oil and injected dispersants spread over hundreds of square miles. A lot of the oil that did float to the surface subsequently sank back down. Oil-covered plankton and particles of marine snow stuck together and fell much faster than normal, in what came to be known as a dirty blizzard.

"We saw this dark line on the seafloor," Nunnally said, recalling the 2017 dive to the *Deepwater Horizon*. The abyssal plain had been the regular, pale beige color except for this meandering mark. The submersible followed the line and at the end found a crab crawling hesitantly along, leaving a trail exposing the black oil just below the surface. In the seven years that had passed since the waters above had cleared of oil, only a thin layer of clean marine snow had fallen and covered over the blackened seabed. All it took was one crab to scratch the surface and show what lay below.

In the months immediately after the *Deepwater Horizon* disaster, the surrounding seafloor transformed into what many have described as a toxic waste dump. Dead bodies of sea cucumbers, sponges, and sea pens lay scattered around. Deepwater corals were smothered and poisoned by a mix of oil and dispersant. During the cleanup, some 766,000 gallons of chemical dispersants were injected directly into the wellhead, something that had never been done before. The dispersants boosted bacterial decomposition of the oil, stripping oxygen from the water and suffocating deep ecosystems. The dispersants also turned out to be more toxic to deepwater corals than oil.

Seven years after the spill, the ecosystem had barely begun to recover, and alarming, unexpected things are still happening. The oily chemicals are proving to be toxic enough to keep many animals away. Around the wellhead are none of the species that are common in other, healthier parts of the Gulf: no flytrap anemones, no sea cucumbers, no giant isopods. The sunken wreckage of the *Deepwater Horizon* drilling rig itself remains chillingly devoid of life. Usually, when a hard structure appears on the oozy abyss, a flock of animals swoops in to take advantage of the firm footing. Something is keeping them away from the *Deepwater Horizon*, likely a combination of the decomposing oil and dispersants.

During the 2017 dive, the only animals McClain and Nunnally saw near the wreckage were evidently not doing well. Crabs with festering shells, as if they hadn't molted properly for some time, were clustered around the wellhead in much higher numbers than normal and shuffling around like zombies. McClain and Nunnally's theory is that crustaceans are attracted by degrading hydrocarbons, which mimic the chemical signals of natural sex hormones. Once the crabs are drawn to the wellhead, the toxic environment makes them too frail to leave. McClain likens it to La Brea Tar Pits in Los

Angeles, which millions of years ago entrapped mammoths, giant sloths, and saber-toothed cats.

Despite the dangers, the oil and gas industry is reaching deeper underwater than ever before. Oil wells 330 feet or more below the surface are already commonplace and ultra-deep wells, 5,000 feet and deeper, are increasing. With greater depth comes a greater probability of accidents and oil spills, especially in US waters since the rollback of regulations introduced after *Deepwater Horizon*. In response to the disaster, President Barack Obama signed an executive order creating a commission to study the spill, which recommended new safety rules, accountability standards, and environmental regulations for drilling in US waters. The administration of Donald Trump, however, prioritized making offshore oil drilling cheaper and easier over protecting human lives, protecting the environment, and avoiding another catastrophic oil spill.

⌒

While the deep sea has absorbed unintentional pollutants, people have also used the enormous space of the deep to deliberately sink unwanted items and inconvenient substances, with the express purpose of forgetting all about them. Often it has proven to be the cheaper or easier, but rarely safer, option to use the deep as a dump site. Lying at the bottom of the sea is an odd assortment of things that hold a record of changing times in the human world.

Beneath busy shipping lanes once plied by steamships lie glassy lumps of clinker, the stony residues left over from burnt coal that were shoveled from the furnaces and dumped over the side. In some places, more than half the stones in the abyss are these man-made leftovers that a few animals will cling to, anemones and brachiopods and others that don't mind the melted chemical mix.

More recently, numbers of dead livestock have been showing up in the deep. With growing demand for cheap meat worldwide, and cultural requirements for local slaughter, more than two billion live animals are now loaded onto ships each year and sent across the oceans, and accidents happen. In 2019, a livestock carrier overturned in the Black Sea on its way from Romania to Saudi Arabia, drowning most of the 14,600 sheep reported to be on board (180 live sheep were rescued). A few months later, it transpired that far more sheep may have in fact been on board, packed into hidden decks. Poor conditions and heat stress often kill thousands of onboard animals. In July 2002, four shipments from Australia heading for the Middle East collectively pitched overboard into the Arabian Sea the carcasses of 15,156 sheep, which were reported to have died in the heat. The bone-eating worms must have feasted.

Some parts of the deep have received more than their fair share of human effluent, in the form of raw sewage. It doesn't happen anymore, but in the not-too-distant past, waste-disposal programs routinely loaded ships with sewage sludge, motored offshore, and dumped it overboard. Deep Water Dumpsite 106, off New York, was used for twenty years and received around 40 million tons of sewage, which wafted in brown plumes for miles until 1992, when DWD-106 was closed to further offerings. I was once told that a good way to know where human sewage has been poured into the sea is to look in the sediments for undigested tomato seeds.

Far more harmful substances have been left in the deep to try to keep humans safe from them. The Caribbean island of Puerto Rico used to give tax breaks to pharmaceutical companies and in the 1970s they were allowed to dump hundreds of thousands of tons of toxic waste at a site in the Puerto Rico Trench, close to four miles down.

There have also been unusual, one-off consignments to the deep. In April 1970, Apollo 13 failed to become the third crewed mission to land on the moon when an oxygen tank exploded. The three astronauts used the lunar module as a life raft and were making their way back to Earth, when staff at mission control began to worry about something the astronauts were bringing with them. The radioisotope thermoelectric generator was supposed to have been left behind on the surface of the moon to power a series of science experiments, with electricity produced from the heat of decaying plutonium-238. It was encased in a protective canister designed to withstand reentry and stay intact for eight hundred years, ten times the plutonium's half-life. Even so, just in case, as the lunar module headed for splash-down in the South Pacific, NASA nudged its course to make sure it landed above the Tonga Trench. Everything went according to plan: the astronauts returned safely, and the radioactive cask is presumed to be lying somewhere inside the world's second-deepest hadal trench, maybe all the way at the bottom, more than 35,000 feet down.

Later that same year, on a calm, sunny day in August, a short way off the coast of Cape Canaveral, Florida, US naval officers watched a military ocean liner tip its bow to the sky and slowly sink into 16,000 feet of water. The USS *Le Baron Russell Briggs* held a controversial cargo—24,000 tons of unwanted Cold War chemical weapons, including mustard gas and the nerve agents VX and sarin—that had been brought to the coast by train, passing crowds of protestors. It was the thirteenth and final ship since 1964 scuttled in a secret military campaign, code name Operation CHASE, the acronym standing for "Cut Holes and Sink 'Em."

The Americans weren't the only ones who were routinely dumping chemical weapons at sea. In the mid-twentieth century, it became standard military practice around the world to dispose of obsolete or unwanted nerve agents either by loading them into metal drums and pushing them off the side of ships or by scuttling entire, laden fleets. Beginning after the First World War, containers of a German blister agent, lewisite, were dropped into the North Atlantic; after the Second World War, Allied forces dumped more than 300,000 tons of Nazi chemical agents at sea; in the 1950s, off Northern Ireland and Scotland, British forces sank old merchant ships filled with nerve agent. Estimates suggest that around 1 million tons of chemical weapons have been sunk, all of them a long way out of sight.

The Operation CHASE incident brought the issue of deep-sea dumping to the public's attention after details were leaked by a Democratic congressman, triggering a national outcry. Original plans for the thirteenth CHASE sinking were put on hold, and in a series of government hearings, US Navy scientists admitted they couldn't locate any of the twelve ships already sunk, nor could they provide any proof the procedure was safe for people or the environment. Various alternatives were rejected, including disposing of the remaining weapons in underground nuclear explosions, but eventually the military ran out of options and time, as the corroding containers of deadly chemicals grew more unstable, and the sinking of *LeBaron Russell Briggs* went ahead. Public outrage continued, and the following year, in 1972, the US Ocean Dumping Act* came into effect, making it illegal, for the first time, to tip toxic wastes into the oceans. An international ban also came into force that year, with the adoption of the United Nations' London Convention.† It had taken decades of unchecked dumping to bring about regulations that still protect the oceans and the deep today.

Fifty years later, the mid-century munitions, along with consignments of nuclear waste, are still scattered through the deep, and still nobody knows the full scale of their impacts. Human tragedies have occurred: chemical weapons dumped in the seas around Japan by US forces after the Second World War have caused at least 820 accidents, including the deaths of ten fishermen who hauled up the sunken ordnance in their nets; between 1946 and 1996, more than two hundred Italian fishermen were hospitalized after exposure to nerve agents leaking from rusting bombshells trawled up from the Adriatic. But there have been only a few ecological studies. At a dump site off the Italian coast, between 600 and 1,000 feet down, two fish species, the blackbelly rosefish and the European conger eel,

---

* Known in full as the Marine Protection, Research, and Sanctuaries Act.

† Known in full as the Convention on the Prevention of Marine Pollution by Dumping of Wastes and Other Matter.

were found to contain higher than normal levels of arsenic, a residue of the chemical agent lewisite. Near Pearl Harbor in Hawaii, traces of mustard gas have been found in sediments at 1,500 feet, where weapons canisters and unexploded bombs were sunk. Chemicals lying in the deep may have formed a coagulated crust that seals in the active agent. Nobody knows how long those seals might last, how much more contamination might eventually leak out, and where it will spread.

American author Rachel Carson wrote about the threats of dumped pollutants pervading the oceans in the preface to the 1961 edition of her best-selling book *The Sea around Us*. "The truth is that disposal proceeded far more rapidly than our knowledge justifies," she wrote. "To dispose first and investigate later is an invitation to disaster." It's a disaster that could still be unfolding, as precious little is understood about how pollutants flow through marine ecosystems or what the eventual consequences of decades of historical dumping will be.

∽

The original London Convention, which entered into force in 1975, provided a blacklist of banned substances, including high-level radioactive wastes and chemical weapons, plus a gray list of materials that required special care when released at sea. In 1996, the black and gray lists were scrapped, and the convention was turned on its head; the parties to the revised protocol sought to fully embrace what is known as the precautionary principle. The core idea is to assume that dumping *anything* in the oceans may cause unwanted trouble—until proven otherwise. Instead of declaring what can and cannot be dumped at sea, everything is now banned, except for a handful of substances and objects that can still be disposed of but only under strict license and controls; these include fish and agricultural waste, vessels, and oil platforms.

In 2013, a ban was introduced on a new type of ocean dumping that has come to be highly controversial. Over the past few decades, teams of scientists and a few private companies have dumped tons of iron into the oceans—not because they wanted to get rid of the iron but to see whether it would help dispose of a different substance of which there is far too much in the world.

Ocean fertilization experiments essentially aim to mimic the effect of defecating sperm whales and hydrothermal vents. Adding iron to the sea triggers plankton blooms and speeds up the biological pump, drawing more carbon down into the deep, where it will stay away from the atmosphere for hundreds and thousands of years—that's the theory, anyway. So far, thirteen studies have shown that the first step of this process does indeed happen; dumping iron at sea, usually the cheap agricultural fertilizer iron sulfate, has triggered plankton blooms. But only one of those studies witnessed the crucial later stages following through, with a measurable increase in carbon sinking into the deep.

Even though it's not clear whether this approach actually works, by the early 2000s businesses had latched onto the idea and begun planning to make money by dumping all sorts of fertilizers at sea and selling carbon credits. Customers could then pay to offset their own emissions against the carbon allegedly sunk into the deep. Scientists, meanwhile, grew increasingly concerned about the unknown side effects of iron dumping, including the spread of toxic algae and the loss of oxygen when the blooms decompose.

Amid all this uncertainty and worries that companies would start cashing in on deluded carbon-credit schemes, the parties to the London Convention introduced a moratorium on corporations deliberately trying to fertilize the oceans. The UN's Convention on Biological Diversity also decided that the world is not ready for industrial-scale ocean fertilization. Legitimate scientific studies are still allowed, although researchers seem to have been largely put off by a few controversial experiments.

An alternative strategy is to pump carbon dioxide straight into the deep; ways of doing so include a highly contentious method that so far has not been put to the test. If carbon dioxide is pumped down deep enough, the pressure will compress it into a slushy liquid that's denser than seawater. Below 10,000 feet on the abyssal seabed, the unwanted gas would theoretically settle into lakes of liquid carbon dioxide. Some people have even pondered using oceanic trenches as a dumping place for carbon emissions. A back-of-the-envelope calculation showed the potential for dozens of these enormous V-shaped chasms to become a monstrously huge carbon dump: the Java Trench near Indonesia could apparently take 20,000 billion tons of liquid carbon dioxide, and a similar amount would fit in the Puerto Rico Trench. To put all that into perspective, humanity's estimated annual carbon dioxide emissions from burning fossil fuels and cement production is approaching 40 billion tons.

For now, pouring liquid carbon dioxide into deep trenches is not permitted under the London Convention—although that could change, making for a chilling prospect that the hadal zone could one day be used to stash our hellish waste. The costs and practicality of sucking carbon out of the air or diverting it from power-station chimney stacks have yet to be calculated. And the impacts on the living deep are untold. Trenches are not empty receptacles but homes to rich mixes of endemic animals, swarms of amphipods, snailfish, sea cucumbers, snails, and shrimp. Lakes of carbon dioxide would wipe out trench-dwelling creatures and disrupt microbial communities, most likely destroying countless new medical cures before they've been found, along with who knows what else that might prove useful in the human world. And in time, maybe in centuries to come, all that carbon dioxide could begin to dissolve, and the resulting acidified water could leak from those sunken lakes, adding to the problems of ocean acidification and suppressing the amount of carbon the oceans can naturally absorb.

The deep ocean is already in line to get hit hard by the climate crisis. A major study in 2017 made a suite of shocking predictions of what lies in store for the deep by the end of this century.

Temperatures in the twilight and midnight zones could rise by 7.2 degrees Fahrenheit above the current average temperature of around 39 degrees; farther down, waters could warm by 0.9 to 1.8 degrees Fahrenheit, which will be an equally big shock for organisms accustomed to the constant chill of the abyss. The sharpest increase in acidity throughout all the oceans is expected to hit between 650 and 10,000 feet down, where deep-sea corals, sea urchins, and others will struggle to make their calcium carbonate skeletons. In some places flurries of marine snow could decrease by half, due to declining plankton in the shallows, making the deep even hungrier. As waters warm, much of the deep will lose oxygen. An indication of what lies ahead comes from the northeast Pacific, off the coast of Vancouver Island, where oxygen levels in the upper 10,000 feet of the ocean have already fallen by 15 percent in the last 60 years, threatening midwater animals and those growing on clusters of seamounts that reach into this suffocating zone.

Willfully adding carbon to the deep by pumping it down there would not be a problem solved but just hidden away; it would be like the chemical weapons, nuclear waste, and everything else people have disposed of, except on a far bigger and more dangerous scale. All that carbon would still exist, and its impact on the atmosphere and the living planet would simply be postponed for future generations to deal with.

Humanity is not good at learning from past mistakes, but in this one case we should celebrate the fact that within a matter of decades, it has become unacceptable to flagrantly dump poisons and toxins into the sea, and regulations have been put in place to stop it from happening. It would be a pitiful outcome if, in the years ahead, humanity were to reach a stage where there is so much carbon to deal with that nobody can think of anything better to do than shove it into the deep and hope for the best.

What's Mine Is Yours

Walking through the docks in Southampton, Britain's second-largest container port, I felt my sense of scale shifting and bending around me. Cranes stood like headless, metal giraffes against a backdrop of shipping containers neatly stacked like Lego blocks. A cargo ship moored at the eastern dock looked more like a colossal cliff face than a vessel capable of moving. Just across from Berth 44, from which the *Titanic* sailed, is the National Oceanography Centre, the largest ocean science institution in the United Kingdom. I went through the glass entrance hall, under the mustachioed knight figurehead from the historic ship HMS *Challenger*, along the corridors and out into the back lot, where I stepped into a windowless shed. A tang of preserving alcohol hit my nostrils as the strip lights flickered on, revealing a modest-size room packed with shelves and glassware. I had come to see a collection of creatures that once roamed a much wider realm. Crammed on the shelves was a miscellany of animals from the abyss.

My guide was deep-sea biologist Daniel Jones, and together we snooped along the shelving, peering at the preserved creatures floating in jars. I spied five-pointed starfish, coiling snail shells, spiny crabs, and gangly sea spiders with their legs folded to fit in the jar.*

---

* A note for arachnophobes: these are not true spiders but creatures called pycnogonids.

There were dumbo octopuses and piglet squid, both smaller than I expected, not much more than a handful, floating in their tiny captive ocean. I rummaged through the jars and found large coral polyps resembling flowers made of stone, bamboo corals with finely branching twigs, giant barnacles, plump, pink shrimp that looked fresh from the barbecue, and lots of sea cucumbers. There was *Oneirophanta*, "the one who appears in dreams,"★ a sea cucumber with a cloak of long, white tentacles and dozens of stubby tube feet, like nipples, for walking across the seabed. Some sea cucumbers were so big each one occupied its own large Kilner jar, and some preserved together looked like fistfuls of caterpillars.

One species in particular I was curious to behold in the flesh after seeing photographs of its intriguing form in the wild abyss. Nicknamed the gummy squirrel (and officially called *Psychropotes longicauda*), this six-inch-long sea cucumber has a translucent lemon-yellow body with an unusual appendage sprouting from its rear end that looks like a squirrel's tail. "I don't think you're going to like it," Jones said, pulling a jar off a shelf and showing me a pallid, shapeless blob. The animal in the jar was certainly no longer beautiful, although still useful; DNA taken from snippets of preserved specimens has helped show there are in fact numerous species that look rather alike but are nevertheless genetically distinct.

Up in Jones's office, I saw arranged along a bookcase a selection of black lumpy rocks that were also collected from the abyss. One was the size and texture of a large head of broccoli; some looked like nuggets of coal, and some were smooth, disk-shaped pebbles. Jones passed me a fist-sized chunk, and for a moment it felt wrong. It was far too heavy for its size, like the rock my grandmother found long ago in her garden that my family has always thought might be a meteorite. Jones's rocks didn't fall from space but grew right

---

★ The name comes from Greek words *oneiro*, meaning "dream," and *phainomai*, "to appear."

where they were, lying on the deep seabed. At the heart of each rock is a tooth dropped by a shark millions of years ago or a chip of whale ear bone or some other small, hard fragment. As eons passed, waterborne minerals and metals settled in thin layers onto the solid nucleus, in the way a pearl forms, and the rocks gradually became bigger and heavier.

I remember being told in high school science classes about these rocky nodules that lie on the abyssal plains and how one day they could be mined for metals inside them. Back then, the image I held in my mind was of a blank flatland of oozy mud and rocks, not a place where marvelous things live and grow, including bright yellow sea cucumbers with tails.

The first time these deep-sea rocks were trawled up from the abyss was in the mid-nineteenth century, by the British scientists on board HMS *Challenger* as they circled the planet and learned so much about the oceans. The abyssal nodules were put on display to the public and treated like exotic curiosities, as if they had come from outer space. Not until much later did people begin to ponder the weighty metals inside them and wonder whether it might be worth going back to gather more.

As I write this, midway through 2020, no commercial mines are operating on the deep seafloor. But there is a possibility that by the time you read this, the first mines will have opened or at least been given the go-ahead.

In the past few years, mining corporations have been making plans to mine nodules several miles beneath the sea surface and across thousands of square miles of the abyss. What they're after are the metals that lie inside those rocks. Though composed roughly of 30 percent manganese, a metal that's not in great demand, the rocks also contain traces of other, more desirable elements, such as nickel, copper, and cobalt.

Besides abyssal nodules, two other targets have come into view for aspiring deep-sea miners. Some operations plan to mine seamounts.

In a way similar to the layering of the nodules, metal-rich crusts settle onto the tops and flanks of these underwater mountains. It takes millions of years for a finger-thick layer to form, yet it would probably take only hours for those deposits to be drilled and scraped away by mining machinery and dispatched to the surface. Mining corporations also have plans to knock down and demolish the chimneys of hydrothermal vents. As scorching fluids collide with cold seawater, quickly cooling and precipitating, they deposit a mix of metals, such as iron, lead, zinc, silver, and gold.★

The proposed mining ventures bear the hallmarks of extractivism, a centuries-old economic model commonly associated with colonialism and latterly with transnational corporations that extract natural raw materials for export. The goal is to mine a resource on a one-shot basis, then move on elsewhere and repeat. This has traditionally included such practices as gold and gem pit mining, mountain-top removal for coal, and clear-felling of old-growth forests. Central to the model are so-called sacrifice zones, those places that would inevitably be destroyed in the name of economic gain. Huge swaths of the deep sea—hundreds of square miles per mine per year—are in line to become such sacrificial zones.

There are, no doubt, mineral riches to be found in the deep, and many people are in favor of cashing them in now, but numerous peer-reviewed research papers warn of the dangers of doing so. At this point, what the science is saying—loud and clear—is that the deep-sea mining industry would pose dangerous risks to biodiversity and the environment, on timescales and intensities that cannot yet be fully quantified but could be catastrophic and permanent.

Still, there are important choices to make as we stand at a turning point in humanity's dealings with the deep sea, and with it the entire planet. The story leading to where we are now is filled with

---

★ The mining industry commonly refers to hydrothermal vent deposits as "seafloor massive sulfides" or "polymetallic sulfides" and seamount deposits as "cobalt-rich ferro-manganese crusts." I will call them what they are: hydrothermal vents and seamounts.

a mix of truths and lies, integrity and greed, mistakes and misfortunes. Interest in deep-sea mining has risen and fallen with the push and pull of changing metal prices and all the while driven by the inflating demands of mass consumerism. This is not a sudden rush for the deep but the culmination of a contemplation of the seabed that's been going on for more than fifty years.

∽

At the headquarters of the United Nations in New York, on November 1, 1967, the General Assembly listened to a long, impassioned speech about the oceans. "The dark oceans were the womb of life," they heard from the Maltese representative, Arvid Pardo. "From the protecting oceans life emerged. We still bear in our bodies—in our blood, in the salty bitterness of our tears—the marks of this remote past." As Pardo saw it, humans had recently begun to return to the ocean and were looking deeper to benefit from this huge realm. This could, he warned, mark the beginning of the end for life as we know it on earth. Alternatively, he said, it could be a chance to lay the foundations for a "peaceful and increasingly prosperous future for all peoples."

A debate had been scheduled for that morning's agenda at the United Nations, but in the end only Pardo spoke. For three hours, he delivered not so much a speech as a long, detailed lecture about the seas and the way people use them. He spoke of the troubles of chemical pollution, the possibility of stationing nuclear weapons at the peaks of seamounts, and of advances in ocean exploration, evoking the memory of the descent seven years earlier of Jacques Piccard and Don Walsh inside the bathyscaphe *Trieste* to the bottom of the Mariana Trench. Pardo spoke at length about the riches people could reap from the oceans. A revolutionary type of ocean food would come from a newly opened American factory that rendered down unpopular types of fish into "fish-protein concentrate," a forerunner of the fish meal used in farm animal feeds today. Just ten grams (about a third of an ounce) of this fishy supplement would, Pardo said, meet the daily nutritional requirements of a human child at the cost of less than one cent. He also predicted that by the 1980s, scientists would crack the techniques of fish husbandry and set up ocean-based farms; air-bubble curtains would corral the fish, tended by dolphins trained to work as sheepdogs.

Commercial ocean farming, Pardo thought, lay firmly in the future, but in 1967, mining the seabed seemed imminent. Rocky nodules lying on the Pacific seabed between 5,000 and 20,000 feet down held estimated reserves of metals that would supply the world for thousands of years to come. At then-current global consumption rates, the seabed held copper reserves that would last for 6,000 years, 150,000 years' worth of nickel, and cobalt enough to last for 200,000 years, all compared to less than a century's supply in the known reserves on land.

Pardo had gleaned these figures from a 1965 book by American mining engineer John Mero called *The Mineral Resources of the Sea*. Mero's book is largely responsible for transforming the view of seabed nodules from curiosities into a potential resource to be mined. Pardo told the UN General Assembly that these rocks not only were phenomenally abundant but would keep growing back, producing so many in a year that people wouldn't know what to do with them all.

What concerned Pardo most was who would get their hands on these precious seabed treasures first. Following the end of the Second World War, countries with coastlines had been gradually expanding their territories beyond the horizon, claiming more of the adjacent sea as their own. The original ambition of such moves, led by US president Harry Truman in 1945, was chiefly to exploit offshore oil and gas reserves. Facilitating this territorial shift was the lack of a firm definition of the maritime boundaries between a country's national waters and the high seas, those areas that belong to nobody in particular. With growing interest in seabed mining, coastal states seemed likely to continue edging their borders seaward until they divided the entire seabed among them. It was also plain to see that technologically advanced countries were closest to being able to mine the deep, excluding other, poorer countries from the seabed jackpot.

At the climax of Pardo's address, he made a plea that the seabed beneath the high seas should be declared the common heritage belonging to all of humanity, now and in the future. He proposed that the tremendous mineral wealth of the seabed should be exploited with "harm to none and benefit to all," and that no single country should be allowed to mine seabed metals without sharing the proceeds with the rest of the world, especially with poorer countries. In an interview years later, Pardo said, "I thought it could serve as sort of a bridge to the future and unite the world community in its quest to preserve our planet for generations to come."

Pardo received a predictably mixed response to his speech before the UN General Assembly. Developing countries were naturally in favor of a system that would entitle them to a share of the deep's wealth. Pardo had smartly garnered their support by likening the situation on the seabed to the nineteenth-century colonial scramble for land-based resources across Africa. The idea also appealed to Eastern Bloc countries, which opposed capitalist claims on the seabed. Even a few Western European states backed Pardo's plans. By and large, though, the rich and powerful industrialized states were less keen, but they were outnumbered, and the notion of the common heritage of the seabed was placed firmly on the United Nations' agenda.

What followed was more than a decade of difficult negotiations over how to govern the oceans with this idea in mind. At the same time, important developments were taking place out at sea, as major players in the mining industry were learning more about the alleged treasures of the deep.

∽

A commodity boom in the early 1970s fueled interest in seabed mining as ore prices soared. Western industrialized states grew increasingly uncomfortable at their reliance on raw materials exported from countries in the Global South. The seabed offered the possibility of securing supplies while sidestepping countries considered to be politically unstable. And within the legal system at the time, as Pardo had outlined, a lack of ownership and regulation in the high seas made it all the more appealing for mining companies to explore the possibilities of moving into the deep. They could do pretty much whatever they wanted.

Given the high costs and high risks involved in operating in distant and deep waters, several multinational consortia were formed between the world's leading mining corporations, including familiar names such as British Petroleum, Rio Tinto, Lockheed Martin, Standard Oil, and Mitsubishi. The consortia spent millions of dollars developing prototype mining equipment. In the late 1970s, the first successful tests were carried out on the metal-rich nodules of the Pacific Ocean floor. The mining consortia brought up a few hundred tons of nodules, showing that at least in theory seabed mining could work.

International interest was also stoked by what turned out to be a Cold War cover-up. In 1974, the US vessel *Glomar Explorer* set off from California, allegedly to gather nodules from the Pacific and investigate the practicalities of seabed mining. Inside the ship's hull was a huge hatch that would open to reveal a moon pool, an interface with the ocean through which deep-diving submersibles could be lowered to survey the seabed for nodules, or so the public was led to believe. In fact, that hatch was intended to receive the remains of a Soviet ballistic missile submarine, *K-129*, lost six years previously. The Americans had found the wreck site, 1,500 miles northwest of Hawaii and more than three miles underwater. The CIA launched a secret mission, code-named Project Azorian, spending $500 million on the ship and equipment to salvage the Soviet submarine. The *Glomar Explorer* arrived above the wreck, opened up its moon pool, lowered a giant mechanical claw, and grabbed the stricken submarine. But partway through the salvage mission, the claw broke, and the submarine tore in half, sending the all-important nuclear missiles and secret code books tumbling back into the deep. After that, the Americans abandoned their plans, but in the meantime the CIA had constructed a convincing smoke screen, dispatching geologists to talk at mining conferences, show off the handful of nodules grabbed from the seabed, and make out as if they were legitimately planning to go mining in the deep.

By the time the truth about Project Azorian came out a year later, interest in seabed mining was already beginning to subside. Findings from the genuine seabed surveys were not matching up to the early promises. The figures in John Mero's book had been based on just forty-five samples of nodules. More extensive studies found that the nodules may be as abundant as Mero suggested, but the metal concentrations inside them were not uniformly as high. Crucially, the nodules won't be growing back anytime soon. The formation of abyssal nodules is one of the slowest-known geological processes; it takes ten million years for a nodule to grow from the size of a pea to a golf ball.

Economic and political factors further deflated the initial euphoria surrounding seabed mining. Metal prices had slumped, and there was growing uncertainty as negotiations were ongoing at the United Nations over the issue of seabed ownership. As long as the mining consortia couldn't be sure of holding on to all their profits, the deep sea remained a much less attractive prospect. In the 1980s, most of the seabed mining projects were shelved.

၁

Arvid Pardo's idea of portioning out the riches of the deep had played a central role in starting and then stalling the first wave of interest in seabed mining. It also initiated rolling discussions at the United Nations over who owns and uses the oceans.

Eventually, in 1982, the United Nations adopted the Convention on the Law of the Sea, a great raft of an international agreement that firmly established jurisdictions over the blue parts of the planet. Coastal states' territorial waters now reach 12 nautical miles from shore;* another 200 nautical miles beyond that is an exclusive economic zone, to which a state has sovereign rights to exploit the living and mineral resources of the seabed.† Everything else is officially the high seas, a vast area covering more than half of the planet. The seabed below those waters has come to be known in UN parlance as "the Area," and here Pardo's proposal of sharing the seabed came to fruition. Article 136 of the Convention on the Law of the Sea simply states:

The Area and its resources are the common heritage of mankind.

To administer the common heritage of the Area, a new organization was founded. The International Seabed Authority (ISA) has the duty to oversee all extraction and mining activities on the seabed of the high seas while acting on behalf of the rest of humanity. This puts the ISA in a unique and powerful position. The Area is the largest part of the planet that falls under the purview of a single, global organization.

The role of the ISA has become all the more crucial because seabed mining is back on the international agenda. With rising metal prices and advances in deepwater mining technologies, companies have once again started entertaining the possibility of mining the deep seabed—especially now that a protocol is in place to begin that process. Any ISA member state can choose a piece of seabed inside the Area and, for a fee of half a million US dollars, apply for a mining-exploration permit. This permit allows the state to prospect the metal reserves in its contract area and test its mining

---

* 1 nautical mile is equal to 1.15 miles.

† Where the continental shelf extends naturally beyond 200 nautical miles, a state can submit a claim to expand this zone, for example in Ireland as featured in "The Real Map of Ireland."

equipment, but commercial mining is not authorized—not until the ISA finalizes and releases a set of regulations governing the planning and operation of seabed mines and how profits should be shared, known as the Mining Code.

The ISA set a self-imposed deadline of 2020 for the release of the code, which was delayed due to the coronavirus pandemic. As and when the code is finalised, companies will be able to apply to switch their exploration permit for a mining permit. Only then can full-scale mining begin. In anticipation of that milestone, the ISA has been granting exploration permits on what appears to be a first-come, first-served basis.* By 2019 China had five permits, more than any other country, granting it access to 92,000 square miles of seabed, roughly the size of the United Kingdom. Between them, three Chinese companies have acquired permits for all three types of seabed mine: they are surveying hydrothermal vents in the Indian Ocean, seamounts in the western Pacific, and nodules in the central Pacific, in a region known as the Clarion Clipperton Zone (CCZ).

Stretching thousands of miles between Mexico in the east and the islands of Kiribati in the west, the CCZ is an undulating abyssal plain scattered with metallic nodules, in places so dense it looks like a cobbled street. It's not the only part of the abyss studded with these metallic rocks, but it's thought to be one of the most commercially valuable deposits. More than a dozen countries have piled in alongside China and obtained exploration permits for the CCZ. A map of the claimed areas looks like a giant game of Tetris, with a convoluted arrangement of odd-shaped geometric blocks fitting together, most of them around 30,000 square miles, the standard size for an exploitation zone. Blocks have been claimed by France, South Korea, Japan, Russia, Belgium, Germany, Singapore, and the United Kingdom, and one block is being explored jointly by

---

* When this book went to press, the ISA had issued thirty-one mining-exploration permits covering more than 600,000 square miles. https://isa.org.jm/deep-seabed-minerals-contractors.

Bulgaria, Russia, Slovakia, Czech Republic, and Cuba. The United States is missing from this list because it has not ratified the Convention on the Law of the Sea and as such is not a member state to the ISA. However, there are mining claims in the CCZ held by the British company UK Seabed Resources, a wholly owned subsidiary of Lockheed Martin UK, the British arm of the US aerospace and weapons manufacturing giant Lockheed Martin.

Among the claimed blocks are areas set aside for the ISA itself to mine. The Enterprise, yet another United Nations moniker, is a mining company that would be run by the ISA. The idea is that it would use technology from mining countries, part of the deal to help share the benefits of the deep, and any profits it makes would be divided among the ISA members. So, from the moment the ISA opened its doors in Kingston, Jamaica, in 1994, its very reason for existence was to facilitate seabed mining, to oversee mining activities, and eventually to open its own mines.

The incumbent secretary general to the ISA in 2022, Michael Lodge, has shown ample signs of his pro-mining stance. He has appeared in publicity videos for the seabed mining corporation DeepGreen Metals. In a journal article published in 2018, Lodge wrote that it is useless and counterproductive to conduct an "existential debate" about whether deep-sea mining should or should not go ahead. As far as Lodge is concerned, mining the deep seabed is a foregone conclusion.

Nevertheless, mining is not the ISA's only responsibility. Under the Law of the Sea, the ISA is also legally bound to safeguard ocean ecosystems. The text of the convention is emphatic on this point. Various articles lay out how the ISA shall take steps to effectively protect the marine environment from any harmful effects of seabed mining, to avoid upsetting the oceans' ecological balance, and to prevent damage to marine fauna and flora. General provisions of the Law of the Sea also call for the protection of rare and fragile ecosystems and the habitats of depleted, threatened, or endangered species.

These restrictions are perhaps surprising, given that environmental concerns were not prominent during the 1970s when the Law of the Sea was being drafted. The convention focuses entirely on nodules, with no mention of mining seamounts or hydrothermal vents; interest in those has occurred since. At the time it was thought that nodule fields were little more than rocks scattered across empty mud and that minimal ecological harm would come from taking away bare pebbles. The notion that so little was apparently at stake could be why such strong wording was accepted into the convention. Environmental protections would have seemed irrelevant and certainly not something that could stand in the way of the mining industry. So much more is known now about the deep sea, from its mineral riches to its complex ecosystems.

The ISA has become both the exploiter and the protector of the deep seabed, and it will need to satisfy both mandates, to allow mining to proceed while also protecting the marine environment from harm. Time will tell how the overseers of the deep-sea mining industry will respond to this genuine existential crisis.

∽

Up until a few years ago, hardly any biological expeditions had visited the CCZ, because it was so remote and expensive to get to. Now a spotlight is shining brightly on this region, as a result of the interest and money pouring in from the mining industry. Teams of scientists are working on independent expeditions or collaborating with mining companies to get a handle on what the CCZ's seabed ecosystem looks like before mining begins and to try to predict what the likely impacts might be.* Conducting initial environmental assessments is one of the stipulations that come with prospecting

---

* Scientists tend to negotiate contracts for working with mining companies to protect their academic freedom. However, a 2021 article in the *Wall Street Journal* reported that an employee of a leading mining company warned a deep-sea scientist he might lose funding if he continued to publicly criticize seabed mining.

permits from the ISA. Amid their discoveries, scientists are realizing that the CCZ is an unusual, special place, filled with far more life than expected for a stretch of hungry abyss.

Shrimp, sea cucumbers, brittle stars, and starfish roam around the nodule fields. Fish and octopuses swim by. Especially common and diverse in the CCZ are what look like sculpted mud balls, up to a hand-span wide, which in fact are living things known as xeno-phyophores.* The name, which stems from Greek words meaning "one who bears foreign bodies," reflects the way these amoeba-like creatures construct themselves a shelter by gluing together grains of sediments. Dozens of new xenophyophore species are being found in the CCZ, and while they are certainly weird-looking, they form important oases of life in the abyss, creating microhabitats for worms, crustaceans, and other creatures that hunker down inside them.

The nodules themselves create a place to live for all sorts of organisms. In all, between 60 and 70 percent of animals living in the CCZ depend on the rocks, making them as vital to abyssal ecosystems as trees are to forests. Tucked away in the holes and cracks are tiny things like nematode worms and tardigrades, the microscopic "water bears" that have survived being frozen, boiled, and put in the vacuum of outer space, and can also tolerate the crushing pressure miles underwater.

Nodules provide firm footing for anemones, sponges, and corals—including ultra-long-lived black corals—all of which gain a step up from the seabed that helps them reach into the water to catch and filter passing flecks of food. It recently came to light that abyssal rocks, and the tall sponges sprouting from them, are also vital for cephalopods. Until 2016, the only octopuses seen living so deep down were dumbo octopuses, which swim through the water with gentle flaps of two earlike fins on the sides of their heads. Then a

---

* Although a type of foraminifera, common inhabitants of the seabed that are usually tiny, xenophyophores are among the biggest single-celled organisms on the planet; each hand-sized ball is made of just one living cell.

submersible caught sight of an unusual ghost-white octopus sitting on the seabed, 14,075 feet down. The translucent creature peered into the camera with beady black eyes, and people nicknamed it Casper. With no flapping appendages, this was evidently one of the benthic octopuses, which mostly sit or crawl across the seabed and had previously been seen only in waters far shallower. The discovery spawned a hunt for more Caspers in the abyss. Archive footage from submersibles was found to contain dozens more shots of pale and interesting octopuses at abyssal depths. Two were evidently female octopuses, their arms encircling a clutch of eggs laid on the stalk of a tall, dead sponge, which in turn was fixed to a rocky nodule. Nodules, we know now, are the foundation stones for an octopuses' nursery.

Studying the wildlife over vast areas of abyss is not easy; the CCZ is 2,500 miles from one end to the other, covering an area almost as big as Europe. Cataloguing the larger, visible species has become the task of autonomous underwater vehicles sent to fly over the abyss taking millions of photographs. Generally, there is an animal in view in every two or three pictures, or the equivalent of one individual occupying each pool-table-size area of seabed, one gummy squirrel sea cucumber, one coral, one anemone. Life is relatively sparse in the nodule fields, but across this vast region of abyssal plain, the numbers soon add up. The CCZ's diversity in species of megafauna—animals bigger than about a half inch—is among the highest across the deep sea.

～

Life is evidently abundant across the abyssal nodule fields, and it's hard to imagine how seabed mines could feasibly operate without devastating species and ecosystems. Indeed, deep-sea experts widely agree on the obvious impacts nodule mining would cause. As one paper quite simply puts it, mining would "erase the biota" that depends on nodules for habitat.

Even if the mining machines merely picked up each individual rock delicately—which they won't—still they would be removing habitat that would take millions of years to grow back. And seabed mining machines would do plenty more besides removing rocks.

The abyss is normally a quiet, still place, especially the Clarion Clipperton Zone, where the waters are crystal clear. That would suddenly change if mining begins. Mining companies are developing various designs for nodule-collecting machines that would be operated remotely by pilots on a ship at the surface; resembling enormous electric bulldozers, they are giant, destructive versions of the submersibles used by scientists. A common design would crawl along on caterpillar tracks, trampling and flattening the animals unable to get out of the way. Some of the contraptions would push rows of metal teeth a few inches into the soft seabed, to scrape and scoop up nodules as they go, like a potato harvester; others would work more like vacuum cleaners, with hydraulic pumps that suck up a mixture of nodules, water, and any living thing within reach. Nodules would then be pumped along a riser pipe, rattling and clattering all the way to the surface, several miles up.

As the mining machines thunder across the seabed, they would kick up fine, muddy clouds that would hang in the water because no strong currents are there to disperse them. Delicate animals caught in those clouds and unable to swim away, like corals and sponges, would be smothered and choked.

Warnings over the likely impacts of seabed mining are made all the more terrifying by the colossal scale at which the seabed disruption could realistically take place. Nodule mines would operate horizontally and advance over huge expanses of seabed. Each individual mine would be expected to exploit hundreds of square miles of the abyss every year, a footprint as big as the Isle of Wight, or several times the area of Manhattan. Since more than a dozen countries and corporations are bidding to mine the CCZ, multiple mining projects are likely to be approved and to operate continuously for thirty years or longer, working over more and more of the abyss.

Predictions are no less chilling for the impacts of mining on seamounts and hydrothermal vents. Those metal-rich deposits are not lying around loose on the seabed but would require cutting and digging out. Convoys of enormous crushing and drilling robots would scrape the crusts from the tops of seamounts and demolish vent chimneys. The noise would be like that of a road being jack-hammered, only much louder underwater and heard much farther away. Mining operations could be loud enough to scare off sea-mount visitors; spawning fish and migrating sharks and turtles may decide to stay away. Toxic dust storms would billow into the water from the drilling sites and spread as huge plumes before settling and blanketing the seabed.

Seamounts won't be removed wholesale; they would end up just being a few yards shorter than they were. Those once covered in sponge and coral forests would be stripped bare. The impacts would be comparable to the passing of a trawl net, only mining would be more methodical and thorough. Once the costly machines have been sent down to the mountaintops, guided from above, they would extract everything within reach.

Hydrothermal vent chimneys, on the other hand, would be flat-tened, taking with them the habitat for whichever subset of unique vent species happens to be living in that spot; the sequin-clad fighting worms, purple sock creatures, hairy-armed crabs, or any of the other as yet unknown, unnamed species.

A prevailing misconception is that the living communities on hydrothermal vents would recover rapidly from mining. Knocking down a vent chimney to mine the metals inside would doubtless have devastating effects, similar to those when eruptions strike these volcanic sites, when living creatures are wiped out by lava flows and tall chimneys are obliterated by seismic quakes. In regions hit by frequent volcanic activity, ecosystems tend to have evolved to be fast-paced and resilient, occupied by species that can potentially bounce back within a few years following an eruption as larvae arrive from nearby vents to kick-start the lost populations. It's dangerous to assume that all vents operate like this, but it's a premise that arose from the nature of the vents most commonly studied by scientists. Over the past forty years, by far the highest concentration of deep-sea research has been conducted on vents of the Northern Hemisphere within closest reach of major centers for deep-sea research. Numerous expeditions have visited the Mid-Atlantic Ridge between the Woods Hole Oceanographic Institution in Massachusetts and IFREMER in Brittany, the French research institute for exploitation of the sea. Vents in the northwestern Pacific are frequently visited by researchers from the Japanese research institute JAMSTEC, while North American scientists on the Pacific coast tend to visit the Juan de Fuca Ridge west of Vancouver Island or the Galápagos Rift off Ecuador. The best-studied Northern Hemisphere vents also happen to be among the most volatile in the ocean, located on mid-ocean ridges where tectonic plates are dragged fiercely apart.

While most scientists explore northerly vents, mining corporations are looking south. In 2019, of all the existing exploration permits granted for hydrothermal vent fields, in both national and international waters, nine were in the Northern Hemisphere and thirty-six in the Southern Hemisphere. Most of those southerly vents are not on mid-ocean ridges but associated with subduction zones, which form the type of deposits mining companies are most eager to exploit. These vents are long-lived and have built up substantial metal deposits from fluids pouring through them for hundreds and thousands of years. In addition, vents at subduction zones are enriched with metals brought into the mix as tectonic plates collide and one of the huge slabs of metal-rich oceanic crust sinks into the mantle and melts. They are also far more stable and less volatile than northerly vents on mid-ocean ridges, as seen in a rare study of a vent field in the Southern Hemisphere, when scientists made repeated visits to the Polynesian island of Tonga, one of several South Pacific countries that have granted exploration permits for the seabed within their national waters. Over the course of the ten-year study, there was little change in either geology or biology at the vents: there was no sign of an eruption or lava flow; vent chimneys stayed standing tall, with scorching fluids pouring through the same culverts at the same temperatures; dense populations of chemosynthetic mussels and baseball-size snails were still growing in the same places.

Such a stable environment creates favorable conditions for classic *K*-strategists, as ecologists label them, species with long life spans and slow reproduction; these aren't well suited to withstand recurrent explosions and eruptions—or mining. It's been widely assumed that vents are occupied by *r*-strategists, species that are weedy in comparison and can cope better with fast-changing conditions because they grow quickly and produce masses of offspring before dying young. The stability of the Tongan vents contradicts the popular story of vents being wildly erratic and universally colonized by *r*-strategists with inbuilt resilience. It's not clear whether ecosystems on volatile northern vents would be able to recover from the impacts of vent mining, because so much would depend on how mining is conducted and which vents would be left intact and undamaged, in order to ensure the sustained influx of drifting larvae. But it's quite obvious that ecosystems occupying the quieter southern vents would be hit even harder and take far longer to recover from mining, if at all.

Extinction is a distinct risk posed by seabed mining, especially on hydrothermal vents. In 2019, the scaly-foot snail became the first animal to be officially classified as an endangered species due to the threat of deep-sea mining. This followed an Indian Ocean research cruise three years previously, when deep-sea malacologist Julia Sigwart and her colleagues dived on the Kairei hydrothermal vent field. This was a known part of the snail's range, measuring only 100 by 260 feet (around half the area of a football field), but scientists failed to find a single gastropod with a black shiny shell and armor-clad foot. Eventually, on a second dive, they found two lonely snails in a spot where previously there had been thousands. More snails were later found, but by then Sigwart had realized just how difficult snails can be to spot—even at a vent like Kairei that has not yet been mined—and how easily a mining operation could wipe out an entire, rare population of scaly-foots without anyone even comprehending what had happened.

Returning from the Indian Ocean, Sigwart set out to translate that risk into something that could be widely recognized; she contacted experts at the International Union for the Conservation of Nature (IUCN), the global authority on species endangerment. The IUCN's Red List is a catalogue of the world's living species, organized according to their risk of extinction. At one end of the scale are thousands of species that are doing fine—common toads, Eurasian badgers, coyotes, and American robins; these are classified as Least Concern. Leading on from there is a spectrum of increasing peril, from Vulnerable to Endangered to Critically Endangered. In these categories are tigers and polar bears, sugarfoot moth flies and purple pitcher plants, Madam Berthe's mouse lemurs and Catarina pupfish. Beyond them is one more threat category that explains itself: Extinct.

A file of information was assembled for the IUCN to assess the threatened status of scaly-foot snails. Estimates of the total population size are unknown, but the total area of their habitat is at most five acres (or four football fields), split between three sites: the Longqi vent field, 1,200 miles southeast of Madagascar; the Solitaire vent field, within the waters of Mauritius; and the Kairei vent field, 470 miles to the south. The species' biology gives it little to no ability to recover from mining, as revealed by genetic studies showing that very few larvae drift the hundreds and thousands of miles between the three populations; if one population is wiped out by mining, there won't be squadrons of snail larvae coming to the rescue. Crucially, the International Seabed Authority has granted mining-exploration permits for the two vents located in the high seas: Kairei vent to a German mining company, Longqi vent to the Chinese. The evidence was enough to add the scaly-foot snail to the Red List in the Endangered category. It has since been joined by dozens of other hydrothermal vent mollusks assessed by Sigwart and her colleagues, some Vulnerable, some Endangered, and some Critically Endangered. The mollusks will likely be just the beginning and other endemic vent species, as well as those living on seamounts and on abyssal plains, could likewise be assessed for the threats they face from deep-sea mining.

No automatic legal protection comes with a species being labeled as threatened with extinction. The IUCN's Red List is, however, a powerful tool for drawing attention to the species most in trouble and most in need of urgent attention, to help guide conservation actions and international policies.* There are, as noted, obligations under the Law of the Sea to protect the habitats of endangered species. The IUCN assessments for vent species also reveal a simple but vital truth: it would be a relatively straightforward matter to take animals like the scaly-foot snail off the endangered list. All this would require is for mining on those vents not be given the go-ahead. Mining is the single, most urgent threat looming over vents, and it could quite feasibly be called to a halt. Some vents are already protected, and seabed mining not permitted, although they are mostly in the Northern Hemisphere, where miners aren't interested anyway, including the Endeavour vent field in Canadian waters; occasional spots in the south, like the Antarctic vents where Hoff crabs live, are also protected. In these places, few if any species will

---

* When the scaly-foot snail's endangered status was first announced, attempts were made to rebrand it. "Scaly does not sound attractive," says Julia Sigwart. The snail was renamed "sea pangolin," after the endearing scaly mammals that resemble animated pinecones and are also highly threatened with extinction, but it turned out that the public wasn't familiar with land pangolins either, and the nickname was dropped.

be flagged as highly threatened because they are already protected from mining, and the same could happen elsewhere.

Mining the vents also risks demolishing ecosystems that have fundamentally transformed the view of life on earth. In 2017, the International Seabed Authority granted a fifteen-year exploration permit to a Polish mining company for a region of the Mid-Atlantic Ridge including the TAG (Trans-Atlantic Geotraverse) and Broken Spur hydrothermal vent fields, which have been the subject of decades-long scientific research programs. Lost City also falls within this mining concession, the unique white smoker that could be a contemporary analogue of the conditions that allowed the first biological cells to spark into life. One of the most important scientific, not to mention cultural, sites in the deep sea, it has been proposed as a potential World Heritage Site, meeting UNESCO's standards for outstanding, universal value.

ℂ

Besides the immediate footprint of mining operations, a major concern over their impacts has to do with the tailings, the contaminated waste materials and seawater that would be left over after the valuable ore is processed on a ship at the surface. Tailings would either be pumped back down to the mining site to mingle with the plumes already disturbed or, if that is deemed too expensive, piped down 3,000 feet or so into deep open waters, where they would cause troubles of their own. Flakes of marine snow are normally the only particles that drift through the twilight and midnight zones. Plumes of mining tailings would inject dust storms into their midst, including fine sediments that would hang suspended for years and get carried by ocean currents for hundreds of miles. Delicate animals of so many kinds—ctenophores and siphonophores, gossamer worms and bomber worms, larvaceans and jellyfish—would be smothered and dragged down by particles settling on them, their gills and delicate feeding apparatuses clogged so they can't breathe or eat. Dust clouds would substantially absorb blue light, selectively blocking the most common color the bioluminescent animals use to communicate. Their blinking lights and messages to lure and warn would be muted and erased in the murk.

Those gritty clouds would also be laced in toxic metals released from crushed seabed ores. In the open water, the contaminants could easily seep into the tangled food web that connects the deep with the surface seas. Snow-catching zooplankton and jellyfish would likely pick up the tainted particles and pass them on up the food web and into shallower seas on their nocturnal migrations to the surface.

Whale sharks have been tracked as they swim across the Pacific, passing right through the Clarion Clipperton Zone. If nodule mining goes ahead, the long-lived sharks would unavoidably begin to absorb and accumulate toxins from the polluted plankton they sift from the sea each time they swim by. Leatherback turtles make similar transoceanic treks and also dive down to 3,000 feet to feed on jellyfish, potentially right in the middle of the mining plumes. While we don't know at this stage exactly how badly the toxins might affect turtles and sharks, as well as seabirds, whales, and many other animals that pass through, these creatures clearly would be harmed in some way.

Another major concern, with more big unknowns, is how toxins stirred up by mines could contaminate fisheries. Half the world's tuna supplies come from the Pacific, including fisheries that operate in and around the CCZ. Various tuna species are highly migratory and would likely swim through polluted zones. Bigeye and yellow-fin tuna go on long foraging dives into the twilight zone, where, like leatherbacks, they could get directly exposed to mining wastes. The fisheries support thousands of jobs and bring important revenue to Pacific island nations, all of which could be at risk if pollutants from seabed mining end up inside tuna fish sandwiches and salads. Only very few people would ever directly see the impacts of deep-sea mining, but it would become difficult to ignore if those toxic impacts are let loose on the whole ocean and make their way into the human food chain.

৵

Terrestrial mining regulations often require that biodiversity loss, ideally, should be avoided or minimized; lost populations should somehow be replaced afterward or even replenished elsewhere. In the deep, avoiding the loss of biodiversity would be impossible, for the obvious reason that seabed mines would directly demolish species and habitats. Losses away from the mining sites could perhaps be minimized by controlling where the sediment plumes drift, with some kind of baffle around mining machinery and by designing machines that trample less heavily across the abyss. Impacts could also be reduced by setting aside substantial portions of the abyss as no-mining zones. In the Clarion Clipperton Zone, the ISA has allocated areas where mining would not be allowed, but most are located at the fringes of the nodule fields, where the density of rocks is lower and corporations are less interested in mining. Where there are naturally fewer nodules, the abundance of abyssal species is naturally lower too, so protecting these areas is unlikely to achieve the desired protection of biodiversity. It would be like protecting only the very edges of a rain forest, not its dense, luxuriant heart.

Replacing lost species in the deep is near impossible. The theory of remediation suggests that animals and plants can be reintroduced to a mined site once operations have finished to help kick-start the ecosystem's recovery, for instance by replanting a felled forest with saplings grown elsewhere. The costs of doing something like this in the deep would be astronomical and could well cause more harm than good. It's difficult to imagine how thousand-year-old corals plucked from healthy seamount ecosystems and fixed to the sides of mined mounts would survive, or how tube worms in their thousands would be glued, one by one, in places where hydrothermal vent fluids still pour through the seabed.

Suggestions have been made that after nodule-mining operations have ceased, artificial nodules could be manufactured and placed on the seabed to give animals back the hard substrate they need. However, a rough calculation, based on a price of ten cents per rock (which needs to include the cost of transporting them offshore and putting them in the abyss), estimates that rebuilding a single mined concession area in the CCZ would come to more than US$20 billion, a major chunk of the projected mining revenue of US$60 billion over thirty years. We also have no way of knowing whether the living creatures and their larvae from surrounding, non-mined areas would accept those replacement rocks and move in.

The strategy of offsetting is also problematic in the deep sea. This involves attempting to cancel out the destruction of an ecosystem by protecting and restoring a similar ecosystem somewhere else. As scientists are increasingly discovering, shuffling bargaining chips in this way is not a reliable option for the deep sea. For instance, studies show that no two hydrothermal vent ecosystems are alike; each contains its own unique assemblage of species, depending on the mix of geological and chemical conditions; so, protecting one vent field is no guarantee species will be saved from destruction at another.

Some have proposed that mining the deep could be offset by restoring coral reefs in shallow waters, by way of an ecological apology to the planet. This does, however, assume there is some equivalency of species, an *Iridogorgia* deep-sea coral traded, for example, for a tropical *Acropora*. Moreover, this approach to accounting for a net benefit to global biodiversity is so ambiguous as to be scientifically meaningless.

There is also talk of mining only inactive or dormant hydro-thermal vents, areas where chimneys have naturally stopped pouring out hot fluids. However, these areas are not empty of life but contain their own ecosystems about which even less is known.

～

The apparently unavoidable loss of biodiversity from seabed mines casts serious doubt over whether it is possible to sustainably mine the deep. The stakes soar even higher when we look at the possible impacts on the planet as a whole. Plans for mining the seabed are accelerating, and at the same time our awareness is growing of how the deep sea plays a critical role in regulating the earth's life-support systems.

Numerous deep-sea experts advise that seabed mining has the potential to worsen the climate crisis. Stores of carbon in the abyss could get disrupted by mining activities that churn up delicate microbial communities that are vital for the carbon cycle and have taken millions of years to evolve. It's also not clear how vent mining would upset chemosynthetic microbes that mop up methane that bubbles through the seabed. Released to the atmosphere, methane becomes a greenhouse gas twenty-five times more potent than carbon dioxide. Whether mined vents would burp more methane is another unresolved matter.

With all of this in mind, if the International Seabed Authority gives commercial mines permission to open before the full impacts of mining are well understood, it risks tragically failing in its responsibilities to safeguard life in the abyss—not to mention threatening the rest of the planet.

⌀

Efforts are being made to answer the most pressing questions regarding the impacts of deep-sea mining, some by scientists sponsored by mining corporations to study proposed mining sites. Several relatively small-scale simulated mining experiments have been conducted in the abyss, giving some clues as to the possible outcomes. The most ambitious, which started in 1989, took place in the Peru Basin off the Pacific coast of South America, where a team of German researchers selected a four-square-mile block of an abyssal nodule field (tiny compared to the size of future mines) and dragged a twenty-six-foot-wide plow harrow across it seventy-eight times. The plow didn't remove the nodules but pushed them aside and buried them in the soft sediment. Scientists have been back at intervals to survey the site, and in 2015 an autonomous submersible photographed the whole area. The resulting photomosaic showed the plow tracks still clearly visible, crisscrossing the seabed, almost three decades later. Even these modest disturbances to the sediments have barely changed in all that time in the calm and still abyss. Mobile animals such as crabs and sea cucumbers had begun to move back in, but the sedentary animals—the corals, sponges, and anemones—were still missing.

Troubles stirred up by scraping over the abyss extend beyond visible animals. Another team of researchers visited the Peru Basin and made some fresh seabed tracks to compare to the decades-old scars. In this part of the abyss, the seabed is covered in a thin layer of sediments that acts like an intricately structured living skin, crawling with microbes. This microscopic community processes the raw organic matter that falls from above as marine snow, incorporating this carbon into the seabed ecosystem. When this delicate skin was experimentally turned over, the microbes were thrown into disarray; immediately half were lost. In the thirty-year-old tracks, the abundance of microbes was still at least 30 percent lower than in undisturbed areas. The study, published in 2020, predicted that microbial life and carbon flux in the seabed would take at least fifty years to return to normal, strengthening concerns over the climate impacts of seabed mining.

A few other mining-simulation studies have been carried out, all with worrying outcomes for biodiversity, but they all share one important shortcoming—they are academic trials, not industrial enterprises. The impacts of full-scale mining would likely be far worse than anything they have shown. In 2022 and 2023 scientists and miners plan to return to the Clarion Clipperton Zone to study what happens as prototype mining machines of the designs that would be used in commercial-scale mining are deployed. However, the time frames for exploitation and good science do not necessarily match. Scientists will need time to reach conclusions, and it remains to be seen whether officials at the International Seabed Authority will be patient and wait for the science to properly assess the impacts before deciding whether or not mines should go ahead. There is a tangible sense within the scientific community of the unstoppable momentum of an industry backed by powerful lobbies against which scientists can't do battle.

"Even if we found unicorns living on the seafloor," says Daniel Jones, of the British National Oceanography Centre, "I don't think it would necessarily stop mining."

PART FOUR

PRESERVE

PART FOUR

PRESERVE

Green vs Blue

A new argument is emerging for mining the deep. Seabed mines, we're being told, are going to save the planet.

In April 2018, a 300-foot Maersk offshore supply vessel left the dock in San Diego, California, heading west. Among the well-wishers at the prelaunch party were Baron Waqa, president of Nauru, the tiny island state in Micronesia northeast of Australia, and Michael Lodge, the secretary-general of the International Seabed Authority (ISA). The men took turns sitting in a large chair surrounded by buttons and levers on the ship's bridge, each of them sporting a hard hat with the logo of DeepGreen Metals. This is what the latest wave of interest in deep-sea mining looks like.

The Maersk ship was heading for the Clarion Clipperton Zone on one of five planned research trips to parts of the nodule fields that DeepGreen has permits to explore. To prospect the seabed in the high seas, DeepGreen, as with all independent corporations, can't work directly with the International Seabed Authority but must operate via a state-sponsored company, which is why the president of Nauru was involved.★

The eight-square-mile island country, in the central Pacific to the west of the Clarion Clipperton Zone, has a tragic history of mining

---

★ Any country would do, as long as it is party to the Convention on the Law of the Sea, so that's most states, except the United States.

on land. What used to be a tropical idyll was transformed in the early twentieth century into a desolate, lunar wasteland. Open cast mines stripped away deposits of phosphate, the fossilized remains of seabird droppings (or guano), used to make cheap agricultural fertilizer. Much of Nauru's interior has been rendered uninhabitable, nothing left but the jagged limestone peaks of ancient corals on which the island was formed. After the country gained independence in 1968, it amassed substantial royalties from phosphate mining, and for a while Nauru was one of the richest countries per capita in the world. However, by the 1990s, the guano had run out, and a string of corrupt politicians had squandered the profits on bad investments, including a 1993 West End musical about a fictitious love affair between Leonardo da Vinci and Mona Lisa.* Since then, Nauru has been a money-laundering haven with links to the Russian Mafia and al-Qaeda and became the base for Australia's notorious, prison-like refugee detention center. Seabed mining is the latest idea for digging the country out of financial trouble.

If deep-sea mining starts anywhere in the high seas, Nauru stands to gain a share of the proceeds, regardless of whether it sponsors a mining corporation—although not a great deal. In 2018, the ISA contracted a team from the Massachusetts Institute of Technology (MIT) to look into the economics of nodule mining. Rough calculations indicate that a seabed mine collecting 3.3 million tons of nodules could generate revenue each year of around US$2 billion. Complying with the notion of the deep seabed being the common heritage of humanity, the ISA plans to impose a royalty tax on all high-seas mines and share those proceeds equally among its member states. At a royalty rate of 10 percent (the upper end of recent ISA negotiations), that would yield $200 million—or a royalty of around $1 million annually to each of the ISA's 168 members. The ISA would keep the rest for operating and regulatory costs. Even

---

* *Leonardo the Musical* was a flop and closed within a month.

if several mines were operating, each member state would receive only a modest revenue.

The figures look different, however, for countries like Nauru that decide to sponsor mining corporations, because the government can charge capital gains tax on the income generated. The MIT study predicted that after all operating costs, capital costs, and royalty payments to the ISA are deducted, profits from one seabed mine could be between $500 million to $1 billion per year. From those profits, if a government were to levy a corporate tax of 20 or 25 percent, it would provide an annual tax revenue of $100 million to $250 million. This is how Nauru hopes to bring fortunes back to a government that keeps falling on hard times.

When Arvid Pardo made his speech to the United Nations in 1967, he did not envision national taxation as the way to allow low-income countries to gain a substantial share of the common heritage of the seabed. In any case, for that to happen, each low-income country would have to sponsor its own mines, which would add up to a lot of mining, especially if all members of the ISA, rich and poor alike, decide to do the same.

For companies like DeepGreen Metals, working with impoverished countries like Nauru adds a touch of legitimacy to their plans, offering some sort of proof that the seabed's wealth would be shared with those most in need. And Nauru is proving to be especially helpful in the process. With backing of the Nauru government, DeepGreen has become a prominent voice at the ISA, pushing hard for the release of the Mining Code, which would pave the way for commercial mines to open. The ISA has come under mounting pressure from pro-mining states and companies like DeepGreen, who insist that mining must be allowed to proceed now, or it might not happen at all.

This sense of urgency to hold an exploitation permit comes not just from the need to start mining. Being given the green light could be enough to stimulate further investment, at which point the companies could float on the stock market, and executives and others would stand to make a fortune even before their first mine opens.

In the course of DeepGreen's involvement with Nauru and the ISA, its chief executive officer, Gerard Barron, has been given some remarkable platforms. In February 2019, he was allowed to address the ISA council, an unprecedented appearance for a forum reserved for member states, not commercial entities. Barron took the Nauru government's seat and delivered a speech promoting his company and his vision for the imperative to mine the seabed.★

"Personally, I get very uncomfortable when people describe us as deep-sea miners," Barron said in his address to the ISA. "We don't think of ourselves as developing a mining business," he continued. "We are in the transition business—we want to help the world transition away from fossil fuels."

Barron constantly repeats the message to potential investors and in marketing materials that the most sustainable way to meet future demand for metals will be to gather nodules from the abyss in the Clarion Clipperton Zone. He argues that harvesting nodules would have less impact than land-based mines, which are running out of high-grade ores and causing ever more damage to the environment, and that seabed nodules, sitting there waiting to be picked up, contain all the necessary metals to manufacture the wind turbines, solar panels, and electric cars needed for a low-carbon future. The choice laid down is one of green or blue: the greening of global economies pitted against the health and integrity of the blue oceans.

Since the full and long-term impacts of nodule mining are matters that scientists are only just beginning to gauge, claiming that mining impacts on land and in the deep sea can be meaningfully

---

★ The CEO of the Belgian company DEME, Alain Bernard, was also allowed to address the ISA council at the same meeting in 2019. He spoke about the vision of his subsidiary company Global Sea Mineral Resources and described the progress they had been making in testing a nodule-collecting device called Patania II.

compared is ludicrous. And while the metal content of the nodules may incorporate the predicted elements, whether or not those particular metals will be the ones most needed in a fossil-fuel-free world is another question entirely.

❧

In order to avoid the most catastrophic forecasts of the climate crisis, radical changes need to take place in the way global economies operate—the way food and energy are produced, the way vehicles are powered, the way buildings are built, heated, and cooled. Power stations burning coal, oil, and gas need to be switched off. Internal combustion engines, fed by liquid fossil fuels, need to become things of the past.

To give up fossil fuels and bring greenhouse gas emissions crashing down will require enormous quantities of metals. Wind turbines, solar panels, and batteries for electric cars and trucks (maybe even one day for electric container ships and airplanes) will all be made from a blend of metallic elements, some in smaller but vital amounts, others in huge quantities. Our need for fossil fuels will be replaced by a new need for metals, but whether those elements need to come from the deep seabed, as DeepGreen Metals and other mining corporations claim, is debatable.

Predicting which raw materials will be used in the years ahead, and where they will come from, is incredibly complex. For metals, it's not just a case of calculating the size of known, minable reserves around the world, because economic and political factors influence what is mined and refined, as well as the cost and availability of materials. In addition, no single, set pathway leads toward a low- or zero-carbon future for the global economy. Future demands for metals will depend on the particular technologies and machines that are used to decarbonize everyone's daily lives. Already, there are multiple ways of producing, storing, and using renewable energy, each drawing on different parts of the periodic table.

Two main options exist for harnessing energy from the wind: onshore and offshore turbines. Onshore, turbines are usually built with a gearbox that converts the graceful spinning of the blades into a much higher speed to drive an electrical generator. The key metal for the manufacture of the generator coil is copper, one of the elements that could be mined from deep-sea nodules and seamounts.

For wind farms built out at sea, conditions are usually much windier, and the moving parts of a turbine's gearbox are not suited to the wear and stress of faster-spinning blades. Thus, offshore turbines don't have gearboxes but instead use a direct-drive mechanism, which contains a complex generator incorporating rare earth metals. Also known as rare earth elements or just rare earths, most of these seventeen elements are in fact not especially rare; the impression of their rarity comes from the fact that they don't occur in concentrated deposits, making them difficult and expensive to mine and extract compared to most other metals. Trace amounts are used in various technologies, from smartphones and plasma screens, to night-vision goggles, radar, and precision-guided weapons; the bulk of rare earths are currently used in ceramic and glass manufacture and catalytic converters in cars. In offshore wind turbines, alloys of the rare earths neodymium and dysprosium are used to build powerful magnets.

China is by far the world's biggest producer of rare earths, making these some of the more contentious metals. Following a territorial dispute in 2010, China stopped exporting rare earths to Japan, causing a spike in global metal prices. More recently, in 2019, rare earths have been caught up in the US–China trade war, as China hinted it might restrict exports to the United States. With geopolitical concerns over securing supplies, Chinese and other mining companies are naturally showing a lot of interest in the rare earths contained within deep-sea deposits, including the nodules lying scattered across the Pacific.

New turbine designs with different metal requirements may also soon be available. In 2019, a Denmark-based consortium conducted successful full-scale field trials of a direct-drive turbine whose neodymium magnets were replaced by a superconductor. Compared to conventional machines, turbines with superconductors will be cheaper to make and run, being lighter, more efficient, and containing far less rare earth metal. A single such turbine would contain around two pounds of the rare earth gadolinium, while the original magnets being replaced each contain roughly a ton of neodymium.

Therefore, important questions for the renewables market concern whether the future lies in onshore or offshore turbines and in which designs. Currently, geared, onshore wind turbines make up 70 percent of the global market. Government support, local planning regulations, and many other factors will influence whether more onshore or offshore wind farms will be built in the years ahead and hence which metals will be in highest demand.

In contrast, the solar power industry is dominated by a single technology, one it began with more than sixty years ago. The silicon-based photovoltaic cell is first-generation solar technology, with panels made of thin slices of silicon, which release electrons when hit by photons of light. Silver paste loaded into the silicon wafer then conducts those electrons into a circuit, as silver is the best-known electrical conductor. Recent analysis has linked rising demand for solar panels with an increase in the price of silver. And while some silver could be mined from hydrothermal vents, this is not an element that would come from the large-scale mining of Pacific nodules.

Second-generation solar cells are already available, including cadmium telluride cells, which use less silver but need tellurium, a metal that could potentially be mined from seamounts. So far, these and various other solar cells have made only small inroads into global markets, chiefly because the original cells are hard to beat. Since their invention in the 1950s, silicon-based solar cells have gone from

6 percent to over 20 percent efficient,* and they cost less than a fifth of the price they did in the 1990s. To compete with that would either take a huge price shift or the invention of a solar cell that does something completely new.

A third-generation of solar technologies has the potential to disrupt the renewables scene. One design showing particular promise is for solar cells made from minerals known as perovskites. In 2019, more than a dozen companies around the world were working to commercialize this technology, which functions in a similar way to first-generation silicon solar cells, but the current perovskite cells are efficient only at the size of a postage stamp. If they can be upscaled and made more stable, perovskites could eventually become a kind of spray-on solar ink, generating electricity in unconventional places, on walls and windows, car roofs and airplane wings, even clothing. And they can be made from various cheap, abundant materials. Commonly, perovskites contain organic molecules (made of carbon, hydrogen, and nitrogen), one of the halogens (often iodine or chlorine), and lead, a metal not in short supply and not a major target for deep-sea mining.

✌

Arguments in favor of seabed mining commonly focus on the need to electrify the world's fleet of cars and trucks. Abandoning fossil fuel vehicles makes a lot of sense environmentally. A standard internal combustion engine works via an orchestrated sequence of explosions that are only 30 percent efficient. The roar of highways and the burning heat of a car's radiator are signs of all the wasted heat and sound energy that are lost to the air. Electric cars are much cooler and quieter and typically over 90 percent efficient. Charge an electric car from a source of renewable electricity, and overall

---

* Solar cell efficiency refers to the portion of the sun's energy that is converted to electricity. For example, on an average sunny day in London or New York, the sun delivers around four kilowatt-hours of energy to every square yard of ground; a panel with 20 percent efficiency would harness roughly 20 kilowatts per square yard per day.

carbon emissions will be much lower than from a tank filled with gasoline or diesel. And regardless of how the electricity is generated, electric cars have zero tailpipe emissions and do away with problems of local air pollution in cities.

However, most current designs for rechargeable batteries require a lot of cobalt—the average electric car requires around twenty pounds to make the battery's electrodes—and this highly controversial metal happens to occur in the deep sea.

Currently, more than half of the global cobalt supply comes from the Democratic Republic of the Congo (DRC), in central Africa, one of the poorest and most politically unstable countries in the world. The cobalt industry in the DRC is dominated by massive, open-cut mines, which compete with an additional two hundred thousand unauthorized, hand-dug mines. Using chisels and mallets, people scrape into the dirt, dig pits and tunnels, sometimes in their backyards and right below their houses, searching for cobalt-rich seams. Such tunnels have no support to stop them collapsing, and the miners have nothing in the way of safety gear; they don't have face masks, gloves, or even boots. Accidents and fatalities are rife. In June 2019, forty-three miners died inside a collapsed tunnel they were working illegally at the edge of a huge commercial mine.

Amnesty International reports widespread child labor in DRC's hand-dug mines, including children under seven. They carry huge sacks of rocks and inhale harmful cobalt dust. One boy told Amnesty International that when he was twelve, he would stay down in the mines for twenty-four hours at a time. The atrocious human rights record of these land-based mines is one inducement to mine cobalt from the seabed. A further incentive comes from the volatile price of cobalt on global markets.

In the mid-2000s, cobalt prices shot up as demand grew from the tech industry to make rechargeable batteries for smartphones and laptops, but they crashed back down following the 2008 global recession. Then in 2017 and 2018, dozens of countries and cities around the world pledged to phase out fossil fuel vehicles, leading to a feverish rise in interest in electric cars and coinciding with a spike in the price of cobalt, which more than tripled within two years, from under US$30,000 to more than US$95,000 per ton. Partly driving this price jump was the fact that China—which owns eight of the fourteen biggest cobalt mines in the DRC and refines 80 percent of the global cobalt supply—had been stockpiling supplies in anticipation of burgeoning demand from car manufacturers. It was a perfect time for deep-sea mining companies to push their message of problematic cobalt supplies and the urgent priority—and potential profitability—of extracting it from the seabed. However, by 2019, escalating demand for cobalt had yet to materialize and carmakers still hadn't begun churning out electric vehicles. China released its supplies, and by early 2020 the price of cobalt had slumped.

The basic design for rechargeable batteries hasn't changed a great deal since they were originally developed in the 1970s. Rechargeable lithium-ion batteries were first used commercially by the Sony Corporation in 1991 inside handheld video cameras. The same battery technology now powers our entire digital age. It's the black box that most of us interact with via the charging symbol on smartphones. Switch on a phone, and electrons flow through a circuit between two electrodes, from the negative anode to the positive cathode, discharging a current. At the same time, positively charged ions flow between the electrodes passing through a liquid electrolyte. Plug in the phone, and electricity entering the battery reverses this process, shuffling ions back to the anode and building up stored charge.

Early versions of the battery had a lithium anode and a titanium disulfide cathode, which had the unfortunate habit of exploding. Replaced with a cathode of cobalt oxide, the batteries packed more charge and were less likely to catch on fire. These rechargeable batteries work well enough for small electronics, but the race is now on to develop the next generation of electric car batteries that aren't too big and heavy and won't run out miles from the next charging station. Part of the rethink, amid the volatile prices and growing concerns of unethical Congolese mining, involves reducing and even entirely eliminating cobalt.

Already, lithium-ion batteries have been tweaked to reduce their cobalt content. Panasonic, which supplies batteries to electric car-maker Tesla, produces cathodes containing less than half the cobalt of other car batteries.

The cobalt cathode can be entirely replaced with something else, although existing alternatives don't yet always work as well. In China, most electric buses have iron cathodes, but they hold less charge and wouldn't work as well for private cars, which may need to go greater distances on a single charge.

Promising alternatives to the original cobalt-laced designs include solid-state batteries, which are attracting strong interest; car companies investing in their research include Toyota, Mitsubishi, BMW, and Mercedes-Benz. They aim to replace the liquid electrolyte with some kind of nonflammable solid material that works with cobalt-free electrodes. Trailblazing research is also exploring novel solutions for zero-emission cars, including hydrogen fuel cells and superca-pacitors that store energy as static charge. Neither of those would require substantial quantities of cobalt.

To claim that deep-sea cobalt is indispensable for building electric cars, or neodymium for wind turbines, or tellurium for solar panels, is to ignore the fact that technologies can and must be allowed to innovate. It calls to mind the astronomers who build cutting-edge space probes and send them off to explore the edges of the solar system and beyond, knowing only too well that technologies on board, the cameras and sensors, will soon be outdated but that reaching into space and updating the hardware on those space probes is impos-sible.* Manufacturing here on earth has strong momentum, much of it imposed by powerful industrial lobbies defending their way of

---

* Unless somehow faster probes are developed that could catch up with them.

doing things and maintaining profits. But factories are not stuck on a probe hurtling ever farther out of reach through the galaxy. Industries must make room for innovations and swiftly adapt to the needs of people and the available resources, without putting other parts of the human and non-human world at risk.

∽

Technological advances are not going to fix all of humanity's problems and heal over our turbulent relationship with our living planet. Technology, however, could help to wean economies off their fossil fuel dependency and establish a new way of using the earth's resources.

Reserves of the metals needed for electric vehicles, solar panels, and wind turbines are finite, just like the fossil fuels they will replace. Unlike single-use fossil fuels, metals can be recycled and used again and again. These metals form a precious resource that must not be wasted making different versions of old mistakes.

Various studies have attempted the complicated, uncertain task of predicting metal use, and many forecast that in the decades to come, some elements could become scarce, expensive, and difficult to mine on land. Those projections vary, depending on a suite of assumptions, and they don't list the same so-called critical metals. Most do at least agree on one point: the need to reclaim and recycle.

If manufacturers keep reusing the same key metals, there should be no need to deplete land-based reserves and no justification for mining the deep sea. However, recycling will not be a straightforward matter.

Currently, the main industrial way of extracting metals from the rechargeable batteries in portable devices, including old phones and laptops, is to toss them into a furnace and melt them down into a mixed alloy. Individual metals can then be extracted from the mix by reacting them with chemicals such as sulfuric acid. It's an expensive and toxic process.

A more sophisticated approach, albeit far away, would involve an automated process for pulling apart devices into components for separate recycling. In 2018, in a step toward such automation, tech giant Apple proudly unveiled a robotic disassembly line, which, in a matter of seconds and via dozens of manipulations, can break down an iPhone into its major parts. However, it doesn't know what to do with anything except a recent iPhone model.

Recycling electric car batteries is going to be a much more complicated and dangerous process; even opening up the casing can deliver a lethal shock. They will need very careful, expert processing, offering one option for job creation as part of a new, green economy. A wide variety of battery cell packs and chemistries inside car batteries already exists, and each design will need its own method of disassembly. So, while many start-ups and research teams are seeking ways to make new types of rechargeable batteries, others have begun to think about how to unmake them, including unconventional ideas involving bacteria that can selectively chew away at metal oxides from a battery's cathode and turn them into nanoparticles of pure metal.

As the automotive industry scales up production of electric vehicles, more of the first-generation electric cars will reach the end of their lives, their batteries will be recycled, and demand for new materials should begin to drop. This idea has been adopted by Deep-Green Metals, which claims it will mine just enough metals from the seabed to build all the cars, wind turbines, and everything else the world needs—and then stop.

This might appear to be an admirable sentiment, but who will decide when enough is enough? And when DeepGreen's mines are in full swing, money is being made, and shareholders are demanding profits, can production realistically be called to a halt?* Even if DeepGreen did decide to stop mining, it is absurd to imagine that

---

* CEO Barron demonstrated just how obligated his company is to the demands of investors when, at the height of the Covid-19 pandemic, he declared DeepGreen's mines would commence operation by 2023, if necessary by invoking a loophole in the ISA's legislation allowing mining to go ahead two years after an exploration permit is granted, even without the release of the Mining Code. In 2021, Nauru's president went ahead and triggered this "two-year rule."

any other mining company would follow suit and likewise opt to halt production. In the meantime, DeepGreen would have helped to stimulate a new industry, one which other mining corporations would surely carry on. In time, global economies and technologies could easily come to depend on abundant and cheap supplies of deep-sea ores. It risks triggering a global addiction to virgin metals that would be very hard to give up, and which could be avoided in the first place.

∽

Plans for mining hydrothermal vents come with no grand promises of halting the climate crisis or helping "green" economies. The metals they contain are mainly precious elements, like zinc and gold, which nobody is forecasting will be important in the global effort to give up fossil fuels. And it's disingenuous to claim that mining vents would replace brutal, polluting mines on land; both types of mining would continue. That leaves financial gain as the only real benefit to be had from vent mining, but the likelihood of turning a substantial profit from the practice could be a long shot.

Over the past decade, there have been times when it seemed likely the world's first deep-sea mines would open in Papua New Guinea, targeting hydrothermal vents at a site in the Bismarck Sea known as Solwara 1. In 2011, Canadian company Nautilus Minerals was granted the first ever permit to prospect the deep seabed within a country's territorial waters. In 2018, mining seemed imminent when a trio of enormous mining machines arrived in Papua New Guinea from a factory in the United Kingdom and were tested in shallow water, flashing their jaws of swirling teeth and enormous spiked rollers, giving a chilling impression of what the reality of vent mining would entail. By then local support in Papua New Guinea for the project was already dwindling, amid growing fears over widespread environmental impacts in a country that depends on its healthy seas for food and livelihoods. Then, in early 2019, escalating costs and financial troubles brought Nautilus's plans to a halt, and the company declared bankruptcy, leaving the vents intact and the Papua New Guinean government wondering what its 15 percent stake in the company had got it, besides US$125 million in debt, a sum equivalent to a third of the country's health-care budget.

Despite Nautilus Minerals' failure to usher in a new era of deep-sea mining, and its inability to demonstrate that vent mining can turn a profit, the rest of the world hasn't given up on the idea. Other countries have sold exploration permits for vents within their waters; test mines have already been carried out on hydrothermal vents as well as seamounts in Japanese waters. And several countries, including France, South Korea, Russia, and China, are prospecting vents in the high seas. It's possible that vent mining may never be profitable, because the sites are too deep, too remote, and too technically challenging to exploit. Nevertheless, vent mining could conceivably go ahead anyway, if a government or corporation with enough power, money, and egotism decides it simply wants to be able to claim it did it first.

A Sanctuary in the Deep

The deep is the final frontier, the last, vast place left on Earth to open up and exploit. Doing so would be to repeat the centuries-old story of resource extraction. Whether it's gold mines or oil wells, the near extinction of bison on the Great Plains of North America, or deep-sea trawlers destroying ancient ecosystems on seamounts, the story is essentially the same: natural resources become scarce; new frontiers are found and exploited until they too are depleted; as one frontier closes the next opens until there is nowhere else to go. The frontier story has always been one of destruction and loss, and increasingly it's becoming a desperate tale of the race to grab what's left. It is naive to assume that the process would play out any differently in the deep.

Everything about the deep points toward it being an impossible place for sustainable exploitation to happen. Mining activities are challenging enough to control and manage on land, so how will this be done any better in the remote, inaccessible deep? Fisheries in the deep already contend with those same problems of control and management. In theory, it is possible to fish sustainably in shallow seas, but in practice it rarely happens, for mostly political and economic reasons. How will that dismal track record be miraculously changed for fisheries in deeper waters? Not only is enforcement far more problematic, but deep ecosystems operate in fundamentally different ways than the shallow seas: deepwater fish live for hundreds of years and have relatively low reproductive rates; vital habitat is created by corals and sponges that live for millennia. The slow, hungry world of the deep is so desperately unsuited to exploitation, any semblance of sustainability will quickly tip into depletion.

Time and again, opportunities have been missed to protect the planet and its natural resources and to find truly sustainable ways of supporting the human population. The deep offers an unrivaled opportunity to do things differently and write a bold, new story into the pages of human history. There are no compelling reasons for exploiting the deep, just industry and politics vying to push into that last frontier. Instead, there are strong, logical motivations to declare the entire realm off limits—no mining, no fishing, no drilling for oil and gas, from the top of the twilight zone to the deepest trenches, no extraction of any kind.

That's not to say that no one should go to the deep. With exploitation brought to a halt, scientists would be free to continue finding out more about what lives in the deep and discovering in ever more detail how this whole intricate living system works. That includes the continued search for bioactive molecules and the inspiration for new medicines. If humans are to use the deep in any way, then let it be this way; not fishing, drilling, or mining, but copying molecular ideas that stand a genuine chance of reducing human suffering and saving lives, without directly threatening the health of the planet in the process. This is a zero-sum game. We can't have both. Extractive industries will erode those biodiverse ecosystems and all the medic-inal riches they contain.

How, then, can preservation of the deep be brought into effect? The closest precedent for such ambitious preservation is the Antarctic Treaty, an international agreement that declares the entire frozen southern continent as a natural reserve, devoted to peace and science. Just like the deep, Antarctica has no native human population, and many countries are eager to secure access to its resources, including potential reserves of oil, gas, and minerals. And yet, amid various Cold War conflicts, an original group of twelve countries was able to agree to set aside territorial claims and ratify the treaty, which prohibits all military activities and mining—at least for now. Cracks in the agreement have since started showing, as dozens more states have signed up, and many have their eyes on resources that could become available in the future. In 2048, it's expected the treaty will come up for review, which could bring an end to the anti-mining policy. In the waters surrounding Antarctica, fishing is allowed, including an increasing volume of krill fishing, which has been shown to put penguin populations at risk of going hungry. Nevertheless, Antarctica remains the most pristine continent surrounded by the least exploited ocean, and—just like the deep sea—is uniquely sensitive and plays a critical role in the global climate. To weaken its protection would be a grim pronouncement for the future of the planet.

The deep needs decisive, unconditional protection, and one way to begin is within the countries already involved in deep-sea fishing and in buying and prospecting the abyss. If you live in one of those countries, you can put pressure on your government to divest from those extractive industries.* If you are a citizen of one of the 168 members of the International Seabed Authority, including the European Union, then you can call on your government to fully implement the environmental protections for the deep seabed required under the Law of the Sea.† You can support NGOs that are campaigning for stringent protection in the deep and to bring seabed mining and deep-sea trawling to an end. Consumers of seafood can pay attention to what's on the label, learn where species live and how they are caught, and refuse to eat any animals, and

---

* At the time of publication, countries involved in deep-sea extractive industries are: Australia, Belgium, Brazil, Bulgaria, China, Cook Islands, Cuba, Czech Republic, Denmark, Estonia, Faroe Islands, France, Germany, Iceland, India, Jamaica, Japan, Kiribati, Latvia, Lithuania, Nauru, New Zealand, Norway, Poland, Portugal, Singapore, Slovakia, Solomon Islands, South Korea, Spain, Tonga, United Kingdom, and the United States.

† ISA member states: https://www.isa.org.jm/member-states.

their by-products, that come from the deep. And you can take any opportunity to know about the deep and its hidden living wonders, care about them, talk about them, help make them as beloved and cherished as more familiar animals and wild places on the planet.

Preserving the deep takes place not just within the deep itself. Plentiful food can be harvested sustainably from shallow seas by targeting species that swiftly reproduce and replenish, by adopting fishing techniques that don't wreck ecosystems, by halting bycatch of unwanted species, by eliminating harmful subsidies to fishing industries, and by farming low-impact species of shellfish and seaweed that come with the added bonus of capturing carbon from the atmosphere. Achieve truly sustainable fishing and seafood farming in the surface, sunlit zone and there would be no need to even consider whether the deep can feed the world, because the shallows would already be doing so, supported by intact food web links weaving through the deep and by the nutrients welling up from healthy waters thousands of feet below.

Pollutants sinking into the deep, from carbon to PCBs, come from human activities on land and in surface seas, that much is glaringly obvious. Sources of plastic and other forms of chemical pollution need to be identified, and their escape to the environment minimized and wherever possible stopped altogether. Emissions of carbon dioxide and other greenhouse gases must be drastically cut. What's keeping us from achieving the goal of a low-carbon global economy is not a limited supply of metals to make wind turbines, solar panels, and electric cars—it's the political will to make the transition happen. Urgent action requires large-scale governmental spending: to invest in renewable technologies, ones that don't rely on seabed metals; to move innovative zero-emission vehicles from laboratories to highways; to develop circular economies that reuse and recycle materials; to support innovations that will improve efficiencies in the resources we already have access to, instead of opening up new frontiers. The 2020s is the decade when all of this must happen—otherwise humanity will surrender itself to the worst possible version of the climate crisis.

Any of us can decide to become an active part of that transition toward a new way of doing things and a future that doesn't necessitate the exploitation of the deep and lead to the hastening collapse of ecosystems and climate. Demand better of your elected officials. Protest, if you wish. Show what's possible, in any way you can. Say no to single-use plastics—single-use anything—and be part of reshaping a society that has the aspiration and wherewithal to mend, fix, and make things last. You can choose to fly less, drive a smaller car, or no car at all, and step off the endless treadmill of mass consumerism. And if you can't find the better, ethical options you want, then ask why and urge corporations to provide them.

It becomes more than just a matter of protecting the deep, which is the amazing thing about this: the same kinds of initiatives that protect the parts of the planet we see and live among, directly protect the hidden deep too, by removing any need to exploit it.

Epilogue

I arrive at the top floor of the hotel and step into a large reception room, filled with people and murmurous chat. Floor-to-ceiling windows reveal a panoramic view across the coastal California city of Monterey. Curving to the right is the beach I ran along that morning, where I stepped between the sand crabs, emerging like giant fleas and being pecked at by seabirds. Left is the harbor, where the sea otters romped at dusk, and beyond that Cannery Row, the strip of defunct sardine-packing factories renamed in honor of John Steinbeck's 1945 novel of the same name. In 1940, Steinbeck and Ed Ricketts, the real-life biologist who inspired the book's character Doc, set out together on a 4,000-mile voyage on the sardine boat *Western Flyer* to study marine life in the Sea of Cortez (now generally known as the Gulf of California). Steinbeck wrote a book chronicling their explorations and pondering the connections between humans and oceans. "There is some quality in man," he wrote, "which makes him people the ocean with monsters and one wonders whether they are there or not." Back in Monterey, he told the story of a reporter rushing off to take pictures of a sea serpent that locals said had washed up on a nearby beach, only to find a note pinned to the evil-smelling monster reading:

Don't worry about it, it's a basking shark.

The truthful note came as a blow to the people of Monterey. "They so wanted it to be a sea-serpent," Steinbeck wrote. "When sometimes a true sea-serpent, complete and undecayed, is found or caught, a shout of triumph will go through the world. 'There, you see,' men will say, 'I knew they were there all the time. I just had a feeling they were there.'"

Overlooking the gleaming blue surface of Monterey Bay, stretching to the horizon, I'm surrounded by people who have discovered and studied deep-dwelling animals far more extraordinary than any sea serpent Steinbeck could have imagined. Every two years, several hundred biologists from around the world congregate for a week-long schedule of talks and conference papers to share the latest findings from their studies of the deep. Many of them have found living marvels right here in Monterey Bay, where the continental shelf drops away and the canyon carves into the abyss just a short boat ride offshore from Ed Ricketts's Pacific Biological Laboratories, which are still there on Cannery Row. I can't help but wonder what Ricketts and Steinbeck would have made of it all.

Here at the conference reception are the people who almost twenty years ago bumped into a dead whale lying at the bottom of Monterey Bay, cloaked in a carpet of red worms that were eating its bones. Here are the scientists who watched a vampire squid in the deep packing snowballs to eat, others who spotted an octopus cradling a half-eaten scyphozoan in her arms. There's the team who discovered swimming worms that hurl glowing green bombs and then flee into the ever-night of the midnight zone, and here's the biologist who first contemplated the arrhythmic jiving of hairy-armed crabs, and there the team that found yet more Yeti crabs in places no one was expecting.

In the days ahead, the stories most recently brought back from the deep are passed on; scientists announce the species found, the lives unpicked and understood in new ways, the links traced between hidden parts of ecosystems.

New views of the deep are revealed. A hydrothermal vent recently discovered in the Indian Ocean is displayed as an intricate, three-dimensional computerized model, made from thousands of photographs stitched together. With the press of a button, one can fly around this virtual vent, spinning the chimney or zooming in close to see each individual animal that lives there, each crab, anemone, mussel, and snail. This meticulous map is not simply a record of what the vent looked like at that instant; it also shows how species colonized this extreme ecosystem, pinpointing precisely where they live and how they all get along.

Answers to great mysteries are proposed. For instance, how do packs of human-size Humboldt squid chase after lanternfish in the twilight zone without squabbling over the same prey or bumping into each other? Scientists have watched and analyzed footage of squid filmed in the deep as they repeatedly display patterns that could form a kind of language with at least a dozen phrases: a dark lateral stripe, pale eyes and dark body, dark stripy arms, pale tentacles, and so on. The squid can also make their skin glow, which could provide backlighting to illuminate their messaging in the dark. A cephalopod Rosetta stone has yet to be found to translate what each squid pattern means. "Hey, that's my fish!" seems likely.

So many minutiae are uncovered: the brains of tiny amphipods and the fiber-optic cables that connect thirty-two retinas in each crystalline eye, helping them see through the shadowy dark; the way a gossamer worm maneuvers its bristly legs to wriggle elegantly in tight pirouettes through the water; the life story of one particular species of snail that begins on a hydrothermal vent able to chew and eat, then after a while abandons its stomach, grows a huge pouch to stash microbes, and switches to a chemosynthetic diet (the process is called cryptometamorphosis, because from the outside that transformation is hidden); the glowing colors that ripple along a sea cucumber if you pick one up from the abyss and gently wave it around.

Not so very long ago, the deep sea was a tremendous void containing only myths, legends, and endless unknowns. Today we know a great deal, and tomorrow we'll know more. Whenever and wherever someone explores, the window into the living deep opens a little wider and more details come into view. And yet our accumulated knowledge still shrinks in comparison to what remains to be discovered and learned from this enormous space. And perhaps John Steinbeck would have preferred it that way. "An ocean without its unnamed monsters would be like a completely dreamless sleep," he wrote in his book *The Log of the Sea of Cortez*.

The deep sea will never run out of things for us to dream about. Places will remain unseen and unvisited, fleeting moments will be missed, and nimble creatures, whose existence nobody can guess, will keep slipping out of sight. We need to do all we can to keep it that way.

Acknowledgments

Deep-sea biologists form an inspiring and close-knit community of scientists, who are also explorers and the principal advocates for this distant, vital realm. Among them my particular thanks go to Craig McClain, Clif Nunnally, Shana Goffredi, Greg Rouse, Bob Vrijenhoek, Anela Choy, Alice Alldredge, Karen Osborn, Steven Haddock, Julia Sigwart, Andrew Thurber, Nicolai Roterman, Mackenzie Gerringer, Marcel Jaspars, Kerry Howell, Mat Upton, Louise Allcock, Maria Baker, Malcolm Clark, Kevin Zelnio, Andrew Thaler, Daniel Jones, Erik Simon-Lledó, Frédéric Le Manach, Alan Jamieson, Thomas Linley, Nils Piechaud, Adrian Glover, Diva Amon, Maggie Georgieva, and Michelle Taylor. Thank you also to the captain and crew of the research vessel *Pelican* and the staff of LUMCON, who looked after me so well during my visit to Cocodrie as part of LUMCON's short-term visitor program, especially Virginia Schutte, Amanda Rodriguez, and Tiffany LeBoeuf. My greetings and gratitude for being such good company afloat in the Gulf of Mexico to Emily Young, River Dixon, John Whiteman, Granger Hanks, Mac Winter, Catalina Rubiano, and Sarah Foster. For discussions about the future of the deep sea, my thanks to Anna Heath and Jim Pettiward at Synchronicity Earth and Matthew Gianni of the Deep Sea Conservation Coalition.

My career as an author was first sparked and nurtured by my agent of many years, Emma Sweeney, and this book, too, began with her boundless support, enthusiasm, and creativity, and I was very sad to see her retire while I was writing *The Brilliant Abyss*. However, I'm thrilled her place is now taken by Margaret Sutherland Brown, who has so fabulously cheered this book past the finishing line. My tremendous thanks to George Gibson at Grove Atlantic, who took the chance to leap into the deep with me and bring this book to life, and also Anna MacDiarmid, Angelique Neumann and Jim Martin at Bloomsbury. And my continued thanks and gratitude to Aaron John Gregory, who has created yet more fabulous artwork to accompany my words.

Much of this book was written by the sea in a little stone house called Meriel, which maybe someday I'll write about. To my family and friends, thank you, always. You have seen me through writing enough books that I now have to use my fingers to count and remind myself how many there are. This time around, my heartfelt thanks and appreciation go especially to Ayna Bogdanova and Dorian Gangloff, for all your companionship and support, for the shared waves and snacks delivered to my doorstep when I needed them most. Thanks to Liam Drew for helping me see when my words can be better. Kate, you are my oceanographic ninja and so much more. And my love to Ivan, and thanks for sharing a life that's wrapped up in books.

Notes

HERE IS THE DEEP

4   **If the moon's surface.** The area of the seabed lying beneath waters greater than 660 feet deep is approximately 139 million square miles; the surface area of the moon is approximately 14.6 million square miles.

5   **30 percent more mud.** Eivind O. Straume, Carmen Gaina, Sergei Medvedev, Katharina Hochmuth, Karsten Gohl, Joanne M. Whittaker, Rader Abdul Fattah, Hans Doornenbal, and John R. Hopper, "GlobSed: Updated Total Sediment Thickness in the World's Oceans," *Geochemistry, Geophysics, Geosystems* 20, no. 4 (April 2019):1756–72, doi:10.1029/2018GC008115.

6   **this is the hadal zone.** As well as twenty-seven hadal trenches, there are thirteen non-seismic troughs within abyssal plains and seven trench faults formed by the fracturing of mid-ocean ridge spreading centers perpendicular to the ridge axis. Heather A. Stewart and Alan J. Jamieson, "Habitat Heterogeneity of Hadal Trenches: Considerations and Implications for Future Studies," *Progress in Oceanography* 161 (2018):47–65, doi:10.1016/j.pocean.2018.01.007.

7   **a massive earthquake.** "M9 Quake and 30-Meter Tsunami Could Hit Northern Japan, Panel Says," *Japan Times*, April 21, 2020, https://www.japantimes.co.jp/news/2020/04/21/national/m9-quake-30-meter-tsunami-hit-northern-japan-government-panel/.

8   **150,000 years to fill up the entire deep.** The deep sea contains approximately 240 million cubic miles of water. The River Amazon discharges 7,380,765 cubic feet per second.

8   **half of Earth's water supply.** Ziliang Jin and Maitrayee Bose, "New Clues to Ancient Water on Itokawa," *Science Advances* 5, no. 5 (2019):eaav8106, doi:10.1126/sciadv.aav8106.

8   **primordial water.** Jun Wu, Steven J. Desch, Laura Schaefer, Linda T. Elkins, Tanton Kaveh Pahlevan, and Peter R. Buseck, 2019. "Origin of Earth's Water: Chondritic Inheritance Plus Nebular Ingassing and Storage

of Hydrogen in the Core," *JGR Planets* 123, no. 10 (2019):2691–2712, doi:10.1029/2018JE005698.

9   **beginning to form the oceans.** Bruce Dorminey, "Earth Oceans Were Homegrown," *Science*, November 29, 2010, https://www.sciencemag.org/news/2010/11/earth-oceans-were-homegrown.

9   **microcontinents peeping up.** Benjamin W. Johnson and Boswell A. Wing, "Limited Archaean Continental Emergence Reflected in an Early Archaean 18 O-Enriched Ocean," *Nature Geoscience* 13 (2020):243–48, doi:10.1038/s41561-020-0538-9.

10   **95 percent of the earth's biosphere.** Andrew R. Thurber, Andrew K. Sweetman, Bhavani E. Narayanaswamy, Daniel. O. B. Jones, Jeroen Ingels, and Roberta L. Hansman, "Ecosystem Function and Services Provided by the Deep Sea," *Biogeosciences* 11 (2014):3941–63, doi:10.5194/bg-11-3941-2014.

10   **drop a glass marble.** Calculations of the speed of the falling marble from Dorian Gangloff, in conversation with the author, January 12, 2020.

12   **half of them new to science.** J. Frederick Grassle and Nancy J. Maciolek, "Deep-Sea Species Richness: Regional and Local Diversity Estimates from Quantitative Bottom Samples," *American Naturalist* 139, no. 2 (1992):313–41.

12   **three-year survey.** Brian R. C. Kennedy, Kasey Cantwell, Mashkoor Malik, Christopher Kelley, Jeremy Potter, Kelley Elliott, Elizabeth Lobecker, Lindsay McKenna Gray, Derek Sowers, Michael P. White, Scott C. France, Steven Auscavitch, Christopher Mah, Virginia Moriwake, Sarah R. D. Bingo, Meagan Putts, and Randi D. Rotjan, "The Unknown and the Unexplored: Insights into the Pacific Deep-Sea Following NOAA CAP-STONE Expeditions," *Frontiers in Marine Science* 6 (2019):480, doi:10.3389/fmars.2019.00480.

13   **central inventory of deep-sea life.** Adrian G. Glover, Nicholas Higgs, and Tammy Horton, World Register of Deep-Sea Species (WoRDSS), 2020, accessed October 21, 2020, http://www.marinespecies.org/deepsea, doi:10.14284/352.

17   **living worms and a large basket star.** It was originally reported from the HMS *Isabella* expedition that the worms and basket star had been caught at 800 fathoms (4,800 feet), an overestimation by 200 fathoms that was only recognized 150 years later.

18   **Wallich's discovery.** Thomas R. Anderson and Tony Rice, "Deserts on the Sea Floor: Edward Forbes and His Azoic Hypothesis for a Life-less Deep Ocean," *Endeavour* 30, no. 4 (2006):131–37, doi:10.1016/j.endeavour.2006.10.003.

19   **marine snow.** Noboru Susuki and Kenji Kato, "Studies on Suspended Materials Marine Snow in the Sea. Part I. Sources of Marine Snow," *Bulletin of the Faculty of Fisheries Science Hokkaido University* 4, no. 2 (1953):132–37.

20   **The vampire squid.** Hendrik J. T. Hoving and Bruce H. Robison, "Vampire Squid: Detritivores in the Oxygen Minimum Zone," *Proceedings of the Royal Society B* 279, no. 1747 (2012):4559–67, doi:10.1098/rspb.2012.1357; Alexey V. Golikov, Filipe R. Ceia, Rushan M. Sabirov, Jonathan D. Ablett,

Ian G. Gleadall, Gudmundur Gudmundsson, Hendrik J. Hoving, Heather Judkins, Jónbjörn Pálsson, Amanda L. Reid, Rigoberto Rosas-Luis, Elizabeth K. Shea, Richard Schwarz, and José C. Xavier, "The First Global Deep-Sea Stable Isotope Assessment Reveals the Unique Trophic Ecology of Vampire Squid *Vampyroteuthis infernalis* (Cephalopoda)," *Scientific Reports* 9 (2019):19099, doi:10.1038/s41598-019-55719-1.

23   **Victor Vescovo.** The Five Deeps Expedition, accessed September 7, 2020, https://fivedeeps.com/.

THE WHALE AND THE WORM

24   **thirty-six logs.** Craig McClain and James Barry, "Beta-Diversity on Deep-Sea Wood Falls Reflects Gradients in Energy Availability," *Biology Letters* 10 (2015):20140129, doi:10.1098/rsbl.2014.0129.

27   **sperm whales . . . make regular dives.** Hal Whitehead, *Sperm Whale Societies: Social Evolution in the Ocean* (Chicago, IL: University of Chicago Press, 2003).

27   **ropes 225 fathoms.** Helena M. Rozwadowski, *Fathoming the Ocean: The Discovery and Exploration of the Deep Sea* (Cambridge, MA: Harvard University Press, 2008), 44.

27   **Captain William Scoresby.** George C. Wallich, *The North-Atlantic Seabed: Comprising a Diary of the Voyage on Board H.M.S. Bulldog, in 1860* (London: Jan Van Voorst, 1862), 110.

28   **arteries and veins so big.** George J. Race, W. L. Jack Edwards, E. R. Halden, Hugh E. Wilson, and Francis J. Luibel, "A Large Whale Heart," *Circulation* 19 (1959):928–32.

28   **evolved a form of myoglobin.** Scott Mirceta, Anthony V. Signore, Jennifer M. Burns, Andrew R. Cossins, Kevin L. Campbell, and Michael Berenbrink, "Evolution of Mammalian Diving Capacity Traced by Myoglobin Net Surface Charge," *Science* 340 (2013):1303–11, doi:10.1126/science.1234192.

29   **sperm whales subdue.** Malcom R. Clarke, "Cephalopoda in the Diet of Sperm Whales of the Southern Hemisphere and Their Bearing on Sperm Whale Biology," *Discovery Reports* 37 (1980), 1–324.

29   **Various theories.** Stephanie L. Watwood, Patrick J. O. Miller, Mark Johnson, Peter T. Madsen, and Peter L. Tyack, "Deep-Diving Foraging Behaviour of Sperm Whales (*Physeter macrocephalus*)," *Journal of Animal Ecology* 75 (2006):814–25.

30   **quickens its clicks.** Patrick J. O. Miller, Mark P. Johnson, and Peter L. Tyack, "Sperm Whale Behaviour Indicates the Use of Echolocation Click Buzzes 'Creaks' in Prey Capture," *Proceedings of the Royal Society B* 271 (2004):2239–47, doi:10.1098/rspb.2004.2863.

31   **It twists and turns.** Andrea Fais, Mark Johnson, Maria Wilson, Natacha Aguilar Soto, and Peter T. Madsen, "Sperm Whale Predator-Prey Interactions Involve Chasing and Buzzing, but No Acoustic Stunning," *Scientific Reports* 6 (2016):28562, doi:10.1038/srep28562.

31   **only eight or nine minutes.** Watwood et al., "Deep-Diving Foraging Behaviour."

32   **761,523 were recorded.** R. C. Rocha, Phillip J. Clapham, and Yulia V. Ivashchenko, "Emptying the Oceans: A Summary of Industrial Whaling Catches in the 20th Century," *Marine Fisheries Review* 76, no. 4 (2015):37–48, doi:10.7755/MFR.76.4.3.

33   **estimates of sperm whale numbers.** Hal Whitehead, "Estimates of the Current Global Population Size and Historical Trajectory for Sperm Whales," *Marine Ecology Progress Series* 242 (2002):295–304, doi:10.3354/meps242295.

34   **ruptured penile urethra.** Keith P. Bland and Andrew C. Kitchener, "The Anatomy of the Penis of a Sperm Whale (*Physeter catodon* L., 1758)," *Mammal Review* 3, no. 304 (2008):239–44, doi:10.1111/j.1365-2907.2001.00087.x.

34   **male pilot whale.** "Whale That Died off Thailand Had Eaten 80 Plastic Bags," *BBC News*, June 2, 2018, https://www.bbc.co.uk/news/world-asia-44344468.

35   **phenomena above and beneath the waves were linked.** Klaus H. Vanselow, Sven Jacobsen, Chris Hall, and Stefan Garthe, "Solar Storms May Trigger Sperm Whale Strandings: Explanation Approaches for Multiple Strandings in the North Sea in 2016," *International Journal of Astrobiology* 17, no. 4 (2018):336–44, doi:10.1017/S147355041700026X.

35   **many experts agree.** Matt McGrath, "Northern Lights Linked to North Sea Whale Strandings," *BBC News*, September 5, 2017, https://www.bbc.co.uk/news/science-environment-41110082.

35   **stronger solar activity.** Klaus H. Vanselow and Klaus Ricklefs, "Are Solar Activity and Sperm Whale *Physeter macrocephalus* Strandings around the North Sea Related?," *Journal of Sea Research* 53 (2005):319–27, doi:10.1016/j.seares.2004.07.006.

36   **Nobody will ever.** Bob Vrijenhoek, in conversation with the author, January 22, 2019.

36   **Among us.** Shana Goffredi, in conversation with the author, February 9, 2019.

37   **new genus of polychaete worms.** Greg W. Rouse, Shana Goffredi, and Robert C. Vrijenhoek, "*Osedax*: Bone-Eating Marine Worms with Dwarf Males," *Science* 305, no. 5684 (2004):668–71, doi:10.1126/science.1098650.

37   **I understand it's catchy.** Greg Rouse, in conversation with the author, March 6, 2019.

38   **known as "whale falls."** Craig R. Smith, Adrian G. Glover, Tina Treude, Nicholas D. Higgs, and Diva J. Amon, "Whale-Fall Ecosystems: Recent Insights into Ecology, Paleoecology, and Evolution," *Annual Review of Marine Science* 7 (2015):571–96, doi:10.1146/annurev-marine-010213-135144.

38   **tremendous consignments of food.** Craig R. Smith and Amy R. Baco, "Ecology of Whale Falls on the Deep-Sea Floor," *Oceanography and Marine Biology* 41 (2003):311–54.

38   **"implanted" whale fall.** Bob Vrijenhoek, in conversation with the author, January 22, 2019.

39   **dozens of species of *Osedax*.** Greg W. Rouse, Shana Goffredi, Shannon B. Johnson, and Robert C. Vrijenhoek, "An Inordinate Fondness for *Osedax* (Siboglinidae: Annelida): Fourteen New Species of Bone Worms from California," *Zootaxa* 4377, no. 4 (2018):451–89, doi:10.11646/zootaxa.4377.4.1; in addition, there are many more *Osedax* species that have been discovered but not yet officially named: Greg Rouse, in conversation with the author, March 6, 2019.

40   **worms secrete acid.** Martin Tresguerres, Sigrid Katz, and Greg W. Rouse, "How to Get into Bones: Proton Pump and Carbonic Anhydrase in *Osedax* Boneworms," *Proceedings of the Royal Society B* 280 (2013):20130625, doi:10.1098/rspb.2013.0625.

41   **first examined *Osedax*.** Shana Goffredi, in conversation with the author, February 9, 2019.

41   **broadly referred to as fish.** For more discussion of the origins and definition of the term *fish*, see Helen Scales, *The Eye of the Shoal* (London: Bloomsbury, 2018).

42   **increasingly adapted to an aquatic life.** Riley Black, "How Did Whales Evolve?" *Smithsonian Magazine*, December 1, 2010, https://www.smithsonianmag.com/science-nature/how-did-whales-evolve-73276956/.

42   ***Osedax* may have evolved.** Robert C. Vrijenhoek, Shannon B. Johnson, and Greg W. Rouse, "A Remarkable Diversity of Bone-eating Worms (*Osedax*; Siboglinidae; Annelida), *BMC Biology* 7 (2009):74, doi:10.1186/1741-7007-7-74.

42   **Calibrating a molecular clock.** Bob Vrijenhoek, in conversation with the author, January 22, 2019.

43   **plesiosaur humerus bone.** Silvia Danise and Nicholas D. Higgs, "Bone-eating *Osedax* Worms Lived on Mesozoic Marine Reptile Deadfalls," *Biology Letters* 11 (2015):20150072, doi:10.1098/rsbl.2015.0072.

45   **second alligator.** Clifton Nunnally, in conversation with the author, June 30, 2019.

46   **Greenland shark.** These sharks have shown up rather unexpectedly in the Gulf of Mexico, a long way from their regular range in the Arctic. Jeffrey Marlow, "What Is a Greenland Shark Doing in the Gulf of Mexico?," *Wired*, August 27, 2013, https://www.wired.com/2013/08/what-is-a-greenland-shark-doing-in-the-gulf-of-mexico/.

46   **tackle a whole alligator.** Craig Robert McClain, Clifton Nunnally, River Dixon, Greg W. Rouse, and Mark Benfield, "Alligators in the Abyss: The First Experimental Reptilian Food Fall in the Deep Ocean," *PLoS One* 14, no. 12 (2019):e0225345, doi:10.1371/journal.pone.0225345.

46   **giant squid.** Clifton Nunnally, in conversation with the author, June 30, 2019.

CAUGHT IN A JELLY WEB

49 **"nothing exerted."** Ernst Haeckel, *Monographie der Medusen* (Jena: G. Fischer, 1879-1881), 15, translated in Olaf Breidbach, Irenaeus Eibl-Eibesfeldt, and Richard Hartmann, *Art Forms in Nature: Prints of Ernst Haeckel* (Munich: Prestel, 1998).

53 **harder to catch fragile animals.** Steven H. D. Haddock, "A Golden Age of Gelata: Past and Future Research on Planktonic Ctenophores and Cnidarians," *Hydrobiologia* 530/531 (2004):549–56.

53 **"It is not surprising."** William M. Hamner, "Underwater Observations of Blue-water Plankton: Logistics, Techniques, and Safety Procedures for Divers at Sea," *Limnology and Oceanography* 20 (1975):1045–51.

54 **"When you're floating."** Alice Alldredge, in conversation with the author, April 22, 2019.

54 **creating flurries of marine snow.** Alice L. Alldredge, "Abandoned Larvacean Houses: A Unique Source of Food in the Pelagic Environment," *Science* 177, no. 4052 (1972):885–87, doi:10.1126/science.177.4052.885.

56 **searched through the archive.** C. Anela Choy, Steven H. D. Haddock, and Bruce H. Robison, "Deep Pelagic Food Web Structure as Revealed by in Situ Feeding Observations," *Proceedings of the Royal Society B* 284 (2017):20172116, doi:10.1098/rspb.2017.2116.

56 **"Each line."** Anela Choy, in conversation with the author, April 16, 2019.

58 **"They're supercool."** Karen Osborn, in conversation with the author, May 7, 2019.

59 **almost 10,000 feet down worms.** Karen J. Osborn, Laurence P. Madin, and Greg W. Rouse, "The Remarkable Squidworm Is an Example of Discoveries That Await in Deep-Pelagic Habitats," *Biology Letters* 7, no. 3 (2010), doi:10.1098/rsbl.2010.0923.

60 **pig's-rump worm.** Karen J. Osborn, Greg W. Rouse, Shana K. Goffredi, and Bruce Robison, "Description and Relationships of *Chaetopterus pugaporcinus*, an Unusual Pelagic Polychaete (Annelida, Chaetopteridae)," *Biological Bulletin* 212 (2007):40–54.

59 ***Swima bombiviridis.*** Karen J. Osborn, Steven H. D. Haddock, Fredrik Pleijel, Laurence P. Madin, and Greg W. Rouse, "Deep-Sea, Swimming Worms with Luminescent 'Bombs,'" *Science* 325 (2009):964, doi:10.1126/science.1172488.

60 **76 percent were bioluminescent.** Séverine Martini and Steven H. D. Haddock, "Quantification of Bioluminescence from the Surface to the Deep Sea Demonstrates Its Predominance as an Ecological Trait," *Scientific Reports* 7 (2017):45750, doi:10.1038/srep45750. Bioluminescence also occurs on the deep seabed, although not as commonly as in open water. Martini and Haddock repeated their study for animals on the bottom and found at most 41 percent make light; Séverine Martini, Linda Kuhnz, Jérôme Mallefet, and Steven H. D. Haddock, "Distribution and Quantification of Bioluminescence as an Ecological Trait in the Deep-Sea Benthos," *Scientific Reports* 9 (2019):14654, doi:10.1038/s41598-019-50961-z.

61   **"I call them 'Just So Stories.'"** Steven Haddock, in conversation with the author, May 8, 2020.

62   **he saw an arrow worm.** Ibid. Arrow worms belong to their own phylum, Chaetognatha.

62   **spiny silverfin.** Zuzana Musilova, Fabio Cortesi, Michael Matschiner, Wayne I. L. Davies, Jagdish Suresh Patel, Sara M. Stieb, Fanny de Busse-rolles, Martin Malmstrøm, Ole K. Tørresen, Celeste J. Brown, Jessica K. Mountford, Reinhold Hanel, Deborah L. Stenkamp, Kjetill S. Jakobsen, Karen L. Carleton, Sissel Jentoft, Justin Marshall, and Walter Salzburger, "Vision Using Multiple Distinct Rod Opsins in Deep-Sea Fishes," *Science* 364, no. 6440 (2019):588–92, doi:10.1126/science.aav4632.

63   **collecting samples of black fish skin.** Alexander L. Davis, Kate N. Thomas, Freya E. Goetz, Bruce H. Robison, Sönke Johnsen, and Karen J. Osborn, "Ultra-Black Camouflage in Deep-Sea Fishes," *Current Biology* 30 (2020):1–7, doi:10.1016/j.cub.2020.06.044. Melanin granules in deep-sea fish skin also have the added benefit of forming an antifungal and antibacterial layer, Karen Osborn, in conversation with the author, May 7, 2019.

In a Chemical World

65   ***Kiwa hirsuta.*** Eric MacPherson, William Jones, and Michel Segonzac, "A New Squat Lobster Family of Galatheoidea (Crustacea, Decapoda, Anomura) from the Hydrothermal Vents of the Pacific-Antarctic Ridge," *Zoosystema* 27, no. 4 (2005):709–23.

66   **Isn't the deep ocean?** "Discovering Hydrothermal Vents," Woods Hole Oceanographic Institution, accessed August 21, 2020, https://www.whoi .edu/feature/history-hydrothermal-vents/discovery/1977.html.

66   **650 hydrothermal vent fields.** Andrew D. Thaler and Diva Amon, "262 Voyages beneath the Sea: A Global Assessment of Macro- and Megafaunal Biodiversity and Research Effort at Deep-Sea Hydrothermal Vents," *PeerJ* 7 (2019):e7397, doi:10.7717/peerj.7397.

67   **ocean cycles through hydrothermal vents.** "Discovering Hydrothermal Vents," Woods Hole Oceanographic Institution.

68   **mapped the Endeavour seabed.** David A. Clague, Julie F. Martin, Jennifer B. Paduan, David A. Butterfield, John W. Jamieson, Morgane Le Saout, David W. Caress, Hans Thomas, James F. Holden, and Deborah S. Kelley, "Hydrothermal Chimney Distribution on the Endeavour Segment, Juan de Fuca Ridge," *Geochemistry, Geophysics, Geosystems* 21, no. 6 (2020):e2020GC008917, doi:10.1029/2020GC008917.

69   **Pescadero Basin vents.** Shana K. Goffredi, Shannon Johnson, Verena Tunnicliffe, David Caress, David Clague, Elva Escobar, Lonny Lundsten, Jennifer B. Paduan, Greg Rouse, Diana L. Salcedo, Luis A. Soto, Ronald Spelz-Madero, Robert Zierenberg, and Robert Vrijenhoek, "Hydrothermal Vent Fields Discovered in the Southern Gulf of California Clarify Role of Habitat in Augmenting Regional Diversity," *Proceedings of the Royal Society B* 284 (2017):20170817, doi:10.1098/rspb.2017.0817.

70   **eleven thousand shrimp.** Densities of three thousand shrimp per liter have been measured on the Mid-Atlantic Ridge. Eva Ramirez Llodra, Timothy M. Shank, and Christopher R. German, "Biodiversity and Biogeography of Hydrothermal Vent Species," *Oceanography* 20, no. 1 (2007):30–41.

70   **shining worms picking fights.** Avery S. Hatch, Haebin Liew, Stéphane Hourdez, and Greg W. Rouse, "Hungry Scale Worms: Phylogenetics of Peinaleopolynoe (Polynoidae, Annelida), with Four New Species. *ZooKeys* 932 (2020):27–74, doi:10.3897/zookeys.932.48532.

71   **seven hundred species.** Christopher R. German, Eva Ramirez-Llodra, Maria C. Baker, Paul A. Tyler, and the ChEss Scientific Steering Committee, "Deep-Water Chemosynthetic Ecosystem Research during the Census of Marine Life Decade and Beyond: A Proposed Deep-Ocean Road Map," *PLoS One* 6, no. 8 (2011):e23259, doi:10.1371/journal.pone.0023259.

72   **great pile of egg cases.** Pelayo Salinas-de-León, Brennan Phillips, David Ebert, Mahmood Shivji, Florencia Cerutti-Pereyra, Cassandra Ruck, Charles R. Fisher, and Leigh Marsh, "Deep-Sea Hydrothermal Vents as Natural Egg-Case Incubators at the Galapagos Rift," *Scientific Reports* 8 (2018):1788, doi:10.1038/s41598-018-20046-4.

73   **packed with sulfur-oxidizing bacteria.** Colleen M. Cavanaugh, Stephen L. Gardiner, Meredith L. Jones, Holger W. Jannasch, and John B. Waterbury, "Prokaryotic Cells in the Hydrothermal Vent Tube Worm *Riftia pachyptila* Jones: Possible Chemoautotrophic Symbionts," *Science* 213, no. 4505 (1981):340–42.

73   **enormous heart.** Chong Chen, Jonathan T. Copley, Katrin Linse, Alex D. Rogers, and Julia D. Sigwart, "The Heart of a Dragon: 3D Anatomical Reconstruction of the 'Scaly-Foot Gastropod' (Mollusca: Gastropoda: Neomphalina) Reveals Its Extraordinary Circulatory System," *Frontiers in Zoology* 12 (2015):13, doi:10.1186/s12983-015-0105-1.

74   **nanoscopic tubes.** Satoshi Okada, Chong Chenb, Tomo-o Watsuji, Manabu Nishizawa, Yohey Suzuki, Yuji Sanoe, Dass Bissessur, Shigeru Deguchi, and Ken Takai, "The Making of Natural Iron Sulfide Nanoparticles in a Hot Vent Snail," *Proceedings of the National Academy of Sciences (US)* 116, no. 41 (2019), doi:10.1073/pnas.1908533116.

75   **coat of stringy bacteria.** Nadine Le Bris and François Gaill, "How Does the Annelid *Alvinella pompejana* Deal with an Extreme Hydrothermal Environment?," *Reviews of Environmental Science and Biotechnology* 6 (2007):197–221, doi:10.1007/s11157-006-9112-1.

75   **produces an antibiotic.** Aurélie Tasiemski, Sascha Jung, Céline Boidin-Wichlacz, Didier Jollivet, Virginie Cuvillier-Hot, Florence Pradillon, Costantino Vetriani, Oliver Hecht, Frank D. Sönnichsen, Christoph Gelhaus, Chien-Wen Hung, Andreas Tholey, Matthias Leippe, Joachim Grötzinger, and Françoise Gaill, "Characterization and Function of the First Antibiotic Isolated from a Vent Organism: The Extremophile Metazoan *Alvinella pompejana*," *PLoS One* 9, no. 4 (2014):e95737, doi:10.1371/journal.pone.0095737.

75 **Temperature probes.** Juliette Ravaux, Gérard Hamel, Magali Zbinden, Aurélie A. Tasiemski, Isabelle Boutet, Nelly Léger, Arnaud Tanguy, Didier Jollivet, and Bruce Shillito, "Thermal Limit for Metazoan Life in Question: In Vivo Heat Tolerance of the Pompeii Worm," *PLoS One* 8, no. 5 (2013):e64074, doi:10.1371/journal.pone.0064074.

76 **known as Strain 121.** Kazem Kashefi and Derek R. Lovley, "Extending the Upper Limit For Life," *Science* 301, no. 5635 (2003): 934, doi:10.1126/science.1086823.

77 **constant flow of larvae.** Sara Teixeira, Ester A. Serrão, and Sophie Arnaud-Haond, "Panmixia in a Fragmented and Unstable Environment: The Hydrothermal Shrimp *Rimicaris exoculata* Disperses Extensively along the Mid-Atlantic Ridge," *PLoS One* 7, no. 6 (2012):e38521, doi:10.1371/journal.pone.0038521.

77 **very little mixing.** Chong Chen, Jonathan T. Copley, Katrin Linse, and Alex D. Rogers, "Low Connectivity between 'Scaly-Foot Gastropod' (Mollusca: Peltospiridae) Populations at Hydrothermal Vents on the Southwest Indian Ridge and the Central Indian Ridge," *Organisms Diversity and Evolution* 15, no. 4 (2015): 663–70, doi:10.1007/s13127-015-0224-8.

78 **covered in tube worms.** Surveys of the Pescadero Basin vents counted between 407 and 2,423 *Oasisia* worms per square meter. Goffredi et al., "Hydrothermal Vent Fields Discovered."

79 **chemical-harnessing microbes.** Nicole Dubilier, Claudia Bergin, and Christian Lott, "Symbiotic Diversity in Marine Animals: The Art of Harnessing Chemosynthesis," *Nature Reviews Microbiology* 6 (2008):725–40, doi:10.1038/nrmicro1992.

79 **growing on sacks of beans.** Paul R. Dando, Alan F. Southward, Eve C. Southward, D. R. Dixon, Alec Crawford, and Moya Crawford, "Shipwrecked Tube Worms," *Nature* 356 (1992):667.

79 **decomposing paper.** David J. Hughes and Moya Crawford, "A New Record of the Vestimentiferan *Lamellibrachia* sp. (Polychaeta: Siboglinidae) from a Deep Shipwreck in the Eastern Mediterranean," *Marine Biodiversity Records* 1 (2008):e21, doi:10.1017/S1755267206001989.

79 **ecosystem powered entirely by chemicals.** Mahlon C. Kennicutt II, James M. Brooks, Robert R. Bidigare, Roger R. Fay, Terry L. Wade, and Thomas J. McDonald, "Vent-Type Taxa in a Hydrocarbon Seep Region on the Louisiana Slope," *Nature* 317 (1985):351–53, doi:10.1038/317351a0.

79 **Since they were first spotted.** Jean-Paul Foucher, Graham K. Westbrook, Antje Boetius, Silvia Ceramico, Stéphanie Dupré, Jean Mascle, Jürgen Mienert, Olaf Pfannkuche, Catherine Pierre, and Daniel Praeg, "Structure and Drivers of Cold Seep Ecosystems," *Oceanography* 22, no. 1 (2009):92–109.

80 ***Kiwa puravida.*** Andrew R. Thurber, William J. Jones, and Kareen Schnabe, "Dancing for Food in the Deep Sea: Bacterial Farming by a New Species of Yeti Crab," *PLoS One* 6, no. 11 (2011):e26243, doi:10.1371/journal.pone.0026243.

80   **More specimens brought up.** Andrew Thurber, in conversation with the author, May 21, 2019.

81   **crab crowds were highly segregated.** Leigh Marsh, Jonathan T. Copley, Paul A. Tyler, and Sven Thatje, "In Hot and Cold Water: Differential Life-History Traits Are Key to Success in Contrasting Thermal Deep-Sea Environments," *Journal of Animal Ecology* 84 (2015):898–913, doi:10.1111/1365-2656.12337.

83   **observed in Pompeii worms.** Florence Pradillon, Bruce Shillito, Craig M. Young, and Françoise Gaill, "Developmental Arrest in Vent Worm Embryos," *Nature* 413 (2018):698–99.

83   **how Hoff crabs got where they are.** Christopher N. Roterman, Won-Kyung Lee, Xinming Liu, Rongcheng Lin, Xinzheng Li, and Yong-Jin Won, "A New Yeti Crab Phylogeny: Vent Origins with Indications of Regional Extinction in the East Pacific," *PLoS One* 13, no. 3 (2018):e0194696, doi:10.1371/journal.pone.0194696.

85   **Roterman thinks is no coincidence.** Christopher Nicolai Roterman, in conversation with the author, May 28, 2019

85   **researchers from Korea.** Sang-Hui Lee, Won-Kyung Lee, and Yong-Jin Won, "A New Species of Yeti Crab, Genus *Kiwa* MacPherson, Jones and Segonzac, 2005 (Decapoda: Anomura: Kiwaidae), from a Hydrothermal Vent on the Australian-Antarctic Ridge," *Journal of Crustacean Biology* 36, no. 2 (2016):238–47, doi:10.1163/1937240X-00002418.

86   **new light on the evolution of Yetis.** Roterman et al., "A New Yeti Crab Phylogeny."

Highs and Lows

88   **transmitting real-time images.** "Massive Aggregations of Octopus Brooding near Shimmering Seeps," Nautilus Live, Ocean Exploration Trust, accessed August 18, 2020, https://nautiluslive.org/video/2018/10/24/massive-aggregations-octopus-brooding-near-shimmering-seeps.

89   **scientists went back and she was gone.** Bruce Robison, Brad Seibel, and Jeffrey Drazen, "Deep-Sea Octopus (*Graneledone boreopacifica*) Conducts the Longest-Known Egg-Brooding Period of Any Animal," *PLoS One* 9, no. 7 (2014):e103437, doi:10.1371/journal.pone.0103437.

89   **found the brooding octopuses still there.** "Return to the Octopus Garden in Monterey Bay National Marine Sanctuary," Nautilus Live, Ocean Exploration Trust, accessed August 18, 2020, https://nautiluslive.org/blog/2019/10/13/return-octopus-garden-monterey-bay-national-marine-sanctuary.

90   **Davidson Seamount.** Malcom R. Clark, David A. Bowden, "Seamount Biodiversity: High Variability Both within and between Seamounts in the Ross Sea Region of Antarctica," *Hydrobiologia* 761 (2015):161–80, doi:10.1007/s10750-015-2327-9.

90   **the line went slack.** Albert E. Theberge, "Mountains in the Sea," *Hydro International*, May 19, 2016, https://www.hydro-international.com/content/article/mountains-in-the-sea.

91   **"To our surprise and delight."** Herbert Laws Webb, "With a Cable Expedition," *Scribner's Magazine*, October 1890.

91   **biggest seamounts.** Peter J. Etnoyer, John Wood, and Thomas C. Shirley, "How Large Is the Seamount Biome?," *Oceanography* 23, no. 1 (2010):206–9.

91   **oceanic hot spots.** "Hot Spots," National Geographic Society Resource Library, accessed April 5, 2019, https://www.nationalgeographic.org/encyclopedia/hot-spots/.

92   **high-end estimate.** Paul Wessel, David T. Sandwell, and Seung-Sep Kim, "The Global Seamount Census," *Oceanography* 23, no. 1 (2010):24–33.

93   **more types of coral live in deep, cold seas.** For all background on deep-sea corals: J. Murray Roberts, Andrew J. Wheeler, Andrew Freiwald, and Stephen D. Cairns, *Cold Water Corals: The Biology and Geology of Deep-Sea Coral Habitats* (Cambridge: Cambridge University Press, 2019).

94   **Common on seamounts.** Deep-sea corals are generally defined as those living below 164 feet, where sunlight becomes dim and photosynthesis difficult to sustain. Stephen Cairns, "Deep-Water Corals: An Overview with Special Reference to Diversity and Distribution of Deep-Water Scleractinian Corals," *Bulletin of Marine Science* 81, no. 3 (2007):311–22. This book considers the corals growing in the twilight zone and deeper, but there are distinct coral-associated ecosystems shallower than this: the mesophotic (between 100 and 490 feet) and the more recently identified rariphotic (400 to 1,000 feet). Carole C. Baldwin, Luke Tornabene, and D. Ross Robertson, "Below the Mesophotic," *Scientific Reports* 8 (2018):4920, doi:10.1038/s41598-018-23067-1.

95   **calls for its renaming as *Desmophyllum pertusa*.** Anna Maria Addamo, Agostina Vertino, Jaroslaw Stolarski, Ricardo García-Jiménez, Marco Taviani, and Annie Machordom, "Merging Scleractinian Genera: The Overwhelming Genetic Similarity Between Solitary *Desmophyllum* and Colonial *Lophelia*," *BMC Evolutionary Biology* 16 (2012):108, doi:10.1186/s12862-016-0654-8; Stephen Cairns, "WoRMS Note Details", accessed October 14, 2020 http://www.marinespecies.org/aphia.php?p=notes&id=307194.

95   **We write *Desmophyllum*.** Nils Piechaud on Twitter (@NPiechaud), October 14, 2020.

95   **them growing off the coast of South Carolina.** Caitlin Adams, "The Significance of Finding a Previously Undetected Coral Reef," NOAA, Ocean Exploration and Research, August 24, 2018, https://oceanexplorer.noaa.gov/explorations/18deepsearch/logs/aug24/aug24.html.

95   **growing continuously . . . for fifty thousand years.** Andrea Schröder-Ritzrau, André Freiwald, and Augusto Mangini, "U/Th-Dating of Deep-Water Corals from the Eastern North Atlantic and the Western Mediterranean Sea," in *Cold-Water Corals and Ecosystems*, ed. André Freiwald and Murray J. Roberts (Heidelberg: Springer, 2005), 157–72.

96   **marine species can also go in the opposite direction.** Alberto Lindner, Stephen D. Cairns, and Clifford W. Cunningham, "From Offshore to Onshore: Multiple Origins of Shallow-Water Corals from Deep-Sea Ancestors," *PLoS One* 3, no. 6 (2008):e2429, doi:10.1371/journal.pone.0002429.

96   **sponges behaving in unexpected ways.** Amanda S. Kahn, Clark W. Pennelly, Paul R. McGill, Sally P. Leys, "Behaviors of Sessile Benthic Animals in the Abyssal Northeast Pacific Ocean," *Deep Sea Research Part II: Topical Studies in Oceanography* 173 (2020):104729, doi:10.1016/j.dsr2.2019.104729.

97   **straight out of a Dr. Seuss book.** Dive to the "Forest of the Weird" took place during the 2017 NOAA Laulima O Ka Moana expedition within the Pacific Remote Islands Marine National Monument. "Dive 11: Forest of the Weird" NOAA, accessed October 21, 2020 https://oceanexplorer.noaa. gov/okeanos/explorations/ex1706/logs/photolog/welcome.html#cbpi=/ okeanos/explorations/ex1706/dailyupdates/media/video/dive11-forest/ forest.html.

97   **Bamboo corals can live.** Alex D. Rogers, Amy Baco, Huw Griffiths, Thomas Hart, and Jason M. Hall-Spencer, "Corals on Seamounts," in *Seamounts: Ecology, Fisheries and Conservation*, ed. Tony Pitcher et al. (Oxford: Blackwell, 2007), 141–69.

97   **Individual sea lilies.** Sarah Samadi, Thomas A. Schlacher, and Bertrand Richer de Forges, "Seamount Benthos," in *Seamounts: Ecology, Fisheries and Conservation*, ed. Tony Pitcher et al. (Oxford: Blackwell, 2007), 119–40.

98   **Hexactinellid sponges.** Ibid.

98   **Even longer-lived.** Ages for both the gold coral (*Gerardia* sp.) and black coral (*Leiopathes* sp.) were obtained from samples collected between 1,310 and 1,640 feet down off Hawaii in 2004. E. Brendan Roark, Thomas Guilderson, Robert B. Dunbara, Stewart J. Fallon, and David A. Mucciarone, "Extreme Longevity in Proteinaceous Deep-Sea Corals," *Proceedings of the National Academy of Sciences (US)* 106, no. 13 (2009):5204–8, doi:10.1073/ pnas.0810875106.

98   **Etched into the skeletons.** Laura F. Robinson, Jess F. Adkins, Norbert Frank, Alexander C. Gagnon, Nancy G. Prouty, E. Brendan Roark, and Tina van de Flierdt, "The Geochemistry of Deep-Sea Coral Skeletons: A Review of Vital Effects and Applications for Palaeoceanography," *Deep-Sea Research II* 99 (2014):184–98, doi:10.1016/j.dsr2.2013.06.005.

99   **corals collected off Nova Scotia.** Owen A. Sherwood, Moritz F. Lehmann, Carsten J. Schubert, David B. Scott, and Matthew D. McCarthy, "Nutrient Regime Shift in the Western North Atlantic Indicated by Compound-Specific δ15N of Deep-Sea Gorgonian Corals," *Proceedings of the National Academy of Sciences (US)* 108, no. 3 (2011):1011–15, doi:10.1073/ pnas.1004904108.

99   **cat sharks lay their egg cases.** Alessandro Cau, Maria Cristina Follesa, Davide Moccia, Andrea Bellodi, Antonello Mulas, Marzia Bo, Simonepietro Canese, Michela Angiolillo, and Rita Cannas, "*Leiopathes glaberrima* Millennial Forest from SW Sardinia as Nursery Ground for the Small Spotted Catshark *Scyliorhinus canicula*," *Aquatic Conservation: Marine and Freshwater Ecosystems* 27 (2016):731–35, doi:10.1002/aqc.2717.

99   **carnival of migrants.** Telmo Morato, Divya Alice Varkey, Carla Damaso, Miguel Machete, Marco Santos, Rui Prieto, Ricardo S. Santos, and Tony J.

Pitcher, "Evidence of a Seamount Effect on Aggregating Visitors," *Marine Ecology Progress Series* 357 (2008):23–32, doi:10.3354/meps07269.

100 **Japanese eels.** Katsumi Tsukamoto. "Spawning Eels near a Seamount," *Nature* 439 (2006):929, doi:10.1038/439929a.

100 **Humpback whales.** Solène Derville, Leigh G. Torres, Alexandre N. Zerbini, Marc Oremus, and Claire Garrigue, "Horizontal and Vertical Movements of Humpback Whales Inform the Use of Critical Pelagic Habitats in the Western South Pacific," *Scientific Reports* 10 (2020):4871, doi:10.1038/s41598-020-61771-z.

101 **brand-new seamount.** Simone Cesca, Jean Letort, Hoby N. T. Razafindrakoto, Sebastian Heimann, Eleonora Rivalta, Marius P. Isken, Mehdi Nikkhoo, Luigi Passarelli, Gesa M. Petersen, Fabrice Cotton, and Torsten Dahm, "Drainage of a Deep Magma Reservoir near Mayotte Inferred from Seismicity and Deformation," *Nature Geoscience* 13 (2020):87–93, doi:10.1038/s41561-019-0505-5.

102 **dampening the quake.** Jacob Geersen, César R. Ranero, Udo Barckhausen, and Christian Reichert, "Subducting Seamounts Control Interplate Coupling and Seismic Rupture in the 2014 Iquique Earthquake Area," *Nature Communications* 6 (2015):8267, doi:10.1038/ncomms9267.

102 **hauled back toward the earth's mantle.** Anthony B. Watts, Anthony A. P. Kopper, and David P. Robinson, "Seamount Subduction and Earthquakes," *Oceanography* 23, no. 1 (2010):166–73.

102 **remains of at least four giant seamounts.** James V. Gardner and Andrew A. Armstrong, "The Mariana Trench: A New View Based on Multibeam Echosounding," American Geophysical Union, fall meeting 2011, abstract no. OS13B-1517, https://abstractsearch.agu.org/meetings/2011/FM/OS13B-1517.html.

103 **says Mackenzie Gerringer.** Mackenzie Gerringer, in conversation with the author, February 19, 2020.

103 **named the Mariana snailfish.** Alan Jamieson, in an e-mail to the author, September 24, 2020; Mackenzie E. Gerringer, "On the Success of the Hadal Snailfishes," *Integral Organismal Biology* 1, no. 1 (2019):1–18, doi:10.1093/iob/obz004.

103 **more than five miles down.** Alan Jamieson, in an e-mail to the author, September 24, 2020.

104 **26,900 feet is calculated as the point.** Paul H. Yancey, Mackenzie E. Gerringer, Jeffrey C. Drazen, Ashley A. Rowden, and Alan Jamieson, "Marine Fish May Be Biochemically Constrained from Inhabiting the Deepest Ocean Depths," *Proceedings of the National Academy of Sciences (US)* 111, no. 12 (2014):4461–65, doi:10.1073/pnas.132200311.

105 **worth it on an evolutionary scale.** Mackenzie Gerringer, in conversation with the author, February 19, 2020.

105 **genome of the Mariana snailfish.** Kun Wang, Yanjun Shen, Yongzhi Yang, Xiaoni Gan, Guichun Liu, Kuang Hu, Yongxin Li, Zhaoming Gao, Li Zhu, Guoyong Yan, Lisheng He, Xiujuan Shan, Liandong Yang, Suxiang Lu, Honghui Zeng, Xiangyu Pan, Chang Liu, Yuan Yuan, Chenguang Feng,

Wenjie Xu, Chenglong Zhu, Wuhan Xiao, Yang Dong, Wen Wang, Qiang Qiu, and Shunping He, "Morphology and Genome of a Snailfish from the Mariana Trench Provide Insights into Deep-sea Adaptation," *Nature Ecology and Evolution* 3 (2019):823–33, doi:10.1038/s41559-019-0864-8.

106 **aluminum gel.** Hideki Kobayashi, Hirokazu Shimoshige, Yoshikata Naka-jima, Wataru Arai, and Hideto Takami, "An Aluminum Shield Enables the Amphipod *Hirondellea gigas* to Inhabit Deep-Sea Environments," *PLoS One* 14, no. 4 (2019):e0206710, doi:10.1371/journal.pone.0206710.

106 **Snailfish have very poor vision.** Thomas Linley, in an e-mail to author September 23, 2020.

106 **Mariana snailfish . . . in a CT scanner.** The scanned snailfish was part of the Scan All Fishes project, run by Adam Summers at the Friday Harbor Laboratories marine research station, University of Washington, https:// www.adamsummers.org/scanallfish.

107 **replica snailfish.** Mackenzie E. Gerringer, Jeffrey C. Drazen, Thomas D. Linley, Adam P. Summers, Alan J. Jamieson, and Paul H. Yancey, "Distribution, Composition and Functions of Gelatinous Tissues in Deep-Sea Fishes," *Royal Society Open Science* 4 (2017):171063, doi:10.1098/rsos.171063.

108 **Juveniles have been seen in trenches.** Alan Jamieson, in an e-mail to the author, September 24, 2020.

110 **The brine forming these pools.** Jennifer Frazer, "Playing in a Deep-Sea Brine Pool Is Fun, as Long as You're an ROV," *Scientific American*, June 18, 2015, https://blogs.scientificamerican.com/artful-amoeba/playing-in-a -deep-sea-brine-pool-is-fun-as-long-as-you-re-an-rov-video/.

DEEP MATTERS

115 **Without all the oceans' water.** Callum Roberts, *Reef Life* (London: Profile Books, 2019), 267.

116 **In 2019, this upper layer of the ocean.** Lijing Cheng, John Abraham, Jiang Zhui, Kevin E. Trenberth, John Fasullo, Tim Boyer, Ricardo Locarnini, Bin Zhang, Fujiang Yu, Liying Wan, Xingrong Chen, Xiangzhou Song, Yulong Liu, and Michael E. Mann, "Record-Setting Ocean Warmth Continued in 2019," *Advances in Atmospheric Sciences* 37 (2020):137–42, doi:10.1007/s00376 -020-9283-7.

116 **Argo floats.** Argo website, accessed August 10, 2020, https://argo.ucsd.edu/. The name Argo was chosen because the array of floats works in combination with a satellite, called Jason, which measures the shape of the ocean surface; in Greek mythology, Jason sailed his ship the *Argo* in search of the Golden Fleece.

116 **Ship-based measurements.** Lynne D. Talley et al., "Changes in Ocean Heat, Carbon Content, and Ventilation: A Review of the First Decade of GO-SHIP Global Repeat Hydrography," *Annual Review of Marine Science* 8 (2016):185–215, doi:10.1146/annurev-marine-052915-100829; Sarah G. Purkey and Gregory C. Johnson, "Warming of Global Abyssal and Deep Southern Ocean Waters between the 1990s and 2000s: Contributions to Global Heat

and Sea Level Rise Budgets," *Journal of Climate* 23 (2010):6336–51, doi:10.1175/2010JCLI3682.1.

117 **Cold waters, deeper than 13,000 feet.** Sarah G. Purkey, Gregory C. Johnson, Lynne D. Talley, Bernadette M. Sloyan, Susan E. Wijffels, William Smethie, Sabine Mecking, and Katsuro Katsumata, "Unabated Bottom Water Warming and Freshening in the South Pacific Ocean," *JGR Oceans* 124, no. 3 (2019):1778–94, doi:10.1029/2018JC014775.

118 **getting measurably warmer.** Viviane V. Menezes, Alison M. Macdonald, and Courtney Schatzman, "Accelerated Freshening of Antarctic Bottom Water over the Last Decade in the Southern Indian Ocean," *Science Advances* 3 (2017):e1601426, doi:10.1126/sciadv.1601426.

119 **triggering a big chill.** Daniele Castellana, Sven Baars, Fred W. Wubs, and Henk A. Dijkstra, "Transition Probabilities of Noise-Induced Transitions of the Atlantic Ocean Circulation," *Scientific Reports* 9 (2019):20284, doi:10.1038/s41598-019-56435-6. This portion of the global ocean conveyor belt is known as the Atlantic Meridional Overturning Circulation (AMOC). The Gulf Stream flowing along the American eastern seaboard feeds into the AMOC.

119 **significantly weakened before.** Delia. W. Oppo and William B. Curry, "Deep Atlantic Circulation during the Last Glacial Maximum and Deglaciation," *Nature Education Knowledge* 3, no. 10 (2012):1.

119 **Upwelling waters.** Giulia Bonino, Emanuele Di Lorenzo, Simona Masina, and Doroteaciro Iovino, "Interannual to Decadal Variability within and across the Major Eastern Boundary Upwelling Systems," *Scientific Reports* 9 (2019):19949, doi:10.1038/s41598-019-56514-8.

120 **Snowdrifts build up.** Kirsty J. Morris, Brian J. Bett, Jennifer M. Durden, Noelie M. A. Benoist, Veerle A. I. Huvenne, Daniel O. B. Jones, Katleen Robert, Matteo C. Ichino, George A. Wolff, and Henry A. Ruhl, "Landscape-Scale Spatial Heterogeneity in Phytodetrital Cover and Megafauna Biomass in the Abyss Links to Modest Topographic Variation," *Scientific Reports* 6 (2016):34080, doi:10.1038/srep34080.

120 **Flurries of snow are funneled.** Laurenz Thomsen, Jacopo Aguzzi, Corrado Costa, Fabio De Leo, Andrea Ogston, and Autun Purser, "The Oceanic Biological Pump: Rapid Carbon Transfer to Depth at Continental Margins during Winter," *Scientific Reports* 7 (2017):10763, doi:10.1038/s41598-017-11075-6.

120 **two massive phytoplankton blooms.** Mathieu Ardyna, Léo Lacour, Sara Sergi, Francesco d'Ovidio, Jean-Baptiste Sallée, Mathieu Rembauville, Stéphane Blain, Alessandro Tagliabue, Reiner Schlitzer, Catherine Jeandel, Kevin Robert Arrigo, and Hervé Claustre, "Hydrothermal Vents Trigger Massive Phytoplankton Blooms in the Southern Ocean," *Nature Communications* 20 (2019):2451, doi:10.1038/s41467-019-09973-6.

121 **Every year, sperm whales.** Trish J. Lavery, Ben Roudnew, Peter Gill, Justin Seymour, Laurent Seuront, Genevieve Johnson, James G. Mitchell, and Victor Smetacek, "Iron Defecation by Sperm Whales Stimulates Carbon Export in the Southern Ocean," *Proceedings of the Royal Society B* 277 (2010):3527–31, doi:10.1098/rspb.2010.0863.

121 **Accurately gauging how much carbon.** Stephanie A. Henson, Richard Sanders, Esben Madsen, Paul J. Morris, Frédéric Le Moigne, and Graham D. Quartly, "A Reduced Estimate of the Strength of the Ocean's Biological Carbon Pump," *Geophysical Research Letters* 38, no. 4 (2011):L04606, doi:10.1029/2011GL046735; Craig McClain, "An Empire Lacking Food," *Scientific American* 98, no. 6 (2010):470, doi:10.1511/2010.87.470. The estimated scale of the ocean's biological pump is equivalent to between 18 and around 60 gigatons of carbon dioxide (one ton of carbon being equivalent to 3.67 tons of carbon dioxide).

121 **particle injection pumps.** Philip W. Boyd, Hervé Claustre, Marina Levy, David A. Siegel, and Thomas Weber, "Multi-faceted Particle Pumps Drive Carbon Sequestration in the Ocean," *Nature* 568 (2019):327–35, doi:10.1038/s41586-019-1098-2.

122 **a third of humanity's carbon emissions.** Nicolas Gruber, Dominic Clement, Brendan R. Carter, Richard A. Feely, Steven van Heuven, Mario Hoppema, Masao Ishii, Robert M. Key, Alex Kozyr, Siv K. Lauvset, Claire Lo Monaco, Jeremy T. Mathis, Akihiko Murata, Are Olsen, Fiz F. Perez, Christopher L. Sabine, Toste Tanhua, and Rik Wanninkhof, "The Oceanic Sink for Anthropogenic CO_2 from 1994 to 2007," *Science* 363, no. 6432 (2019):1193–99, doi:10.1126/science.aau5153.

122 **full scale of the biological pump.** Ken O. Buesselera, Philip W. Boyd, Erin E. Black, and David A. Siegel, "Metrics That Matter for Assessing the Ocean Biological Carbon Pump," *Proceedings of the National Academy of Sciences (US)* 117, no. 18 (2020):9679–87, doi:10.1073/pnas.1918114117.

122 **living cells first emerged.** Michael J. Russell, Roy M. Daniel, and Allan J. Hall, "On the Emergence of Life via Catalytic Iron-Sulphide Membranes," *Terra Nova* 5 (1993):343, doi:10.1111/j.1365-3121.1993.tb00267.x; updated in: William Martin and Michael J. Russell, "On the Origins of Cells: A Hypothesis for the Evolutionary Transitions from Abiotic Geochemistry to Chemoautotrophic Prokaryotes, and from Prokaryotes to Nucleated Cells," *Philosophical Transactions of the Royal Society B* 358 (2003):59, doi:10.1098/rstb.2002.1183.

123 **visiting the Atlantis Massif.** Karen L. Von Damm, "Lost City Found," *Nature* 412 (2001):127–28, doi:10.1038/35084297.

123 **oldest known vent field.** Alden R. Denny, Deborah S. Kelley, and Gretchen L. Früh-Green. "Geologic Evolution of the Lost City Hydrothermal Field," *Geochemistry, Geophysics, Geosystems* 17, no. 2 (2015):375–95, doi:10.1002/2015GC005869.

123 **setting the stage for the first living cells.** A key requirement for the hydrothermal vent theory for the origin of life is for the vent fluids to be alkaline, as they are at the Lost City; this could have been vital for setting up proton gradients, a necessary condition for generating energy in all living cells today. For a detailed discussion of the theory see Nick Lane, *The Vital Question* (London: Profile Books, 2015).

123 **successfully generated amino acids.** Laura M. Barge, Erika Floresa, Marc M. Baumb, David G. Vander Veldec, and Michael J. Russell, "Redox and pH Gradients Drive Amino Acid Synthesis in Iron Oxyhydroxide Mineral Systems," *Proceedings of the National Academy of Sciences (US)* 116, no. 11 (2019):4828–33, doi:10.1073/pnas.1812098116.

123 **simple protocells assembled.** Sean F. Jordan, Hanadi Rammu, Ivan N. Zheludev, Andrew M. Hartley, Amandine Maréchal, and Nick Lane, "Promotion of Protocell Self-Assembly from Mixed Amphiphiles at the Origin of Life," *Nature Ecology and Evolution* 3 (2019):1705–14, doi:10.1038/s41559-019-1015-y.

123 **time to call off the search.** Sean Jordan, "Protocells in Deep Sea Hydrothermal Vents: Another Piece of the Origin of Life Puzzle," Nature Research: Ecology and Evolution, November 4, 2019, https://natureecoevocommunity.nature.com/posts/55368-protocells-in-deep-sea-hydrothermal-vents-another-piece-of-the-origin-of-life-puzzle.

124 **microscopic tubes and filaments.** Matthew S. Dodd, Dominic Papineau, Tor Grennec, John F. Slack, Martin Rittner, Franco Pirajnoe, Jonathan O'Neil, and Crispin T. S. Little, "Evidence for Early Life in Earth's Oldest Hydrothermal Vent Precipitates," *Nature* 543 (2017):60–64, doi:10.1038/nature21377.

125 **researchers from Japan announced.** Hiroyuki Imachi, Masaru K. Nobu, Nozomi Nakahara, Yuki Morono, Miyuki Ogawara, Yoshihiro Takaki, Yoshinori Takano, Katsuyuki Uematsu, Tetsuro Ikuta, Motoo Ito, Yohei Matsui, Masayuki Miyazaki, Kazuyoshi Murata, Yumi Saito, Sanae Sakai, Chihong Song, Eiji Tasumi, Yuko Yamanaka, Takashi Yamaguchi, Yoichi Kamagata, Hideyuki Tamaki, and Ken Takai, "Isolation of an Archaeon at the Prokaryote-Eukaryote Interface," *Nature* 577 (2020):519–25, doi:10.1038/s41586-019-1916-6.

DEEP CURES

126 **new tumor-killing medicine.** Danielle Skropeta and Liangqian Wei, "Recent Advances in Deep-Sea Natural Products," *Natural Products Reports* 31, no. 8 (2014):999–1025, doi:10.1039/x0xx00000x.

127 **ideas for new medicines.** Louise Allcock, in conversation with the author, October 15, 2019.

129 **formidable chemical cache.** Lisa I. Pilkington, "A Chemometric Analysis of Deep-Sea Natural Products," *Molecules* 24 (2019):3942, doi:10.3390/molecules24213942.

129 **75 percent of coral and sponge samples.** Peter. J. Schupp, Claudia Kohlert-Schupp, Susanna Whitefield, Anna Engemann, Sven Rohde, Thomas Hemscheidt, John M. Pezzuto, Tamara P. Kondratyuk, Eun-Jung Park, Laura Marler, Bahman Rostama, and Anthony D. Wight, "Cancer Chemopreventive and Anticancer Evaluation of Extracts and Fractions from

Marine Macro- and Micro-Organisms Collected from Twilight Zone Waters around Guam," *Natural Products Communications* 4, no. 12 (2009):1717–28.

130 **lifesaving drugs of the future.** All the examples of bioactive molecules from deep species are taken from Skropeta and Wei, "Recent Advances."

131 **wild bottlenose dolphins were infected.** Adam M. Schaefer, Gregory D. Bossart, Tyler Harrington, Patricia A. Fair, Peter J. McCarthy, and John S. Reif, "Temporal Changes in Antibiotic Resistance among Bacteria Isolated from Common Bottlenose Dolphins (*Tursiops truncatus*) in the Indian River Lagoon, Florida, 2003–2015," *Aquatic Mammals* 45, no. 5 (2019):533, doi:10.1578/AM.45.5.2019.533.

132 **Shigella flexneri.** Kate S. Baker, Alison E. Mather, Hannah McGregor, Paul Coupland, Gemma C. Langridge, Martin Day, Ana Deheer-Graham, Julian Parkhill, Julie E. Russell, and Nicholas R. Thomson, "The Extant World War I Dysentery Bacillus NCTC1: A Genomic Analysis," *Lancet* 384, no. 9955 (2014):1691–97, doi:10.1016/S0140-6736(14)61789-X.

132 **mummies.** Tasha Santiago-Rodriguez, Gino Fornaciari, Stefania Luciani, Scot Dowd, Gary Toranzos, Isolina Marota, and Paul Cano, "Gut Microbiome of an 11th Century A.D. Pre-Columbian Andean Mummy," *PloS One* 10 (2015), doi:10.1371/journal.pone.0138135.

132 **frozen tundra.** Vanessa M. D'Costa, Christine E. King, Lindsay Kalan, Mariya Morar, Wilson W. L. Sung, Carsten Schwarz, Duane Froese, Grant Zazula, Fabrice Calmels, Regis Debruyne, G. Brian Golding, Hendrik N. Poinar, and Gerard D. Wright, "Antibiotic Resistance Is Ancient," *Nature* 477 (2011):457–61, doi:10.1038/nature10388.

133 **colistin.** Ruobing Wang, Lucy van Dorp, Liam P. Shaw, Phelim Bradley, Qi Wang, Xiaojuan Wang, Longyang Jin, Qing Zhang, Yuqing Liu, Adrien Rieux, Thamarai Dorai-Schneiders, Lucy Anne Weinert, Zamin Iqbal, Xavier Didelot, Hui Wang, and Francois Balloux, "The Global Distribution and Spread of the Mobilized Colistin Resistance Gene mcr-1," *Nature Communications* 9 (2018):1179, doi:10.1038/s41467-018-03205-z.

134 **ten million people.** Alessandro Cassini, Liselotte Diaz Högberg, Diamantis Plachouras, Annalisa Quattrocchi, Ana Hoxha, Gunnar Skov Simonsen, Mélanie Colomb-Cotinat, Mirjam E. Kretzschmar, Brecht Devleesschauwer, Michele Cecchini, Driss Ait Ouakrim, Tiago Cravo Oliveira, Marc J. Struelens, Carl Suetens, Dominique L. Monnet, "Attributable Deaths and Disability-Adjusted Life-Years Caused by Infections with Antibiotic-Resistant Bacteria in the EU and the European Economic Area in 2015: A Population-Level Modelling Analysis," *Lancet* 19, no. 1 (2018):56–66, doi:10.1016/S1473-3099(18)30605-4.

134 **specialist in coral and sponge ecosystems.** Kerry Howell, in conversation with the author, September 18, 2019.

135 **tests Howell's sponges and corals.** Mat Upton, in conversation with the author, September 12, 2019.

135 **obligate piezophiles.** Emiliana Tortorella, Pietro Tedesco, Fortunato Palma Esposito, Grant Garren January, Renato Fani, Marcel Jaspars, and

Donatella de Pascale, "Antibiotics from Deep-Sea Microorganisms: Current Discoveries and Perspectives," *Marine Drugs* 16 (2018):355, doi:10.3390/md16100355.

136 **strains capable of killing . . . MRSA.** Mat Upton, conservation with author, September 12, 2019.

136 **pharmacological war chest.** Ibid.

FISHING DEEP

141 **The story of orange roughy.** Kate Evans, "Americans Commonly Eat Orange Roughy, a Fish Scientists Say Can Live to 250 Years Old," *Discover,* September 10, 2019, https://www.discovermagazine.com/planet-earth/americans-commonly-eat-orange-roughy-a-fish-scientists-say-can-live-to-250; M. Lack, K. Short, and A. Willock, *Managing Risk and Uncertainty in Deep-Sea Fisheries: Lessons from Orange Roughy* (N.p.: TRAFFIC Oceania and WWF Endangered Seas Programme, 2003); Trevor A. Branch, "A Review of Orange Roughy *Hoplostethus atlanticus* Fisheries, Estimation Methods, Biology and Stock Structure," *South African Journal of Marine Science* 23 (2001):181–203, doi:0.2989/025776101784529006.

143 **new wave of fishing.** Globally, the mean depth of fishing activity has increased by 1,150 feet; Reg A. Watson and Telmo Morato, "Fishing Down the Seep: Accounting for Within-Species Changes in Depth of Fishing," *Fisheries Research* 140 (2013):63, doi:10.1016/j.fishres.2012.12.004.

143 **"A Deep-Sea Fishery with a Rosy Future."** Nigel Merrett, "Fishing around in the Dark," *New Scientist* 121, no. 16453 (1989):50–54.

143 **Hauls of orange roughies were at first so massive.** Lack et al., *Managing Risk.*

145 **"get the number of zeros correct."** Ibid.

145 **soon they went bust.** Branch, "Review of Orange Roughy."

145 **Recent analysis, piecing together evidence.** Lissette Victorero, Les Watling, Maria L. Deng Palomares, and Claire Nouvian, "Out of Sight, but within Reach: A Global History of Bottom-Trawled Deep-Sea Fisheries from >400 m Depth," *Frontiers in Marine Science* 5 (2018):98, doi:10.3389/fmars.2018.00098.

146 **"It was like dropping a stone."** Matthew Gianni, in conversation with the author, September 18, 2019.

146 **studies were beginning to reveal.** J. Anthony Koslow, Karen Gowlett-Holmes, Jim Lowry, Timothy O'Hara, Gary Poore, and A. Williams, "Seamount Benthic Macrofauna off Southern Tasmania: Community Structure and Impacts of Trawling," *Marine Ecology Progress Series* 213 (2001):111–25, doi:10.3354/meps213111.

147 **One of the longest-running studies.** Malcolm R. Clark, David A. Bowden, Ashley A. Rowden, and Rob Stewart, "Little Evidence of Benthic Community Resilience to Bottom Trawling on Seamounts after 15 Years," *Frontiers in Marine Science* 6 (2019):63, doi:10.3389/fmars.2019.00063.

148 **persistent, depleted state.** Alan Williams, Thomas A. Schlacher, Ashley A. Rowden, Franziska Althaus, Malcolm R. Clark, David A. Bowden, Robert Stewart, Nicholas J. Bax, Mireille Consalvey, and Rudy J. Kloser, "Seamount Megabenthic Assemblages Fail to Recover from Trawling Impacts," *Marine Ecology* 31 (2010):183–99, doi:10.1111/j.1439-0485.2010.00385.x.

148 **study from farther north in the Pacific.** Amy R. Baco, E. Brendan Roark, and Nicole B. Morgan, "Amid Fields of Rubble, Scars, and Lost Gear, Signs of Recovery Observed on Seamounts on 30- to 40-Year Time Scales," *Science Advances* 5 (2019):eaaw4513, doi:10.1126/sciadv.aaw4513.

150 **reducing their chance for long-distance recovery.** Malcom Clark, in conversation with the author, October 17, 2019.

152 **expanding footprint of deep trawlers.** Victorero et al., "Out of Sight."

152 **the deep has provided less than half of one percent.** Ibid.

152 **Government subsidies.** Ussif Rashid Sumaila, Ahmed Khan, Louise Teh, Reg Watson, Peter Tyedmers, and Daniel Pauly, "Subsidies to High Seas Bottom Trawl Fleets and the Sustainability of Deep-Sea Demersal Fish Stocks," *Marine Policy* 34 (2010): 495–97, doi:10.1016/j.marpol.2009.10.004.

153 **governments propping them up.** Ibid.

153 **"Because some boats."** Matthew Gianni, in conversation with the author, September 18, 2019.

154 **"It doesn't surprise me."** Frédéric Le Manach, in conversation with the author, September 27, 2019.

154 **turns even a slim profit.** Matthew Gianni, in conversation with the author, September 18, 2019.

154 **A 2012 study estimated.** Rainer Froese and Alexander Proelss, "Evaluation and Legal Assessment of Certified Seafood," *Marine Policy* 36, no. 6 (2012):1284–89, doi:10.1016/j.marpol.2012.03.017.

155 **published a peer-reviewed paper in 2013.** Claire Christian, David Ainley, Megan Bailey, Paul Dayton, John Hocevar, Michael LeVine, Jordan Nikoloyuk, Claire Nouvian, Enriqueta Velarde, Rodolfo Werner, and Jennifer Jacquet, "A Review of Formal Objections to Marine Stewardship Council Fisheries Certifications," *Biological Conservation* 161 (2013):10–17, doi:10.1016/j.biocon.2013.01.002.

156 **certification for Atlantic bluefin tuna.** Marine Stewardship Council, "Japanese Bluefin Tuna Fishery Now Certified as Sustainable," August 12, 2020, https://www.msc.org/media-centre/press-releases/japanese-bluefin-tuna-fishery-now-certified-as-sustainable; World Wildlife Fund, "MSC Certification of Bluefin Tuna Fishery before Stocks Have Recovered Sets Dangerous Precedent," July 31, 2020, https://wwf.panda.org/wwf_news/?364790/MSC-certification-of-bluefin-tuna-fishery-before-stocks-have-recovered-sets-dangerous-precedent.

156 **dumping and underreporting.** Details of missing orange roughy fishery data from Deep Sea Conservation Coalition's lawyer, Duncan Currie, quoted

in "Orange Roughy Furore," World Fishing and Aquaculture, December 9, 2016, https://www.worldfishing.net/news101/industry-news/orange-roughy-furore.

156 **40 percent of the natural population size.** "Orange Roughy: The Extraordinary Turnaround." Marine Stewardship Council, December 2016, http://orange-roughy-stories.msc.org/

156 **thousands of teenage or younger orange roughies.** Malcom Clark, in conversation with the author, October 17, 2019.

157 **fishing lobby from New Zealand.** High Seas Fisheries Group Incorporated, "Objection by the High Seas Fisheries Group to the Proposed SPRFMO Draft—Bottom Fishing CMM (COMM6-Prop05)," January 3, 2018, https://www.sprfmo.int/assets/COMM6/COMM6-Obs01-NZHSFG-Objection-to-Prop05.pdf.

158 **new global ocean treaty.** Technically, the treaty will be an international legally binding instrument, often referred to as an implementing agreement, to the UN's Convention on the Law of the Sea.

159 **new estimates of the abundance of twilight-zone fish.** Xabier Irigoien, Thor A. Klevjer, Anders Røstad, Udane Martinez, G. Boyra, José L. Acuñã, Antonio Bode, Fidel Echevarria, Juan Ignacio Gonzalez-Gordillo, Santiago Hernandez-Leon, Susana Agusti, Dag L. Aksnes, Carlos M. Duarte, and Stein Kaartvedt, "Large Mesopelagic Fishes Biomass and Trophic Efficiency in the Open Ocean," *Nature Communications* 5 (2014):3271, doi:10.1038/ncomms4271. The upper figure of around 20 gigatons of fish in the twilight zone comes from extending the data collected on the Malaspina expedition between 40°N and 40°S to higher latitudes (70°N and 70°S).

160 **1.25 gigatons of farmed seafood.** Michael A. St. John, Angel Borja, Guillem Chust, Michael Heath, Ivo Grigorov, Patrizio Mariani, Adrian P. Martin, and Ricardo S. Santos, "A Dark Hole in Our Understanding of Marine Ecosystems and Their Services: Perspectives from the Mesopelagic Community," *Frontiers in Marine Science* 3 (2016):31, doi:10.3389/fmars.2016.00031.

161 **adding to the abyssal stores of carbon.** Jeanna M. Hudson, Deborah K. Steinberg, Tracey T. Sutton, John E. Graves, and Robert J. Latou, "Myctophid Feeding Ecology and Carbon Transport along the Northern Mid-Atlantic Ridge," *Deep-Sea Research II* 93 (2014):104–16, doi:10.1016/j.dsr.2014.07.002.

161 **1 million tons of carbon dioxide each year.** Clive N. Trueman, Graham Johnston, Brendan O'Hea, and Kirsteen M. MacKenzie, "Trophic Interactions of Fish Communities at Midwater Depths Enhance Long-term Carbon Storage and Benthic Production on Continental Slopes," *Proceedings of the Royal Society B* 281 (2014):20140669, doi:10.1098/rspb.2014.0669.

162 **A 2019 study reinterpreted.** Roland Proud, Nils Olav Handegard, Rudy J. Kloser, Martin J. Cox, and Andrew S. Brierley, "From Siphonophores to Deep Scattering Layers: Uncertainty Ranges for the Estimation of Global Mesopelagic Fish Biomass," *ICES Journal of Marine Science* 76, no. 3 (2019):718–33, doi:10.1093/icesjms/fsy037.

THE ETERNAL JUNKYARD

163 **wreck will crumble into dust.** Brandon Spector, "The Titanic Shipwreck Is Collapsing into Rust, First Visit in 14 Years Reveals," Live Science, August 21, 2019, https://www.livescience.com/titanic-shipwreck-disintegrating-into-the-sea.html.

163 **Two studies published in 2014.** Andrés Cózara, Fidel Echevarría, J. Ignacio González-Gordillo, Xabier Irigoien, Bárbara Úbeda, Santiago Hernández-León, Álvaro T. Palma, Sandra Navarro, Juan García-de-Lomas, Andrea Ruiz, María L. Fernández-de-Puelles, and Carlos M. Duarte, "Plastic Debris in the Open Ocean," *Proceedings of the National Academy of Sciences (US)* 111, no. 28 (2014):10239–44, doi:10.1073/pnas.1314705111; Marcus Eriksen, Laurent C. M. Lebreton, Henry S. Carson, Martin Thiel, Charles J. Moore, Jose C. Borerro, Francois Galgani, Peter G. Ryan, Julia Reisser, "Plastic Pollution in the World's Oceans: More Than 5 Trillion Plastic Pieces Weighing over 250,000 Tons Afloat at Sea," *PLoS One* 9, no. 12 (2014):e111913, doi:10.1371/journal.pone.0111913.

164 **Victor Vescovo.** Rebecca Morelle, "Mariana Trench: Deepest-Ever Sub Dive Finds Plastic Bag," *BBC News*, May 13, 2019, https://www.bbc.co.uk/news/science-environment-48230157.

164 **a 2020 study announced.** Ian A. Kane, Michael A. Clare, Elda Miramontes, Roy Wogelius, James J. Rothwell, Pierre Garreau, and Florian Pohl, "Seafloor Microplastic Hotspots Controlled by Deep-Sea Circulation," *Science* 368, no. 6495 (2020):1140–45, doi:10.1126/science.aba5899.

164 **eat or get tangled in plastic fibers.** Michelle L. Taylor, Claire Gwinnett, Laura F. Robinson, and Lucy C. Woodall, "Plastic Microfibre Ingestion by Deep-Sea Organisms," *Scientific Reports* 6 (2016):33997, doi:10.1038/srep33997.

164 **Amphipods living at the bottom . . . *Eurythenes plasticus*.** Alan J. Jamieson, Lauren S. R. Brooks, William D. K. Reid, Stuart B. Piertney, Bhavani E. Narayanaswamy, and Thomas D. Linley, "Microplastics and Synthetic Particles Ingested by Deep-Sea Amphipods in Six of the Deepest Marine Ecosystems on Earth," *Royal Society Open Science* 6 (2019):180667, doi:10.1098/rsos.180667; Johanna, N. J. Weston, Priscilla Carillo-Barragan, Thomas D. Linley, William D. K. Reid, and Alan J. Jamieson, "New Species of *Eurythenes* from Hadal Depths of the Mariana Trench, Pacific Ocean (Crustacea: Amphipoda)," *Zootaxa* 4748, no. 1 (2020):163–81, doi:10.11646/zootaxa.4748.1.9.

165 **Starfish and brittle stars from the Rockall Trough.** Winnie Courtene-Jones, Brian Quinn, Ciaran Ewins, Stefan F. Gary, and Bhavani E. Narayanaswamy, "Consistent Microplastic Ingestion by Deep-Sea Invertebrates over the Last Four Decades (1976–2015), a Study from the North East Atlantic," *Environmental Pollution* 244 (2019):503–12, doi:10.1016/j.envpol.2018.10.090.

165 **tracking microplastics in Monterey Bay.** C. Anela Choy, Bruce H. Robison, Tyler O. Gagne, Benjamin Erwin, Evan Firl, Rolf U. Halden, J. Andrew Hamilton, Kakani Katija, Susan E. Lisin, Charles Rolsky, and Kyle S. Van Houtan, "The Vertical Distribution and Biological Transport of

Marine Microplastics across the Epipelagic and Mesopelagic Water Column," *Scientific Reports* 9 (2019):7843, doi:10.1038/s41598-019-44117-2.

165 **Giant larvaceans have been found.** Kakani Katija, C. Anela Choy, Rob E. Sherlock, Alana D. Sherman, and Bruce H. Robison, "From the Surface to the Seafloor: How Giant Larvaceans Transport Microplastics into the Deep Sea," *Science Advances* 3 (2017): e1700715, doi:10.1126/sciadv.1700715.

165 **Impacts of microplastics.** Natalia Prinz and Špela Korez, "Understanding How Microplastics Affect Marine Biota on the Cellular Level Is Important for Assessing Ecosystem Function: A Review," in *YOUMARES 9—The Oceans: Our Research, Our Future*, ed. Simon Jungblut, Viola Liebich, and Maya Bode-Dalby (Berlin: Springer, 2019), doi:10.1007/978-3-030-20389-4_6.

166 **In 2019, scientists at Scripps.** Jennifer A. Brandon, William Jones, and Mark D. Ohman, "Multidecadal Increase in Plastic Particles in Coastal Ocean Sediments," *Science Advances* 5 (2019):eaax0587, doi:10.1126/sciadv.aax0587.

166 **This time capsule revealed.** Plastic particles found in the sediment core dating to before 1945, and hence prior to plastic manufacture, were contaminants from later settlement; Brandon et al., "Multidecadal Increase," considered this rate of contamination to be constant and subtracted it from post-1945 particle counts in order to calculate actual changes in deposition year on year.

167 **A huge oil slick formed.** Charles R. Fisher, Paul A. Montagna, and Tracey T. Sutton, "How Did the Deepwater Horizon Oil Spill Impact Deep-Sea Ecosystems?," *Oceanography* 29, no. 3 (2016):182–95, doi:10.5670/oceanog.2016.82.

167 **Oil-covered plankton.** Ibid.

168 **Deepwater corals were smothered and poisoned.** Danielle M. DeLeo, Dannise V. Ruiz-Ramos, Iliana B. Baums, and Erik E. Cordes, "Response of Deep-Water Corals to Oil and Chemical Dispersant Exposure," *Deep-Sea Research Part II: Topical Studies in Oceanography* 129 (2016):137–47, doi:10.1016/j.dsr2.2015.02.028.

168 **Crabs with festering shells.** Craig R. McClain, Clifton Nunnally, and Mark C. Benfield, "Persistent and Substantial Impacts of the Deepwater Horizon Oil Spill on Deep-sea Megafauna," *Royal Society Open Science* 6 (2019):191164, doi:10.1098/rsos.191164. McClain and Nunnally's 2017 dive to the seabed around *Deepwater Horizon* had not been part of a funded research program but an opportunistic add-on that the weather had permitted. McClain has since been applying for grants to go back, but none have been forthcoming. The funding agencies seem to consider the follow-up work done and dusted. The only funded submersible dive to the site was shortly after the disaster, in 2010.

169 **glassy lumps of clinker.** Eva Ramirez-Llodra, Paul A. Tyler, Maria C. Baker, Odd Aksel Bergstad, Malcolm R. Clark, Elva Escobar, Lisa A. Levin, Lenaick Menot, Ashley A. Rowden, Craig R. Smith, and Cindy L. Van

Dover, "Man and the Last Great Wilderness: Human Impact on the Deep Sea," *PLoS One* 6, no. 7 (2011):e22588, doi:10.1371/journal.pone.0022588.

170 **livestock carrier overturned.** "*Queen Hind*: Rescuers Race to Save 14,000 Sheep on Capsized Cargo Ship," *BBC News*, November 25, 2019, https://www.bbc.co.uk/news/world-europe-50538592.

170 **packed into hidden decks.** Saeed Kamali Dehghan, "Secret Decks Found on Ship That Capsized Killing Thousands of Sheep," *Guardian*, February 3, 2020, https://www.theguardian.com/environment/2020/feb/03/secret-decks-found-on-ship-that-capsized-killing-thousands-of-sheep.

170 **carcasses of 15,156 sheep.** Brian Morton, "Slaughter at Sea." *Marine Pollution Bulletin* 46, no. 4 (2003):379–80.

171 **Operation CHASE.** Simone Müller, "'Cut Holes and Sink 'Em': Chemical Weapons Disposal and Cold War History as a History of Risk," *Historical Social Research* 41, no. 1 (2016):263–84, doi:10.12759/hsr.41.2016.1.263-284.

171 **1 million tons of chemical weapons have been sunk.** Andrew Curry, "Weapons of War Litter the Ocean Floor," *Hakai Magazine*, November 10, 2016, https://www.hakaimagazine.com/features/weapons-war-litter-ocean-floor/

172 **two hundred Italian fishermen.** Ezio Amato, L. Alcaro, Ilaria Corsi, Camilla Della Torre, C. Farchi, Silvia Focardi, Giovanna Marino, A. Tursi, "An Integrated Ecotoxicological Approach to Assess the Effects of Pollutants Released by Unexploded Chemical Ordnance Dumped in the Southern Adriatic (Mediterranean Sea)," *Marine Biology* 149, no. 1 (2006):17–23, doi:10.1007/s00227-005-0216-x.

173 **higher than normal levels of arsenic.** Ibid.

173 **Near Pearl Harbor.** Christian Briggs, Sonia M. Shjegstad, Jeff A. K. Silva, and Margo H. Edwards, "Distribution of Chemical Warfare Agent, Energetics, and Metals in Sediments at a Deep-Water Discarded Military Munitions Site," *Deep Sea Research Part II: Topical Studies in Oceanography* 128 (2016):63–69, doi:10.1016/j.dsr2.2015.02.014.

174 **Ocean fertilization experiments.** Joo-Eun Yoon, Kyu-Cheul Yoo, Alison M. Macdonald, Ho-Il Yoon, Ki-Tae Park, Eun Jin Yang, Hyun-Cheol Kim, Jae Il Lee, Min Kyung Lee, Jinyoung Jung, Jisoo Park, Jiyoung Lee, Soyeon Kim, Seong-Su Kim, Kitae Kim, and Il-Nam Kim, "Reviews and Syntheses: Ocean Iron Fertilization Experiments—Past, Present, and Future Looking to a Future Korean Iron Fertilization Experiment in the Southern Ocean (KIFES) Project," *Biogeosciences* 15 (2018):5847–89, doi:10.5194/bg-15-5847-2018.

175 **monstrously huge carbon dump.** Steve Goldthorpe, "Potential for Very Deep Ocean Storage of CO_2 without Ocean Acidification: A Discussion Paper," *Energy Procedia* 114 (2017):5417–29.

175 **estimated annual carbon emissions.** Hannah Ritchie and Max Roser. "CO_2 Emissions," *Our World in Data*, accessed October 16, 2020, https://ourworldindata.org/co2-emissions.

175 **the impacts on the living deep are untold.** Ken Caldeira and Makoto Akai, "Ocean Storage," in *Carbon Dioxide Capture and Storage*, ed. Bert Metz, Ogunlade Davidson, Heleen de Coninck, Manuela Loos, and Leo Meyer (Cambridge: Cambridge University Press, 2005), 277–318, https://www .ipcc.ch/report/carbon-dioxide-capture-and-storage/.

175 **A major study in 2017.** Andrew K. Sweetman, Andrew R. Thurber, Craig R. Smith, Lisa A. Levin, Camilo Mora, Chih-Lin Wei, Andrew J. Gooday, Daniel O. B. Jones, Michael Rex, Moriaki Yasuhara, Jeroen Ingels, Henry A. Ruhl, Christina A. Frieder, Roberto Danovaro, Laura Würzberg, Amy Baco, Benjamin M. Grupe, Alexis Pasulka, Kirstin S. Meyer, Katherine M. Dunlop, Lea-Anne Henry, and J. Murray Roberts, "Major Impacts of Climate Change on Deep-Sea Benthic Ecosystems," *Elementa Science of the Anthropocene* 5 (2017):4, doi:10.1525/elementa.203.

176 **oxygen levels . . . fallen by 15 percent.** Tetjana Ross, Cherisse Du Preez, and Debby Ianso, "Rapid Deep Ocean Deoxygenation and Acidification Threaten Life on Northeast Pacific Seamounts," *Global Change Biology* 00 (2020):1-21, doi: 10.1111/gcb.15307.

WHAT'S MINE IS YOURS

178 **DNA taken from snippets of preserved specimens.** Chrysoula Gubilia, Elizabeth Ross, David M. Billett, Andrew Yool, Charalampos Tsairidis, Henry A. Ruhl, Antonina Rogacheva, Doug Masson, Paul A. Tyler, and Chris Hautona, "Species Diversity in the Cryptic Abyssal Holothurian *Psychropotes longicauda* (Echinodermata)," *Deep Sea Research Part II: Topical Studies in Oceanography* 137 (2017):288–96, doi:10.1016/j.dsr2.2016.04.003.

179 **traces of other, more desirable elements.** *Future Ocean Resources: Metal-Rich Minerals and Genetics Evidence Pack* (London: Royal Society, 2017), https://royalsociety.org/-/media/policy/projects/future-oceans-resources/ future-of-oceans-evidence-pack.pdf.

180 **numerous peer-reviewed research papers.** Selection of academic literature warning of the impacts of deep-sea mining: Holly J. Niner, Jeff A. Ardron, Elva G. Escobar, Matthew Gianni, Aline Jaeckel, Daniel O. B. Jones, Lisa A. Levin, Craig R. Smith, Torsten Thiele, Phillip J. Turner, Cindy L. Van Dover, Les Watling, and Kristina M. Gjerde, "Deep-Sea Mining with No Net Loss of Biodiversity—An Impossible Aim," *Frontiers in Marine Science* 5 (2018):53, doi:10.3389/fmars.2018.00053; Antje Boetius and Matthias Haeckel, "Mind the Seafloor: Research and Regulations Must Be Integrated to Protect Seafloor Biota from Future Mining Impacts," *Science* 359, no. 6371 (2018):34–36, doi:10.1126/science.aap7301; Bernd Christiansen, Anneke Denda, and Sabine Christiansen, "Potential Effects of Deep Seabed Mining on Pelagic and Benthopelagic Biota," *Marine Policy* 114 (2019):103442, doi:10.1016/j.marpol.2019.02.014.

181 **impassioned speech about the oceans.** Arvid Pardo, Official Records of the United Nations General Assembly, 22nd Session, 1,515th meeting, November 1, 1967, New York, agenda item 92: "Examination of the question of the

reservation exclusively for peaceful purposes of the sea-bed and the ocean floor, and the subsoil thereof, underlying the high seas beyond the limits of present national jurisdiction, and the use of their resources in the interest of mankind."

182 **exploit offshore oil and gas reserves.** Luc Cuyvers, Whitney Berry, Kristina Gjerde, Torsten Thiele, and Caroline Wilhem, *Deep Seabed Mining: A Rising Environmental Challenge* (Gland, Switzerland: IUCN and Gallifrey Foundation, 2018), doi:10.2305/IUCN.CH.2018.16.en.

183 **Pardo said, "I thought it could serve . . ."** Elaine Woo, "Arvid Pardo; Former U.N. Diplomat from Malta," *Los Angeles Times*, July 18, 1999, https://www.latimes.com/archives/la-xpm-1999-jul-18-me-57228-story.html.

183 **notion of the common heritage of the seabed.** Cuyvers et al., *Deep Seabed Mining.*

184 **The seabed offered the possibility.** Ole Sparenberg, "A Historical Perspective on Deep-Sea Mining for Manganese Nodules, 1965–2019," *Extractive Industries and Society* 6 (2019):842–54, doi:10.1016/j.exis.2019.04.001.

184 **brought up a few hundred tons of nodules.** Cuyvers et al., *Deep Seabed Mining.*

184 **US vessel *Glomar Explorer.*** David Shukman, "The Secret on the Sea Floor," *BBC News*, February 19, 2018, https://www.bbc.co.uk/news/resources/idt-sh/deep_sea_mining.

185 **nodules may be as abundant as Mero suggested.** Sparenberg, "Historical Perspective."

185 **one of the slowest-known geological processes.** B. S. Boltenkov, "Mechanisms of Formation of Deep-Sea Ferromanganese Nodules: Mathematical Modelling and Experimental Results," *Geochemistry International* 50, no. 2 (2012):125–32, doi:10.1134/S0016702911120044.

186 **The International Seabed Authority.** The ISA is made up of various UN officials plus an assembly of representatives from all 168 member states (including the European Union) currently signed on to the Convention on the Law of the Sea. A notable absentee is the United States, which hasn't ratified the Law of the Sea. Lisa A. Levin, Diva J. Amon, and Hannah Lily, "Challenges to the Sustainability of Deep-Seabed Mining," *Nature Sustainability*, July 6, 2020, doi:10.1038/s41893-020-0558-x.

186 **entertaining the possibility of mining.** Sparenberg, "Historical Perspective."

187 **Mining Code.** "The Mining Code," *DSM Observer*, accessed August 16, 2020, http://dsmobserver.org/the-mining-code/.

187 **deadline of 2020 for releasing the code.** Amber Cobley, "Deep-Sea Mining: Regulating the Unknown," *Ecologist*, March 15, 2019, https://theecologist.org/2019/mar/15/deep-sea-mining-regulating-unknown.

187 **By 2019 China had five permits.** Todd Woody, "China Extends Domain with Fifth Deep Sea Mining Contract," China Dialogue Ocean, August 15, 2019, https://chinadialogueocean.net/9771-china-deep-sea-mining-contract/.

188 **Lodge wrote that it is useless.** Michael W. Lodge and Philomène A. Verlaan, "Deep-Sea Mining: International Regulatory Challenges and Responses," *Elements* 14, no. 5 (2018):331–36, doi:10.2138/gselements. 14.5.331.

189 **both the exploiter and the protector.** "Editorial: Write Rules for Deep-Sea Mining before It's Too Late," *Nature* 571 (2019):447, doi:10.1038/d41586-019-02276-2.

189 **Scientists tend to negotiate.** https://www.wsj.com/articles/environmental-investing-frenzy-stretches-meaning-of-green-11624554045.

190 **Dozens of new xenophyophore species.** Andrew J. Gooday, Maria Holzmann, Clémence Caulle, Aurélie Goineau, Olga Kamenskaya, Alexandra A. T. Weber, and Jan Pawlowski, "Giant Protists (Xenophyophores, Foraminifera) Are Exceptionally Diverse in Parts of the Abyssal Eastern Pacific Licensed for Polymetallic Nodule Exploration," *Biological Conservation* 207 (2017):106–16, doi:10.1016/j.biocon.2017.01.006.

190 **The nodules themselves create a place to live.** Erik Simon-Lledó, in conversation with the author at the National Oceanography Centre, UK, January 17, 2020.

191 **Two were evidently female octopuses.** Autun Purser, Yann Marcon, Henk-Jan T. Hoving, Michael Vecchione, Uwe Piatkowski, Deborah Eason, Hartmut Bluhm, and Antje Boetius, "Association of Deep-Sea Incirrate Octopods with Manganese Crusts and Nodule Fields in the Pacific Ocean," *Current Biology* 26 (2016):R1247–71, doi:10.1016/j.cub.2016.10.052.

191 **CCZ's diversity in species of megafauna.** Erik Simon-Lledó, Brian J. Betta, Veerle A. I. Huvenne, Timm Schoening, Noelie M. A. Benoista, Rachel M. Jeffreys, Jennifer M. Durden, and Daniel O. B. Jones, "Megafaunal Variation in the Abyssal Landscape of the Clarion Clipperton Zone," *Progress in Oceanography* 170 (2019):119–33, doi:10.1016/j.pocean.2018.11.003.

191 **"erase the biota."** Stefanie Kaiser, Craig R. Smith, and Pedro Martinez Arbizu, "Biodiversity of the Clarion Clipperton Fracture Zone," *Marine Biodiversity* 47 (2017):259–64, doi:10.1007/s12526-017-0733-0.

193 **prevailing misconception.** Craig R. Smith, Verena Tunnicliffe, Ana Colaço, Jeffrey C. Drazen, Sabine Gollner, Lisa A. Levin, Nelia C. Mestre, Anna Metaxas, Tina N. Molodtsova, Telmo Morato, Andrew K. Sweetman, Travis Washburn, and Diva J. Amon, "Deep-Sea Misconceptions Cause Underestimation of Seabed-Mining Impacts," *Trends in Ecology and Evolution* 35, no. 10 (2020):853–57, doi:10.1016/j.tree.2020.07.002.

194 **highest concentration of deep-sea research.** Andrew Thaler and Diva Amon, "262 Voyages beneath the Sea A Global Assessment of Macro- and Megafaunal Biodiversity and Research Effort at Deep-Sea Hydrothermal Vents," *PeerJ* 7 (2019):e7397, doi:10.7717/peerj.7397.

194 **existing exploration permits granted.** Ibid

195 **ten-year study.** Cherisse Du Preez and Charles R. Fisher, "Long-Term Stability of Back-Arc Basin Hydrothermal Vents," *Frontiers in Marine Science* 5 (2018):54, doi:10.3389/fmars.2018.00054.

195 **Extinction is a distinct risk.** Levin et al., "Challenges to the Sustainability."

195 **the scaly-foot snail became the first.** Julia D. Sigwart, Chong Chen, Elin A. Thomas, A. Louise Allcock, Monika Böhm, and Mary Seddon, "Red Listing Can Protect Deep-Sea Biodiversity," *Nature Ecology and Evolution* 3 (2019):1134, doi:10.1038/s41559-019-0930-2.

196 **wipe out an entire, rare population.** Julia Sigwart, in conversation with the author, November 19, 2019.

197 **joined by dozens of other.** Ibid.

197 **Some vents are already protected.** Elisabetta Meninia and Cindy Lee Van Dover, "An Atlas of Protected Hydrothermal Vents," *Marine Policy* 105 (2019):103654, doi:10.1016/j.marpol.2019.103654.

198 **potential World Heritage Site.** David E. Johnson, "Protecting the Lost City Hydrothermal Vent System: All Is Not Lost, or Is It?," *Marine Policy* 107 (2019):103593, doi:10.1016/j.marpol.2019.103593.

199 **contaminants could easily seep into the tangled food web.** For full details of midwater impacts of seabed mining: Jeffrey C. Drazen, Craig R. Smith, Kristina M. Gjerde, Steven H. D. Haddock, Glenn S. Carter, Anela Choy, Malcolm R. Clark, Pierre Dutrieux, Erica Goetzea, Chris Hauton, Mariko Hatta, J. Anthony Koslow, Astrid B. Leitner, Aude Pacini, Jessica N. Perelman, Thomas Peacock, Tracey T. Sutton, Les Watling, and Hiroyuki Yamamoto, "Midwater Ecosystems Must Be Considered When Evaluating Environmental Risks of Deep-Sea Mining," *Proceedings of the National Academy of Sciences (US)* 117, no. 30 (2020):17455–60, doi:10.1073/pnas.2011914117.

199 **Whale sharks.** Hector M. Guzman, Catalina G. Gomez, Alex Hearn, and Scott A. Eckert, "Longest Recorded Trans-Pacific Migration of a Whale Shark (*Rhincodon typus*)," *Marine Biology Records* 11, no. 1 (2018):8, doi:10.1186/s41200-018-0143-4.

199 **Leatherback turtles.** Scott R. Benson, Tomoharu Eguchi, David G. Foley, Karin A. Forney, Helen Bailey, Creusa Hitipeuw, Betuel P. Samber, Ricardo F. Tapilatu, Vagi Rei, Peter Ramohia, John Pita, and Peter H. Dutton, "Large Scale Movements and High Use Areas of Western Pacific Leatherback Turtles, *Dermochelys coriacea*," *Ecosphere* 2, no. 7 (2011):1–27, doi:10.1890/ES11-00053.1.

200 **avoiding the loss of biodiversity.** Cindy Lee Van Dover, Jeff A. Ardron, Elva Escobar, Matthew Gianni, Kristina M. Gjerde, Aline Jaeckel, Daniel O. B. Jones, Lisa A. Levin, H. J. Niner, L. Pendleton, Craig R. Smith, Torsten Thiele, Philip J. Turner, Les Watling, and P. P. E. Weave, "Biodiversity Loss from Deep-Sea Mining," *Nature Geoscience* 10 (2017):464–65.

200 **Replacing lost species in the deep is near impossible.** Kathryn J. Mengerink, Cindy L. Van Dover, Jeff Ardron, Maria Baker, Elva Escobar-Briones, Kristina Gjerde, J. Anthony Koslow, Eva Ramirez-Llodra, Ana Lara-Lopez, Dale Squires, Tracey Sutton, Andrew K. Sweetman, and Lisa A. Levin, "A Call for Deep-Ocean Stewardship," *Science* 344 (2014):696–98, doi:10.1126/science.1251458.

200 **cause more harm than good.** Zaira Da Ros, Antonio Dell'Anno, Telmo Morato, Andrew K. Sweetman, Marina Carreiro-Silva, Chris J. Smith,

Nadia Papadopoulou, Cinzia Corinaldesi, Silvia Bianchelli, Cristina Gambi, Roberto Cimino, Paul Snelgrove, Cindy Lee Van Dover, and Roberto Danovaro, "The Deep Sea: The New Frontier for Ecological Restoration," *Marine Policy* 108 (2019):103642, doi:10.1016/j.marpol.2019.103642.

201 **rebuilding a single mined concession area.** Ibid.

201 **unique assemblage of species.** Shana Goffredi et al., "Hydrothermal Vent Fields Discovered."

201 **scientifically meaningless.** Van Dover et al., "Biodiversity Loss."

201 **inactive or dormant hydrothermal vents.** Andrew Thaler, in conversation with the author, November 20, 2019.

202 **Numerous deep-sea experts advise.** Nathanial Gronewold, "Seabed-Mining Foes Press U.N. to Weigh Climate Impacts," *Scientific American*, July 16, 2019, https://www.scientificamerican.com/article/seabed -mining-foes-press-u-n-to-weigh-climate-impacts/.

202 **churn up delicate microbial communities.** B. Nagender Nath, N. H. Khadge, Sapana Nabar, C. Raghu Kumar, B. S. Ingole, A. B. Valsangkar, R. Sharma, and K. Srinivas, "Monitoring the Sedimentary Carbon in an Artificially Disturbed Deep-Sea Sedimentary Environment," *Environmental Monitoring and Assessment* 184 (2012): 2829–44; Tanja Stratmann, Lidia Lins, Autun Purser, Yann Marcon, Clara F. Rodrigues, Ascensão Ravara, Marina R. Cunha, Erik Simon-Lledó, Daniel O. B. Jones, Andrew K. Sweetman, Kevin Köser, and Dick van Oevelen, "Abyssal Plain Faunal Carbon Flows Remain Depressed 26 Years after a Simulated Deep-Sea Mining Disturbance," *Biogeosciences* 15 (2018):4131–45, doi:10.5194/bg-15-4131-2018.

203 **sedentary animals . . . still missing.** Erik Simon-Lledó, Brian J. Bett, Veerle A. I. Huvenne, Kevin Köser, Timm Schoening, Jens Greinert, and Daniel O. B. Jones, "Biological Effects 26 Years after Simulated Deep-Sea Mining," *Scientific Reports* 9 (2019):8040, doi:10.1038/s41598-019-44492-w.

203 **The study, published in 2020.** Tobias R. Vonnahme, Massimiliano Molari, Felix Janssen, Frank Wenzhöfer, Mattias Haeckel, Jürgen Titschack, and Antje Boetius, "Effects of a Deep-Sea Mining Experiment on Seafloor Microbial Communities and Functions after 26 Years," *Scientific Advances* 6 (2020):eaaz5922, doi:10.1126/sciadv.aaz5922.

203 **A few other mining-simulation studies.** Daniel O. B. Jones, Stefanie Kaiser, Andrew K. Sweetman, Craig R. Smith, Lenaick Menot, Annemiek Vink, Dwight Trueblood, Jens Greinert, David S. M. Billett, Pedro Martinez Arbizu, Teresa Radziejewska, Ravail Singh, Baban Ingole, Tanja Stratmann, Erik Simon-Lledó, Jennifer M. Durden, and Malcolm R. Clark, "Biological Responses to Disturbance from Simulated Deep-Sea Polymetallic Nodule Mining," *PLoS One* 12, no. 2 (2017):e0171750, doi:10.1371/journal.pone.0171750.

203 **scientists and miners plan to return to the Clarion Clipperton Zone**. Erik Simon-Lledó, in conversation with the author at the National Oceanography Centre, UK, January 17, 2020.

204 **"Even if we found unicorns."** Daniel Jones, in conversation with the author at the National Oceanography Centre, UK, January 17, 2020.

GREEN VS BLUE

207 **hard hat with the logo of DeepGreen Metals.** Michael Lodge (@ mwlodge) posted the pictures on Twitter, April 13, 2018, https://twitter .com/mwlodge/status/984626856384221185.

207 **tragic history of mining on land.** Anne Davies and Ben Doherty, "Corruption, Incompetence and a Musical: Nauru's Cursed History," *Guardian*, September 3, 2018, https://www.theguardian.com/world/2018/sep/04/ corruption-incompetence-and-a-musical-naurus-riches-to-rags-tale.

208 **Rough calculations.** Richard Roth, "Understanding the Economics of Seabed Mining for Polymetallic Nodules," presentation at International Seabed Authority council meeting, Kingston, Jamaica, March 6, 2018; also, Matthew Gianni, in conversation with the author, November 4, 2019.

209 **receive only a modest revenue.** Matthew Gianni, in conversation with the author, November 4, 2019.

210 **make a fortune even before their first mine opens.** Gerard Barron, CEO of DeepGreen Metals, has previously taken this approach to making money from deep-sea mining before any mines actually open as an early investor in Nautilus Minerals, the mining company that, for a more than a decade, was poised to mine hydrothermal vents in waters of Papua New Guinea. At a time when mining was looking likely, and share prices were high, Barron sold his stake and made himself millions. *Why the Rush? Seabed Mining in the Pacific Ocean* (Ottawa: Deep Sea Mining Campaign, London Mining Network, Mining Watch Canada, 2019), http://www.deepsea miningoutofourdepth.org/wp-content/uploads/Why-the-Rush.pdf.

210 **"Personally, I get very uncomfortable."** Gerard Barron, address to the International Seabed Authority council, February 27, 2019, https://www .isa.org.jm/files/files/documents/nauru-gb.pdf.

210 **Barron constantly repeats the message.** *DeepGreen: Metals for Our Future*, Vimeo video, 3:49, posted by DeepGreen, 2018, https://vimeo .com/286936275.

211 **Predicting which raw materials.** Daniele La Porta Arrobas, Kirsten L. Hund, Michael S. Mccormick, Jagabanta Ningthoujam, and John R. Drexhage, *The Growing Role of Minerals and Metals for a Low Carbon Future* (Washington, DC: World Bank Group, 2017), http://documents.worldbank. org/curated/en/207371500386458722/The-Growing-Role-of-Minerals-and -Metals-for-a-Low-Carbon-Future.

211 **Future demands for metals.** Indra Overland, "The Geopolitics of Renewable Energy: Debunking Four Emerging Myths," *Energy Research and Social Science* 49 (2019):36–40.

212 **bulk of rare earths.** In 2017, 55 percent of rare earth metals used in the United States were for chemical catalysts, 15 percent for ceramics and glass manufacture. Data from US Geological Survey, quoted in M. Hobart King,

"REE – Rare Earth Elements and Their Uses," Geology.com, accessed August 16, 2020, https://geology.com/articles/rare-earth-elements/.

212 **China stopped exporting rare earths.** Tania Branigan, "Chinese Moves to Limit Mineral Supplies Sparks Struggle over Rare Earths," *Guardian*, October 25, 2010, https://www.theguardian.com/business/2010/oct/25/china-cuts-rare-earths-exports.

212 **rare earths have been caught up.** Kalyeena Makortoff, "US–China Trade: What Are Rare-Earth Metals and What's the Dispute?," *Guardian*, May 29, 2019, https://www.theguardian.com/business/2019/may/29/us-china-trade-what-are-rare-earth-metals-and-whats-the-dispute.

213 **In 2019, a Denmark-based consortium.** Anne Bergen, Rasmus Andersen, Markus Bauer, Hermann Boy, Marcel ter Brake, Patrick Brutsaert, Carsten Bührer, Marc Dhallé, Jesper Hansen, Herman ten Kate, Jürgen Kellers, Jens Krause, Erik Krooshoop, Christian Kruse, Hans Kylling, Martin Pilas, Hendrik Pütz, Anders Rebsdorf, Michael Reckhard, Eric Seitz, Helmut Springer, Xiaowei Song, Nir Tzabar, Sander Wessel, Jan Wiezoreck, Tiemo Winkler, and Konstantin Yagotyntsev, "Design and In-Field Testing of the World's First ReBCO Rotor for a 3.6 MW Wind Generator," *Superconductor Science and Technology* 32 (2019):125006, doi:10.1088/1361-6668/ab48d6.

213 **increase in the price of silver.** Iraklis Apergis and Nicholas Apergis, "Silver Prices and Solar Energy Production," *Environmental Science and Pollution Research* 26 (2019):8525–32, doi:10.1007/s11356-019-04357-1.

214 **One design showing particular promise.** Martin A. Green, Anita Ho-Baillie, and Henry J. Snaith, "The Emergence of Perovskite Solar Cells," *Nature Photonics* 8 (2014):506–14, doi:10.1038/NPHOTON.2014.134.

215 **cobalt industry in the DRC.** Célestin Banza Lubaba Nkulu, Lidia Casas, Vincent Haufroid, Thierry De Putter, Nelly D. Saenen, Tony Kayembe-Kitenge, Paul Musa Obadia, Daniel Kyanika Wa Mukoma, Jean-Marie Lunda Ilunga, Tim S. Nawrot, Oscar Luboya Numbi, Erik Smolders, and Benoit Nemery, "Sustainability of Artisanal Mining of Cobalt in DR Congo," *Nature Sustainability* 1 (2018):495–504, doi:10.1038/s41893-018-0139-4.

215 **Amnesty International reports.** *"This Is What We Die For": Human Rights Abuses in the Democratic Republic of Congo Power the Global Trade in Cobalt* (London: Amnesty International, 2016), https://www.amnesty.org/en/documents/afr62/3183/2016/en/.

216 **spike in the price of cobalt.** "Cobalt on the Rise," *DSM Observer*, November 27, 2017, http://dsmobserver.org/2017/11/cobalt-rising/.

218 **predicting metal use.** Vincent Moreau, Piero Carlo Dos Reis, and François Vuille, "Enough Metals? Resource Constraints to Supply a Fully Renewable Energy System," *Resources* 8 (2019):29, doi:10.3390/resources8010029; Sven Teske, Nick Florin, Elsa Dominish, and Damien Giurco, *Renewable Energy and Deep-Sea Mining: Supply, Demand and Scenarios* (Sydney: Institute for Sustainable Futures, 2016), report prepared for J. M. Kaplan Fund, Oceans 5, and Synchronicity Earth, http://www.savethehighseas.org/publicdocs/

DSM-RE-Resource-Report_UTS_July2016.pdf; Alicia Valeroa, Antonio Valerob, Guiomar Calvob, and Abel Ortego, "Material Bottlenecks in the Future Development of Green Technologies," *Renewable and Sustainable Energy Reviews* 93 (2018):178–200, doi:10.1016/j.rser.2018.05.041; Takuma Watari, Benjamin C. McLellan, Damien Giurco, Elsa Dominish, Eiji Yamasue, and Keisuke Nansai, "Total Material Requirement for the Global Energy Transition to 2050: A Focus on Transport and Electricity," *Resources, Conservation and Recycling* 148 (2019):91–103, doi:10.1016/j.resconrec.2019.05.015; André Månbergera and Björn Stenqvist, "Global Metal Flows in the Renewable Energy Transition: Exploring the Effects of Substitutes, Technological Mix and Development," *Energy Policy* 119 (2018):226–41, doi:10.1016/j.enpol.2018.04.056.

219 **Recycling electric car batteries.** Gavin Harper, Roberto Sommerville, Emma Kendrick, Laura Driscoll, Peter Slater, Rustam Stolkin, Allan Walton, Paul Christensen, Oliver Heidrich, Simon Lambert, Andrew Abbott, Karl Ryder, Linda Gaines, and Paul Anderson, "Recycling Lithium-Ion Batteries from Electric Vehicles," *Nature* 575 (2019):75–86, doi:10.1038/s41586-019-1682-5.

219 **This idea has been adopted by DeepGreen Metals.** Barron, address to the International Seabed Authority council.

221 **troubles brought Nautilus's plans to a halt.** *Why the Rush?* (Deep Sea Mining Campaign).

221 **test mines have already been carried out.** "Japan Just Mined the Ocean Floor and People Want Answers," CBC Radio, October 13, 2017, https://www.cbc.ca/radio/quirks/october-14-2017-1.4353185/japan-just-mined-the-ocean-floor-and-people-want-answers-1.4353198; Japan Oil, Gas, Metals National Corporation, "JOGMEC Conducts World's First Successful Excavation of Cobalt-Rich Seabed in the Deep Ocean," August 21, 2020, http://www.jogmec.go.jp/english/news/release/news_01_000033.html.

221 **vent mining may never be profitable.** Julia Sigwart, in conversation with the author, November 19, 2019.

A SANCTUARY IN THE DEEP

224 **the treaty will come up for review.** Leslie Hook and Benedict Mander, "The Fight to Own Antarctica," *Financial Times*, May 23, 2018, https://www.ft.com/content/2fab8e58-59b4-11e8-b8b2-d6ceb45fa9d0.

224 **increasing volume of krill fishing.** George M. Watters, Jefferson T. Hinke, and Christian S. Reiss, "Long-Term Observations from Antarctica Demonstrate That Mismatched Scales of Fisheries Management and Predator-Prey Interaction Lead to Erroneous Conclusions about Precaution," *Scientific Reports* 10 (2020):2314, doi:10.1038/s41598-020-59223-9.

EPILOGUE

228 **several hundred biologists.** International Deep-Sea Biology Symposium, https://dsbsoc.org/conferences/.

229 **three-dimensional computerized model.** Klaas Gerdes, Pedro Martínez Arbizu, Ulrich Schwarz-Schampera, Martin Schwentner, and Terue C. Kihara, "Detailed Mapping of Hydrothermal Vent Fauna: A 3D Reconstruction Approach Based on Video Imagery," *Frontiers in Marine Science* 6 (2019):96, doi:10.3389/fmars.2019.00096/.

229 **analyzed footage of squid filmed in the deep.** Benjamin P. Burford and Bruce H. Robison, "Bioluminescent Backlighting Illuminates the Complex Visual Signals of a Social Squid in the Deep Sea," *Proceedings of the National Academy of Sciences (US)* 117, no. 15 (2020):8524–31, doi:10.1073/pnas.1920875117.

229 **So many minutiae are uncovered.** Jaimee-Ian Rodriguez, "Many Eyes, Many Perspectives: The Astonishing Visual Systems of Hyperiids," Smithsonian Ocean, January 2020, https://ocean.si.edu/ocean-life/invertebrates/many-eyes-many-perspectives-astonishing-visual-systems-hyperiids.

229 **the process is called cryptometamorphosis.** Chong Chen, Katrin Linse, Katsuyuki Uematsu, and Julia D. Sigwart, "Cryptic Niche Switching in a Chemosymbiotic Gastropod," *Proceedings of the Royal Society B* 285 (2018):20181099, doi:10.1098/rspb.2018.1099.

229 **ripple along a sea cucumber.** Amy Maxmen, "The Hidden Lives of Deep-Sea Creatures Caught on Camera," *Nature* 561 (2018):296–97, doi:10.1038/d41586-018-06660-2.

Photo Credits

Index

Additional Resources

ORGANIZATIONS CAMPAIGNING TO PROTECT THE DEEP

Blue Planet Society: https://blueplanetsociety.org/2020/08/stop-deep
-sea-mining.

Deep-Ocean Stewardship Initiative: https://www.dosi-project.org.

Deep-Sea Conservation Coalition: http://www.savethehighseas.org.

Bloom Association: https://www.bloomassociation.org/en.

Sustainable Ocean Alliance: https://www.soalliance.org/soa-campaign
-against-seabed-mining.

The Ocean Foundation: http://www.deepseaminingoutofourdepth.org.

The Oxygen Project: https://www.theoxygenproject.com.

REPORTS ON DEEP-SEA MINING

Andrew Chin, Katelyn Hari, and Hugh Govan, *Predicting the Impacts of Mining of Deep Sea Polymetallic Nodules in the Pacific Ocean: A Review of Scientific Literature* (np: Deep Sea Mining Campaign and Mining Watch Canada, 2020), https://miningwatch.ca/sites/default/files/nodule_mining_in_the_pacific_ocean.pdf.

Luc Cuyvers, Whitney Berry, Kristina Gjerde, Torsten Thiele, and Caroline Wilhem, *Deep Seabed Mining: A Rising Environmental Challenge* (Gland: IUCN and Gallifrey Foundation, 2018), doi.org/10.2305/IUCN.CH.2018.16.en.

Fauna & Flora International, *An Assessment of the Risks and Impacts of Seabed Mining on Marine Ecosystems* (Cambridge: Flora and Fauna International, 2020), https://cms.fauna-flora.org/wp-content/uploads/2020/03/FFI_2020_The-risks-impacts-deep-seabed-mining_Report.pdf.

Royal Society Future Ocean Resources: Metal-Rich Minerals and Genetics – Evidence Pack. (London: Royal Society, 2017), https://royalsociety.org/future-ocean-resources.

REPORTS ON DEEP-SEA FISHING

Callum M. Roberts, Julie P. Hawkins, Katie Hindle, Rod. W. Wilson, and Bethan C. O'Leary, Entering the Twilight Zone: The Ecological Role and Importance of Mesopelagic Fishes. (np: Blue Marine Foundation, 2020), https://www.bluemarinefoundation.com/wp-content/uploads/2020/12/Entering-the-Twilight-Zone-Final.pdf.

Glen Wright, Kristina Gjerde, Aria Finkelstein, and Duncan Currie, Fishing in the Twilight Zone: Illuminating Governance Challenges at the Next Fisheries Frontier (np: IDDRI Study No. 6, 2020), https://www.iddri.org/sites/default/files/PDF/Publications/Catalogue%20Iddri/Etude/202011-ST0620EN-mesopelagic_0.pdf.

EXPLORING IN THE DEEP

Ocean research organizations broadcast over the Internet live video feed from their ships and submersibles, offering real-time experience of deep-sea exploration:

NOAA, Okeanos Explorer: https://oceanexplorer.noaa.gov/livestreams/welcome.html.

Ocean Exploration Trust, Nautilus: https://nautiluslive.org.

Schmidt Ocean Institute, Falkor: https://schmidtocean.org/technology/live-from-rv-falkor.

FILM AND TELEVISION

Blue Planet II: The Deep, BBC, 2017.

Deep Ocean: Giants of the Antarctic Deep, BBC, 2020.

Deep Planet, Discovery, 2020.

Octonauts and the Yeti Crab, Silvergate Media and BBC, 2013.

Our Planet: The High Seas, Netflix, 2019.

MUSIC

"Abyss Kiss" by Adrianne Lenker, 2018.

"Beyond the Abyss" by Drexciya, 1992.

"How deep is the Ocean" by Aretha Franklin, 1962.

"Weird Fishes/Arpeggi" by Radiohead, 2007.

BOOKS

Maria Baker, Ana Hilário, Hannah Lily, Anna Metaxas, Eva Ramirez-Llodra, and Abigail Pattenden, *Treasures of the Deep* (np: The Commonwealth, 2019), available free to download at https://www.dosi-project.org/wp-content/uploads/TreasuresOfTheDeep_PDF-ebook-small.pdf.

William Beebe, *Half a Mile Down* (Harcourt, Brace and Company: New York, 1934), available freely at the Biodiversity Heritage Library, doi:10.5962/bhl.title.10166.

John D. Gage and Paul A. Tyler, *Deep-Sea Biology: A Natural History of Organisms of the Deep-Sea Floor* (Cambridge: Cambridge University Press, 2012), doi:10.1017/CBO9781139163637.

Ernst Haeckel, *Kunstformen der Nature* (Verlag des Bibliographischen Instituts: Leipzig and Vienna, 1899-1904), available freely at the Biodiversity Heritage Library, doi:10.5962/bhl.title.102214.

Roger Hanlon, Louise Allcock, and Michael Vecchione, *Octopuses, Squid, and Cuttlefish: A Visual Scientific Guide* (Brighton: Ivy Press, 2018).

Imants G. Priede, *Deep-Sea Fishes: Biology, Diversity, Ecology and Fisheries* (Cambridge: Cambridge University Press, 2017), doi:10.1017/9781316018330.

Helena M. Rozwadowski, *Fathoming the Ocean: The Discovery and Exploration of the Deep Sea* (Harvard: Harvard University Press, 2008).

WEBSITES AND BLOGS

Deep Sea News: http://www.deepseanews.com.

Deep-Sea Biology Society: https://dsbsoc.org.

WoRDSS: The World Register of Deep-Sea Species: http://www.marinespecies.org/deepsea.

YOUTUBE CHANNELS

Monterey Bay Aquarium Research Institute: https://www.youtube.com/channel/UCFXww6CrLAHhyZQCDnJ2g2A.

Nekton Mission: https://www.youtube.com/c/NektonMissionOrgDeepOcean.

EDUCATIONAL RESOURCES

Nekton Education: https://nektonmission.org/education.

Okeanos Explorer: https://oceanexplorer.noaa.gov/okeanos/edu/welcome.html.

Nautilus Live: https://nautiluslive.org/education.

Monterey Bay Aquarium Research Institute: https://www.mbari.org/products/educational-resources.

Woods Hole Oceanographic Institution, Education resources for K-12 Students and Teachers: https://www.whoi.edu/what-we-do/educate/k-12-students-and-teachers.